Daniel Defoe's writings have bred controversy since their first appearance in the eighteenth century: *Robinson Crusoe* fuels virulent disagreements among critics, while Defoe's two scandalous women, *Moll Flanders* and *Roxana*, can still shock us and challenge the range of our sympathies.

This essential study:

- takes a fresh look at these intriguing novels and leads the reader into close analysis of Defoe's texts, encouraging an open-minded approach to interpretation
- features chapters on the novels' openings, conscience and repentance, society and economics, women and patriarchy, and the use of 'outsider' narrators
- provides useful sections on 'Methods of Analysis' and 'Suggested Work' to aid independent study
- offers historical and literary background, a sample of critical views, and suggestions for further reading.

Equipping students with the critical and analytical skills with which to approach Defoe's work, this inspiring guide helps readers to appreciate the brilliance of the author's writing and to enjoy the complexity of his fictional creations for themselves.

Nicholas Marsh is a Fellow of the English Association. He is author of the popular *How to Begin Studying English Literature*, now in its third edition, and many titles in the *Analysing Texts* series, of which he is also the General Editor.

Analysing Texts is dedicated to one clear belief: that we can all enjoy, understand and analyse literature for ourselves, provided we know how to do it. Readers are guided in the skills and techniques of close textual analysis used to build an insight into a richer understanding of an author's individual style, themes and concerns. An additional section on the writer's life and work and a comparison of major critical views place them in their personal and literary context.

ANALYSING TEXTS

General Editor: Nicholas Marsh

Published

Jane Austen: The Novels *Nicholas Marsh*
Aphra Behn: The Comedies *Kate Aughterson*
William Blake: The Poems *Nicholas Marsh*
Charlotte Brontë: The Novels *Mike Edwards*
Emily Brontë: Wuthering Heights *Nicholas Marsh*
Chaucer: The Canterbury Tales *Gail Ashton*
Daniel Defoe: The Novels *Nicholas Marsh*
John Donne: The Poems *Joe Nutt*
George Eliot: The Novels *Mike Edwards*
E. M. Forster: The Novels *Mike Edwards*
Thomas Hardy: The Novels *Norman Page*
John Keats: *John Blades*
Philip Larkin: The Poems *Nicholas Marsh*
D. H. Lawrence: The Novels *Nicholas Marsh*
Marlowe: The Plays *Stevie Simkin*
Shakespeare: The Comedies *R. P. Draper*
Shakespeare: The Sonnets *John Blades*
Shakespeare: The Tragedies *Nicholas Marsh*
Shakespeare: Three Problem Plays *Nicholas Marsh*
Mary Shelley: Frankenstein *Nicholas Marsh*
Webster: The Tragedies *Kate Aughterson*
Virginia Woolf: The Novels *Nicholas Marsh*
Wordsworth and Coleridge: Lyrical Ballads *John Blades*

Further titles are in preparation

Analysing Texts
Series Standing Order ISBN 0–333–73260–X
(*outside North America only*)

You can receive future titles in this series as they are published by placing a standing order. Please contact your bookseller or, in case of difficulty, write to us at the address below with your name and address, the title of the series and the ISBN quoted above.

Customer Services Department, Palgrave Ltd
Houndmills, Basingstoke, Hampshire RG21 6XS, England

Daniel Defoe: The Novels

NICHOLAS MARSH

palgrave
macmillan

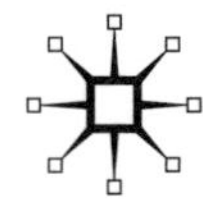

First published 2011 by
PALGRAVE MACMILLAN

Palgrave Macmillan in the UK is an imprint of Macmillan Publishers Limited, registered in England, company number 785998, of Houndmills, Basingstoke, Hampshire RG21 6XS.

Palgrave Macmillan in the US is a division of St Martin's Press LLC, 175 Fifth Avenue, New York, NY 10010.

Palgrave Macmillan is the global academic imprint of the above companies and has companies and representatives throughout the world.

Palgrave® and Macmillan® are registered trademarks in the United States, the United Kingdom, Europe and other countries.

ISBN 978–0–230–24319–4 hardback
ISBN 978–0–230–24320–0 paperback

This book is printed on paper suitable for recycling and made from fully managed and sustained forest sources. Logging, pulping and manufacturing processes are expected to conform to the environmental regulations of the country of origin.

A catalogue record for this book is available from the British Library.

Library of Congress Cataloging-in-Publication Data
Marsh, Nicholas, 1948–
Daniel Defoe, the novels / Nicholas Marsh.
p. cm.
Includes index.
ISBN 978–0–230–24320–0 (pbk.)
1. Defoe, Daniel, 1661?–1731—Criticism and interpretation.
I. Title.
PR3407.M37 2011
823′.5—dc22 2011008497

10 9 8 7 6 5 4 3 2 1
20 19 18 17 16 15 14 13 12 11

Printed and bound in China

For Evie

Contents

General Editor's Preface

This series is dedicated to one clear belief: that we can all enjoy, understand and analyse literature for ourselves, provided we know how to do it. How can we build on close understanding of a short passage, and develop our insight into the whole work? What features do we expect to find in a text? Why do we study style in so much detail? In demystifying the study of literature, these are only some of the questions the *Analysing Texts* series addresses and answers.

The books in this series will not do all the work for you, but will provide you with the tools, and show you how to use them. Here, you will find samples of close, detailed analysis, with an explanation of the analytical techniques utilised.

At the end of each chapter there are useful suggestions for further work you can do to practise, develop, and hone the skills demonstrated and build confidence in your own analytical ability.

An author's individuality shows in the way they write: every work they produce bears the hallmark of that writer's personal 'style'. In the main part of each book we concentrate therefore on analysing the particular flavour and concerns of one author's work, and explain the features of their writing in connection with major themes. In Part II, there are chapters about the author's life and work, assessing their contribution to developments in literature; and a sample of critics' views are summarised and discussed in comparison with each other.

Some suggestions for further reading provide a bridge towards further critical research.

Analysing Texts is designed to stimulate and encourage your critical and analytic faculty, to develop your personal insight into the author's work and individual style, and to provide you with the skills and techniques to enjoy at first hand the excitement of discovering the richness of the text.

NICHOLAS MARSH

A Note on Editions

References to *Robinson Crusoe*, *Moll Flanders*, and *Roxana*, in this book, are to the Penguin Classics editions of all three novels, for no other reason than that they are easily available. As Penguin Classics are sometimes re-edited, this note gives the specific editions used: *Robinson Crusoe*, edited with an introduction and notes by John Richetti (Penguin, 2001); *Moll Flanders*, edited with an introduction by David Blewett (Penguin, 1989); *Roxana*, edited by David Blewett (Penguin English Library, 1982; Penguin Classics, 1987).

Page-references to these editions appear in the text, in brackets, and preceded by '*RC*' for *Robinson Crusoe*, '*MF*' for *Moll Flanders*, and '*R*' for *Roxana*, as for example (*RC* 21–2) for *Robinson Crusoe*, pages 21–2.

PART I

ANALYSING DEFOE'S NOVELS

1

Setting the Agenda

The novels we focus on in this book are *Robinson Crusoe* (1719), *Moll Flanders* (1722), and *Roxana* (1724). The stories of all three remind us of how unpredictable life could be. Defoe's critics are almost equally unpredictable. So Harold Bloom writes that Defoe does not understand Moll; Virginia Woolf writes that Robinson does not believe in nature, God, or death; V. O. Birdsall says the narrators vainly seek 'a significant selfhood';[1] Rousseau saw Robinson as a pre-industrial ideal while for Marx he was an emblem of industry; for Katherine Clark his story is 'a sacred drama that involved the redemption of Crusoe and Friday'[2] while for Michael McKeon Crusoe justifies 'material and social ambition' as 'the way of nature and the will of God'.[3] There is such a wide variety of opinions that it could be hard to maintain our grip on the original experience of reading the novels themselves for the first time.

This book aims to take a fresh look at Defoe's fictions. We will begin with a close examination of that original reading experience, and hope to build our further insights upon a firm understanding of how these texts work. Without more ado, then, let us turn to the analysis of three extracts, one from each novel. We have chosen passages near the start of each text, which may seem to set an agenda for the work in which they appear.

Analysis: *Robinson Crusoe*, pp. 6–8

At the beginning of *Robinson Crusoe*, his father tries to dissuade Robinson from going to sea:

> He bid me observe it, and I should always find, that the calamities of life were shared among the upper and lower part of mankind; but that the middle station had the fewest disasters, and was not expos'd to so many vicissitudes as the higher or lower part of mankind; nay, they were not subjected to so many distempers and uneasinesses either of body or mind, as those were who, by vicious living, luxury and extravagancies on one hand, or by hard labour, want of necessities, and mean or insufficient diet on the other hand, bring distempers upon themselves by the natural consequences of their way of living; *that* the middle station of life was calculated for all kind of vertues and all kinds of enjoyments; that peace and plenty were the handmaids of a middle fortune; that temperance, moderation, quietness, health, society, all agreeable diversions, and all desirable pleasures, were the blessings attending the middle station of life; that this way men went silently and smoothly thro' the world, and comfortably out of it, not embarass'd with the labours of the hands or of the head, not sold to the life of slavery for daily bread, or harrast with perplex'd circumstances, which rob the soul of peace, and the body of rest; not enrag'd with the passion of envy, or secret burning lust of ambition for great things; but in easy circumstances sliding gently thro' the world, and sensibly tasting the sweets of living, without the bitter feeling that they are happy, and learning by every day's experience to know it more sensibly.
>
> After this, he press'd me earnestly, and in the most affectionate manner, not to play the young man, not to precipitate my self into miseries which Nature and the station of life I was born in, seem'd to have provided against; that I was under no necessity of seeking my bread; that he would do well for me, and endeavour to enter me fairly into the station of life which he had been just recommending to me; and that if I was not very easy and happy in the world, it must be my meer fate or fault that must hinder it, and that he should have nothing to answer for, having thus discharg'd his duty in warning me against measures which he knew would be to my hurt: In a word, that as he would do very kind things for me if I would stay and settle at home as he directed, so he would not have so much hand in my misfortunes, as to give me any encouragement to go away: And to close all, he told me I had my elder brother for an

example, to whom he had used the same earnest perswasions to keep him from going into the Low Country wars, but could not prevail, his young desires prompting him to run into the army where he was kill'd; and tho' he said he would not cease to pray for me, yet he would venture to say to me, that if I did take this foolish step, God would not bless me, and I would have leisure hereafter to reflect upon having neglected his counsel when there might be none to assist in my recovery.

I observed in this last part of his discourse, which was truly prophetick, tho' I suppose my father did not know it to be so himself; I say, I observed the tears run down his face very plentifully, and especially when he spoke of my brother who was kill'd; and that when he spoke of my having leisure to repent, and none to assist me, he was so mov'd, that he broke off the discourse, and told me, his heart was so full he could say no more to me.

I was sincerely affected with this discourse, as indeed who could be otherwise; and I resolv'd not to think of going abroad any more, but to settle at home according to my father's desire. But alas! a few days wore it all off; and in short, to prevent any of my father's farther importunities, in a few weeks after, I resolv'd to run quite away from him. However, I did not act so hastily neither as my first heat of resolution prompted, but I took my mother, at a time when I thought her a little pleasanter than ordinary, and told her, that my thoughts were so entirely bent upon seeing the world, that I should never settle to any thing with resolution enough to go through with it, and my father had better give me his consent than force me to go without it; that I was now eighteen years old, which was too late to go apprentice to a trade, or clerk to an attorney; that I was sure if I did, I should never serve out my time, and I should certainly run away from my master before my time was out, and go to sea; and if she would speak to my father to let me go but one voyage abroad, if I came home again and did not like it, I would go no more, and I would promise by a double diligence to recover that time I had lost. (*Robinson Crusoe*, Ed. John Richetti, Penguin Classics, 2003, pp. 6–8)[4]

We can begin by looking at the way Defoe structures his narrative into paragraphs. In this extract there are four, and each serves a purpose. The first paragraph provides an extended and argued account of the elder Crusoe's philosophy, pointing out the disadvantages of extremes and the contentment to be found in the 'middle station in life'. Paragraph 2 then applies this philosophy to the people concerned: Robinson's circumstances are described; the dire consequences of ignoring his father's advice are illustrated by his elder brother's death; and Robinson is promised every comfort if he settles at home, but no support if he persists in going away. The third paragraph focuses on the senior Crusoe, describing the depth of emotion with which he speaks; and the fourth focuses on Robinson, giving his initial and later reactions. The structure, then, has a pleasing methodical quality: first, the 'middle station' philosophy is expounded; then, this is applied to the characters; then, there is a paragraph on each of the participants in the debate. Such a methodical statement of theme, expounded on the second page of the novel, suggests an author setting the agenda: perhaps the 'middle station' in life, together with the errors and horrors of life's higher and lower stations, will prove to be this text's central theme.

This is our first contact with Defoe's writing. How can we describe it? We can start by looking at the sentences. The first paragraph of our extract is a single sentence: it is a very long sentence indeed, and it behoves us to pay attention to its construction. We can do this by summarising each major section of the sentence, taking semicolons and colons to be the usual dividers between sections. So, the sentence that is the first paragraph of our extract can be summarised into sections as follows:

1. High and low in society share life's calamities
2. Those in the middle suffer the least
3. Luxury and poverty bring miseries to the high and the low, respectively
4. Those in the middle live in peace and virtue, comfort, and contentment
5. ... not made miserable and dissatisfied by want, slavery and hard labour, or envy and ambition
6. ... but living in increasing happiness day by day

This summary makes clear the argument and the structure of Defoe's exposition. First, there is a relatively succinct proposition (Sections 1 and 2, from 'He bid me observe ... ' to ' ... lower part of mankind;').

Sections 3 and 4 then repeat the proposition, elaborating each of its two statements. So, from these sections we know, for example, that among the 'calamities' that befall the rich and powerful are 'vicious living, luxury and extravagancies', while the happiness of those in the middle station consists, among other elements, of 'peace and plenty ... temperance, moderation, quietness, health, society, all agreeable diversions'. Sections 5 and 6 are further elaborations of the two statements: prefaced by 'not' and 'but', respectively. These sections contrast violent passions ('enrag'd with the passion of envy, or secret burning lust') against peaceful happiness ('sensibly tasting the sweets of living'), providing us with a final picture of the calamitous existence of rich and poor, in contrast to the contentment of those in the middle.

Defoe's single sentence, then, is carefully constructed.[5] It consists of six sections organised as three pairs, dealing with the two statements of Mr Crusoe's proposition three times. The opening two sections state the proposition; the next two elaborate, expanding on the meaning of each statement; and the final two elaborate again, but this time in terms of emotion, providing a persuasive contrast between violent passion and peaceful contentment as the final impression from the paragraph. In other words, Crusoe's argument is expounded as statement, explanation, and emotion. This is a persuasive order of development, for who could choose violent passion over peaceful happiness, when we know that the former proceeds from so many repugnant aspects of life, while the latter is a consequence of 'vertues' and 'blessings' and suchlike? The emotional choice, on which the paragraph ends, is already made for us.

The second paragraph is again a single sentence, which can be analysed using our summary technique:

1. If I settle at home, I will be well provided for
2. If I am not happy, it will be my fault, not my father's
3. He will be kind to me if I stay, but if I go away, he will not help me
4. My elder brother's death should be an example to me
5. If I go away, God will also abandon me

The subject-matter of this paragraph is twofold: first, the elder Crusoe emphasises the easy life Robinson can expect from settling at home, and the danger and horror to which he will expose himself if he goes abroad; and secondly, he attaches promises and threats – that he will provide or withhold money, and provide or withdraw his blessing, according to Robinson's decision. The final suggestion is that God will also withdraw his blessing if Robinson rejects the 'middle station'. However, the alternation of ideas in this paragraph is more rapid than in the first. So, we are thrown about between 'precipitate my self into miseries' and that 'Nature and the station of life I was born in' which would protect him; or that Mr Crusoe would 'do very kind things for me' but would 'not have so much hand in my misfortunes, as to give me any encouragement'; or, that though he 'would not cease to pray for me', 'God would not bless me'. This paragraph, then, persuades in a more personal manner, and swings from carrot to stick and back again; and is utterly believable as a father's admonition to his son.

Despite the more natural and flowing effect of this paragraph, a formal structure is still discernible. We can say that the paragraph centres on Section 3, which begins after a colon with 'In a word...' and ends with the next colon after '...encouragement to go away:'. This is Mr Crusoe's central and most succinct statement. Sections 1 and 2, leading up to this, maintain a more positive emphasis, with such phrases as 'easy and happy', 'he would do well for me', and 'enter me fairly'; while Sections 4 and 5, with the mention of his brother's death and a picture of desolation, bereft of even God's love, provide a much more threatening mood. So Mr Crusoe's central appeal is preceded by carrot and followed by stick – again, a clear persuasive structure.

The third and shortest paragraph is again one sentence, simply emphasising how the elder Crusoe wept about his eldest son who was killed in the war; and about the prospect of Robinson being in misery and far from help. The fourth paragraph consists of three sentences, which can be summarised as follows:

1. Robinson decides to settle at home
2. A few days pass, and he decides to go away
3. Robinson seeks his mother's aid to obtain his father's consent to his going

The separation of the first part of this paragraph into two comparatively short sentences, put together with what they narrate, has a complicated effect. Robinson is susceptible to the emotion of the moment (he is moved by his father's appeal), but only for the moment: such influences die away, whereupon Robinson reverts to his natural, wilful self. This change of heart is confessed with an exclamatory regret which expresses the old narrator Robinson's retrospective opinion: 'But alas! a few days wore it all off.' The Crusoes are involved in a common generational conflict between a cautious father and an adventurous son. We, as readers, both understand their conflict and notice how the lengthy rhetorical build-up of the elder Crusoe's speech, leading to his tearful climax that leaves Robinson 'sincerely affected', is followed by the bathetic 'a few days wore it all off'. The third, much longer sentence, reports Robinson's attempt at enlisting his mother's support. It is a perfect example of adolescent pleading. Like his father, Robinson uses a carrot and stick strategy, although in his version stick is more apparent than carrot. He will leave home anyway; his father had better consent, or else. And the carrot? Once he has been away and returned, if he does not like the seafaring life, he will work twice as hard, to make up for the time he was not there. We can hear the truculent tone in his way of placing all blame on his father, who 'had better give me his consent than force me to go without it'; and the hopeful offer at the end, which amounts to: *please give me everything I want, and afterwards I promise to be good.*

We have looked at sentences, and used our summary method to appreciate how the longer ones are built up in sections. We should also note that the two long paragraphs, and the long sentence in paragraph 4, are indirect speech. The length and elaborating structure of these sentences give us an impression of persuasive energy: of the participants adding reason to reason and appeal to appeal, in order to bring their interlocutors around to their point of view. So, we are impressed with the emotional importance with which these two characters invest their argument. At the same time, we are amused by the incipient comedy of this family scene, including Robinson's quick recovery from his father's influence, and the pedantic *naïveté* of Mr Crusoe's 'middle-ism' philosophy. This creates an odd effect that we could call 'comic seriousness'.

Defoe's diction is abundant. For example, there is a wide range of terms for the misfortunes Robinson's father warns him of: they are 'calamities', 'disasters', 'vicissitudes', and 'distempers and uneasinesses', all within the first four lines of the extract; then, the long list of terms for the contentment of the 'middle station' includes 'vertues', 'enjoyments', 'peace', 'plenty', 'temperance, moderation, quietness, health, society, all agreeable diversions, and all desirable pleasures', and 'blessings'. This is a rich and varied style, and the elder Crusoe builds and piles up words on each side, each term adding a new detail to his two pictures of misery and happiness. At the same time, the diction emphasises a difference between restless and restful, rough violence and smooth gentleness, which conveys the quality of comfort Mr Crusoe recommends in the life of the 'middle station'. So, high and low are constantly assaulted by the 'passion of envy, or secret burning lust of ambition'; and in contrast, not 'harrast', those of the middle station live 'silently' and 'smoothly' and die 'comfortably', after 'sliding gently' through life. It suits his father's purpose to convey to Robinson that alarms are horrid, and to contrast them against quiet ease; but his speech is doomed. Mr Crusoe's proposal is negative: if you can steer clear of activity, and reach the safety of death before anything has happened to you, then that is happiness. It is ironic because it is delivered to a boy eager for adventure. Robinson, of course, finds 'passion' and 'ambition for great things' attractive, and is put off by the prospect of all that 'sliding gently' and dying quietly. So, the more successful Mr Crusoe's expression, the more unsuccessful his appeal. This, and its negativity, is the fundamental weakness of his case, and the irony is pointed up for us by the contrasting dictions of ease and harassment the father is so keen to emphasise. We notice that Defoe treats the tension between father and son's conflicting outlooks with great delicacy: there is the potential for both sides to appear comic, but at the same time we recognise the insoluble distance between them, and take into account Robinson's retrospective 'Alas!'.

Finally, we can notice two further features of Defoe's writing. First, that the extract is predominantly literal, for there are no prominent images of the author's invention; but that the writing uses common metaphorical expressions freely. So, for example, we hear that 'peace and plenty' are the 'handmaids' of a middle station; that poverty can 'rob' peace from soul and body, that the contented are 'sliding' through the world, 'tasting the Sweets'; and that Robinson should not 'precipitate' himself into 'miseries', and so on. In this extract, then, we find that Defoe does not use imagery to decorate his text, add a subtext or imply a further meaning. Rather, his free use of metaphorical language simply adds to the immediacy of communication. The characters (and the first-person author therefore) are driven by a strong desire to communicate and persuade, and Defoe's expressive use of common metaphor conveys this energy.

Perhaps the most significant image in this extract is also the funniest. When Robinson comments that the effect of his father's talk was short-lived, he says, 'But alas! a few days wore it all off.' We imagine that his father's persuasions have been scoured into Robinson, leaving, as it were, a gouged or scratched surface; then, 'a few days' act like erosion or sandpaper, smoothing Robinson's surface and erasing his father's argument. This idea expresses how time operates to obliterate or change life's impressions. However, it remains only a brief metaphor, hardly more than a common figurative use of language.

The final feature of Defoe's style that we should notice before moving on to another extract is his use of zeugma and of lists. Zeugma occurs where one verb governs two or more clauses. For example, in the first paragraph we read that 'men went silently and smoothly thro' the world, and comfortably out of it', the verb 'went' governs how men go both 'thro'' and 'out of' the world. Earlier in the first paragraph there is a more elaborate example, in which men 'bring Distempers upon themselves' 'by' 'vicious Living etc.', 'hard labour etc.', and 'the natural Consequences etc.' This leads us to noticing the frequency with which Defoe develops lists, ranging from simple lists of terms, such as that beginning with 'temperance, moderation, quietness . . . ' in the first paragraph; to lists of clauses such as the series beginning with 'that' in the fourth paragraph: 'that my thoughts . . . that I should never settle . . . that I was now eighteen . . . that I was sure . . . ' The first of these lists is part of the word-power Robinson's father wields to persuade his son, while the second gives us a rhythmic impression of Robinson's adolescent attempt to browbeat his mother.

We have looked at our first extract from *Robinson Crusoe* in some detail. We can now turn to an extract from *Moll Flanders*, again drawn from near the beginning of the novel, and seeming to set an agenda for the text.

Analysis: *Moll Flanders*, pp. 46–8

In the following extract, the child Moll conceives of her choices as being between a life 'in service' or as a 'gentlewoman':

> I was continu'd here till I was eight years Old, when I was terrified with News, that the Magistrates, as I think they call'd them, had order'd that I should go to Service; I was able to do but very little Service where ever I was to go, except it was to run of Errands, and be a Druge to some Cook-Maid, and this they told me of often, which put me into a great Fright; for I had a thorough Aversion to going to Service, as they call'd it, that is to be a Servant, tho' I was so young; and I told my Nurse, as we call'd her, that I believ'd I could get my Living without going to Service if she pleas'd to let me; for she had Taught me to Work with my Needle, and Spin Worsted, which is the chief Trade of that City, and I told her that if she wou'd keep me, I wou'd Work for her, and I would Work very hard.
>
> I talk'd to her almost every Day of Working hard; And in short, I did nothing but Work and Cry all Day, which griev'd the good kind Woman so much, that at last she began to be concern'd for me, for she lov'd me very well.
>
> One Day after this, as she came into the Room, where all we poor Children were at Work, she sat down just over against me, not in her usual Place as Mistress, but as if she set herself on purpose to observe me, and see me Work: I was doing something she had set me to, as I remember, it was Marking some Shirts, which she had taken to Make, and after a while she began to Talk to me: Thou foolish Child, says she, thou art always Crying; (for I was Crying then) Prithee, What doest Cry for? because they will take me away, *says I*, and put me to Service, and I can't Work House-Work; well Child, says she, but tho' you can't Work House-Work, as you call it, you will learn it in time, and they won't put you to hard Things at first; yes they will, says I, and if I can't do it, they will Beat me, and the Maids will Beat me to make me do great Work, and I am but a little Girl, and I can't do it, and then I cry'd again, till I could not speak any more to her.
>
> This mov'd my good Motherly Nurse, so that she from that time resolv'd I should not go to Service yet, so she bid me not Cry, and she wou'd speak to Mr. *Mayor*, and I should not go to Service till I was bigger.

> Well, this did not Satisfie me, for to think of going to Service, was such a frightful Thing to me, that if she had assur'd me I should not have gone till I was 20 years old, it wou'd have been the same to me, I shou'd have cry'd, I believe all the time, with the very Apprehension of its being to be so at last.
>
> When she saw that I was not pacify'd yet, she began to be angry with me, and what wou'd you have? *says she*, don't I tell you that you shall not go to Service till you are bigger? Ay, says I, but then I must go at last, why what? said she, is the Girl mad? what, would you be a Gentlewoman? Yes *says I*, and cry'd heartily, till I roar'd out again.
>
> This set the old Gentlewoman a Laughing at me, as you may be sure it would: Well, Madam forsooth, says she, *Gibing at me*, you would be a Gentlewoman, and pray how will you come to be a Gentlewoman? what, will you do it by your Fingers Ends?
>
> Yes, *says I again*, very innocently.
>
> Why, what can you Earn, *says she*, what can you get at your Work?
>
> Three-Pence, *said I*, when I Spin, and 4 *d*. when I Work plain Work.
>
> Alas! poor Gentlewoman, *said she again*, Laughing, what will that do for thee?
>
> It will keep me, *says I*, if you will let me live with you; and this *I said*, in such a poor petitioning Tone, that it made the poor Womans Heart yearn to me, as she told me afterwards. (*Moll Flanders*, Ed. David Blewett, Penguin Classics, 1989, pp. 46–8)[6]

The opening paragraph of this extract is a single sentence which sets the terms for the ensuing scene. Our summary method shows that this sentence consists of five sections: Sections 1 and 2 focus on the fear of going 'to Service'; Sections 4 and 5 express Moll's solution – to work for her Nurse; while the middle Section 3 sets out the crux of the matter: the little girl's surprisingly strong emotion: 'for I had a thorough Aversion to going to Service'. So, paragraph 1 is constructed similarly to paragraphs 1 and 2 of our *Robinson Crusoe* extract: as a single sentence structured to be symmetrically balanced; and the focal point is Moll's uncontrollable emotion.

Our third paragraph introduces a fresh technique, where a single sentence is made to contain two exchanges (i.e. four speeches) of a dialogue, written in direct speech. So, the colon after 'began to Talk to me:' introduces 'Thou foolish Child'; 'because they will take me away . . . ', 'well Child . . . ', and 'yes they will . . . ' all change the speaker, but the older narrator's '*says I*' and 'says she' are relegated to the middle of the character's speech. This technique seems to have two effects: first, containing four speeches within one sentence makes the dialogue seem to be a complete event, starting and ending with Moll's tears; second, there is an impression of speed, as if the characters reply without pause. So, when Moll contradicts her Nurse saying 'yes they will', it is as if she cuts into what her elder is saying. This technique for presenting rapid exchanges becomes even more audible as the Nurse's anger spills over. Notice, for example, how we jump, with no indicative punctuation, from Moll's to her Nurse's speech, in 'I must go at last, why, what?'

In the final part of our extract, the dialogue is set out in a manner more familiar to modern readers: each character's speech constitutes a paragraph; speeches are clearly attributed with '*says I*' or '*said she again*', and the characters alternate. This evolution of dialogue, from indirect speech (paragraph 1), through direct speech exchanges contained within one sentence, eventually leading to alternating separate contributions, conveys how the problem first showed itself, and gave rise to some bursts of argumentative talk, before becoming a more formal question and answer session, which steadily reveals Moll's *naïveté*.

These exchanges between Moll and her Nurse are still shorter than the formal persuasive speeches of the elder Crusoe, or Robinson's appeal to his mother, which are more like set-pieces than live talk. Here, the dialogue is shaped and timed so that the two voices emerge in lively counterpoint. We remarked on Defoe's success in rendering indirect speech via paragraph-long sentences in the *Robinson Crusoe* extract. Here, he uses direct speech and we notice how economically the phrasing and diction help us to hear the characters' voices, including slight variations of tone. For example, notice the short phrases each introduced by 'and', which allow us to hear the rhythm of Moll's sobs as she breaks down crying again: 'and if I can't do it, they will Beat me, and the Maids will Beat me to make me do great Work, and I am but a little Girl, and I can't do it'; then, notice the difference between 'is the Girl mad?' and 'Madam forsooth' as the Nurse passes from irritation to ironic amusement. Just the single word 'pray', a respectful term ironically addressed to the childish 'gentlewoman', contains such a wealth of social revelation and – considering Moll's birth – sadness and futility, as fills this dialogue with emotion and meaning.

In our *Robinson Crusoe* extract, the terms of debate were undercut by irony: the recommendation to life's 'middle station' is undermined by its negative presentation; while Robinson's response is expressed as adolescent pleading and emotional blackmail, an attempt to manipulate the sentiments of his mother. In other words, we found a flawed situation with no solution, only irony. Our extract from *Moll Flanders* partakes of the same quality: the situation is both ironic, and not possible to resolve. Clearly, the child Moll has an aversion to 'Service', and she cries in order to get her own way. The Nurse is aware of this: indeed, her first words show annoyance at this manipulative weeping: 'Thou foolish Child . . . thou art always Crying'; and her anger reaches its peak at 'why, what? . . . is the Girl mad?' When, eventually, the Nurse gives in and says 'you shan't go to Service, you shall live with me' (*MF* 49), it is a victory for the child but a defeat for reality. It is clear that Moll has no practical idea of money; and at the end of the dialogue, she offers to do without food. The resolution of this scene, then, only postpones Moll's encounter with a harsher reality. Is the Nurse culpably irresponsible when she gives in to Moll's tears, or should we rather praise her human sympathy? Whichever aspect of the Nurse's capitulation we emphasise, however, the bind into which Moll has been born has not changed.

Both of the extracts we have looked at so far happen to focus on arguments between adults and the young. Both Robinson and Moll are shown as driven by an absolute determination to have their own way. Robinson sets aside his parents' wishes, his brother's death, and even his own emotional response to his father, and resolves to desert his family. Moll sets aside, and her persistent weeping forces her Nurse to set aside, all the determining social and economic facts of her situation. We have noticed that Robinson's father presents a flawed, negative philosophy to his son. We should also notice that the circumstances determining Moll's future – that is, the Nurse's case for her to go to service – are equally negative and repugnant: Moll is a victim of her birth in an unjust and pitiless society. So, ironic but unsolved, this extract leaves us sympathetic but fearful; angry at the system, yet partly regretful that Moll still denies reality.

Moll's avowed desire, in this extract, is to become a 'gentlewoman': she has heard this title used with approval and therefore regards it as enviable. Moll's *naïveté* is the subject of indulgent ridicule from her Nurse, who sarcastically imitates genteel address with 'Madam forsooth' and 'pray'; and over the succeeding pages this patronising amusement at Moll's innocence entertains the Mayoress, other gentlewomen, and their daughters. What emerges for the reader, however, is the question whether the title 'gentlewoman' has any substantive meaning at all, or is it merely a false concept like the 8-year-old Moll's misapprehension. Some other claims to being a 'gentlewoman' may be as ridiculous as Moll's: so, for example, the Lady Mayoress, surely a 'gentlewoman', laughs at Moll (whom she addresses using the derogatory 'Miss'), makes joke of her hands, and is generally indelicate in her behaviour (see *MF* 49).

Analysis: *Roxana*, pp. 39–40

Our third extract is Roxana's account of her first marriage:

> At about Fifteen Years of Age, my Father gave me, *as he called it in* French, 25000 Livres, *that is to say*, two Thousand Pounds Portion, and married me to an Eminent Brewer in the City; *pardon me if I conceal his Name, for tho' he was the Foundation of my Ruin, I cannot take so severe a Revenge upon him.*
>
> With this Thing call'd a Husband, I liv'd eight Years in good Fashion, and for some Part of the Time, kept a Coach, *that is to say*, a kind of Mock-Coach; for all the Week the Horses were kept at Work in the Dray-Carts, but on *Sunday* I had the Privilege to go Abroad in my Chariot, either to Church, or otherways, as my Husband and I cou'd agree about it; which, *by the way*, was not very often: But of that hereafter.
>
> Before I proceed in the History of the Marry'd Part of my Life, you must allow me to give as impartial an Account of my Husband, as I have done of myself: He was a jolly, handsome Fellow, as any Woman need

> wish for a Companion; tall, and well made; rather a little too large, but not so as to be ungentile; he danc'd well, which, *I think*, was the first thing that brought us together: he had an old Father, who manag'd the Business carefully; so that he had little of that Part lay on him, but now-and-then to appear, and show himself; and he took the Advantage of it, for he troubl'd himself very little about it, but went Abroad, kept Company, hunted much, and lov'd it exceedingly.
>
> After I have told you that he was a Handsome Man, and a good Sportsman, I have, indeed, said all; and unhappy was I, like other young People of our Sex, I chose him for being a handsome, jolly Fellow, as I have said; for he was otherwise a weak, empty-headed, untaught Creature, as any Woman could ever desire to be coupled with: And here I must take the Liberty, whatever I have to reproach myself with in my after-Conduct, to turn to my Fellow-Creatures, the Young Ladies of this Country, and speak to them, by way of Precaution, If you have any Regard to your future Happiness; any View of living comfortably with a Husband; any Hope of preserving your Fortunes, or restoring them after any Disaster; Never, Ladies, marry a Fool; any Husband rather than a Fool; with some other Husbands you may be unhappy, but with a Fool you will be miserable; with another Husband you *may*, I say, be unhappy, but with a Fool you *must*; nay, if he wou'd, he cannot make you easie; every thing he does is so awkward, every thing he says is so empty, a Woman of any Sence cannot but be surfeited, and sick of him twenty times a-Day: what is more shocking, than for a Woman to bring a handsome, comely Fellow of a Husband, into Company, and then be oblig'd to Blush for him every time she hears him speak? To hear other Gentlemen talk Sence, and he able to say nothing? And so look like a Fool, or, which is worse, hear him talk Nonsence, and be laugh'd at for a Fool. (*Roxana*, Ed. David Blewett, Penguin Classics, 1987, pp. 39–40)[7]

This extract begins the narrative of what Roxana calls the 'Marry'd Part' of her life. The first two paragraphs tell us that she was married with a two-thousand-pound dowry and lived in comfort for about 8 years. These two narrative statements give a smooth, superficial account of the marriage; but the paragraphs set up much more besides. Each is a single sentence, as we might expect; and in each case the final section teases the reader. In paragraph 1 we hear that Roxana's husband was 'the Foundation of my Ruin'; in paragraph 2, that they did not agree 'very often'. These tidbits of information undercut Roxana's account of her 'Mock-Coach' and her sizeable dowry and tell us that there was much wrong with the marriage. Defoe then adds a second teasing tidbit at the very end of each paragraph. First, we learn that Roxana 'cannot take so severe a Revenge' on the author of her ruin, and we wonder what residue of affection hinders her? Then, she postpones an account of their arguments, saying 'But of that hereafter'. In these two paragraphs, then, Defoe has insinuated a complex situation into what purports to be a plain narrative. There is one further element to remark: Roxana describes herself as living with 'this Thing call'd a Husband' – a very disrespectful phrase – and when we have read on, we recognise this as a reference to his stupidity. However, at this stage, the phrase also conveys the inexperience of a 15-year-old girl, one who suddenly has a 'thing' called a 'Husband', without any clear idea of what marriage might mean. The phrase 'this Thing call'd a Husband' seems to resonate a sad truth about the marriage system, just as the Nurse's mock-respectful 'Madam forsooth' and 'pray' carried a sad resonance concerning Moll's obscure birth.

The third and fourth paragraphs of our extract are longer, and both are punctuated as single sentences. The first addresses the reader directly, and offers the 'impartial . . . Account' of Roxana's husband which effectively fills both paragraphs: a list of his positive qualities fills one, and the statement of his stupidity fills the other. Roxana's claim to be 'impartial' is therefore borne out by her division of his characteristics into positives and negatives. However, it is clear by the end that his negative quality – his foolishness – far outweighs the superficial jollity and good looks for which Roxana chose him. She tells us that being a 'handsome, jolly Fellow' is all he amounts to, and in saying so she has 'said all'. She does her best for him by listing his having 'an old Father, who manag'd the Business carefully' as an advantage, but she soon drops all pretence of impartiality, and in her address to 'my Fellow-Creatures, the Young Ladies of this Country' the vexation and shame she has to bear from her 'Fool' husband are obvious.

The 'positive' sentence/paragraph has a simple structure: Section 1 asks permission to describe her husband, then a colon leads, depending how you divide the rest, to between five and seven sections saying what

'He was': that 'He was' handsome, a good dancer, son of a careful businessman, a keen huntsman, and so on. This paragraph, then, is set out in a plain manner, and makes obvious use of the satirical technique of the list, where one inappropriate item is included. In this case, the father's care in business is the 'odd-one-out' – it has nothing to do with the husband's own character and so hints at his incompetence.

The long sentence/paragraph developing Roxana's advice against marrying fools is more loosely constructed. It consists of numerous sections, but falls into three main parts. The opening part, where she finally reveals what was wrong with this husband, comes in three sections:

1. Handsome and a huntsman is all he was
2. It was unfortunate that I chose him for his looks
3. . . . because he was stupid

So, the husband's positive and negative qualities are placed on either side of Roxana's regret at her mistake. The second, central part of the paragraph begins when she takes 'the Liberty' of warning 'the Young Ladies of this Country'. Not only does she elaborate her approach, and delay her statement, with 'take the Liberty', and intervening clauses such as 'whatever I have to reproach myself with . . . etc.' and 'my Fellow-Creatures', but also, even after she has changed to second-person address she inserts four further conditional clauses ('If . . . Happiness; . . . living comfortably with a Husband; . . . preserving your Fortunes, . . . after any Disaster') before finally reaching her categoric advice: 'Never, Ladies, marry a Fool'. This short blunt phrase contrasts with its elaborated surroundings: as we have seen, several parenthetic and conditional clauses lead up to it, delaying its arrival; then, once it has been said, it is underlined in three further clauses: a re-statement, 'any Husband rather than a Fool', followed by two further insistences, distinguishing 'unhappy' from 'miserable' and 'may' from 'must'. The third and final part of the sentence/paragraph pictures the mortifying life she led with this husband. She remembers joining 'Company' with a husband who embarrasses her whether he speaks or is silent. However, even this description leaves us with more complex emotions than we might expect. On the one hand, Roxana is 'sick of him twenty times a-Day', has to 'Blush for him' whenever he speaks, and going into company with him is 'shocking'. On the other hand, she knows that he is unable to change. The harder he tries, the worse it is because the more 'awkward' and 'empty' his efforts; and in company he cannot avoid being laughed at. It is indeed a miserable story: and this final part of Roxana's paragraph leaves us with a more complex appreciation of her complaint. Yes, on the one hand, it was insufferable suddenly to find herself, at the age of 15, married to a fool. On the other hand, he could not stop being a fool, and Roxana does not hide from the misery of both parties to the mistake.

We have now looked at three passages, one from each text. In each case, the passage announces a topic or a debate, and we have found that Defoe's sentences and paragraphs are skilfully constructed, that his ear for speech – whether presented as indirect or in the form of dialogue – is unerringly natural, and that the issues with which each passage deals are presented in an increasingly ironic and complex manner. In particular, we found in *Robinson Crusoe* a tension between potential comedy, and more complex and insoluble underlying elements of the text, which we dubbed 'comic seriousness'; and this quality has appeared again in our other two extracts. So, there is simple comedy in the Nurse's sarcastic 'Madam, forsooth' and 'pray', addressing the common-born 8-year-old Moll; but her sarcasm resonates with futile sadness, as does Moll's offer to do without food. Similarly, Roxana reaches a pitch of magnificent comic burlesque when she announces 'Never, Ladies, marry a Fool'; but the subsequent picture of him trapped in his stupidity, while she is trapped in her shame, resonates to the sadness of their mistaken union, in a more complex manner.

Defoe's 'comic seriousness' does not destroy the comedy of his narratives: we may still laugh at the speed with which a few days were sufficient to 'wore . . . off' Robinson's obedience, and at Roxana's blunt pronouncement 'Never, Ladies, marry a Fool'. However, it does show how quickly elements of the text become complicated, or transform themselves into situations that are more complex than they appeared to be at the outset.

Comparative Discussion

We chose these passages because they occur near the start of each text, and because we thought they might set an agenda for the work in which they appear. In *Robinson Crusoe*, then, we thought the debate between the 'middle station' philosophy and Robinson's adventurous ambitions might prove to be a central theme. In *Moll Flanders*, the little girl's aversion to service, and her aspirations towards becoming a 'gentlewoman', suggests a possible central theme in the novel. Finally, in *Roxana*, we thought the issue of marriage itself, which Roxana calls the 'Foundation of my Ruin', may become a major theme. We can now think about each text in general terms and arrive at a preliminary assessment of the proposed themes.

Robinson argues that he suffers each time he ignores his father's advice: that his first adventure leads him into slavery; then, when he is lucky enough to be set back on his feet, Robinson turns his back on the contentment of a 'middle station' again. His second adventure – leaving the Brasils on a slaving voyage – leads him to be marooned upon his island for 28 years. After 27 of those years, Robinson himself acknowledges that ignoring his father is his 'ORIGINAL SIN', and defines this as 'not being satisfy'd with the station wherein God and Nature hath plac'd' him (both *RC* 154). On the other hand, the elder Crusoe's philosophy is also frequently undercut. So, within another page, Robinson is impatient to escape his island, and tells us that 'all this was the fruit of a disturb'd mind, an impatient temper' (*RC* 156); and even while castigating his 'ORIGINAL SIN', Robinson carelessly suggests that it was Providence which failed him; for had 'Providence . . . bless'd me with confin'd desires', he says he would by now have been very rich indeed; whereupon he enters into a discussion of the cost of negroes in comparison with the cost of being marooned for 28 years (see *RC* 154). Above all, Robinson's narrative seems repeatedly to play upon this theme ironically. Defoe's language when he describes 'sliding gently' and passing 'silently and smoothly' through and then out of the world carries a hint of amusement at such negativity. As a preliminary conclusion, then, we can say that the 'middle station' theme does recur throughout *Robinson Crusoe*. On the other hand, the idea that it was Robinson's 'ORIGINAL SIN' to run away, although regularly argued by Robinson himself, hardly bears investigation. He becomes a very rich man, and each time an idea of 'middle station' is implied, the actual circumstances quickly metamorphose into something else, so that our 'theme' is either transformed or recedes from view. We will also find the 'middle station' idea contributing to Defoe's critique of society in Chapter 3.

With regard to *Moll Flanders*, the suggestion is that becoming a 'gentlewoman' and avoiding 'Service' are central concerns of the novel. Does the passion exhibited by Moll at the age of eight remain a driving force of her character? In this case, even cursory recollection of the novel suggests that we can give a positive answer. Moll's terror of poverty and her attempts to achieve a respectable way of life remain prominent elements of her motivation and of the novel's critique of society. On the other hand, like *Robinson Crusoe*, Moll's narrative also plays a complicated comic game with these ideas. Fear of 'going to Service' only figures for a short time, for example: our theme very quickly metamorphoses into a terror of poverty. Also, Moll's first heartbreak may be seen as equally formative, and as complicating the 'gentlewoman' theme. At the end of the novel, Moll finally achieves respectability and comfort. The comedy is that this respectability is achieved by an ex-thief and an ex-highwayman. It remains difficult to determine how far the gentility theme in *Moll Flanders* has been announced only for all its terms to become devalued.

With regard to *Roxana*, the story does reveal a continuing and important concern with marriage. See, for example, the detailed debates between Roxana and her Dutch merchant. Roxana presents a powerful critique of marriage and gives her reasons for rejecting the merchant's proposals; while his forceful arguments urge her to accept. On the other hand, our knowledge of the story's subsequent events enables us to say that she was both wise and unwise to reject the merchant's first offer. Was she wise or unwise to accept his offer in the end?

In thinking about both *Robinson Crusoe* and *Moll Flanders*, we have found ourselves referring to the text playing 'a complicated comic game' with a theme, or referring to it 'ironically'. We can start to clarify these remarks by looking at the sequel to each of our extracts.

If we re-read the pages succeeding our extract from *Robinson Crusoe*, we find further references to Robinson's error in rejecting his father's advice. Several times, he resolves to return home; his companion and the owner of the first ship in which he embarked both urge him not to tempt Providence further, after their experience in the storm. On the other hand, he does not return home. His first voyage being rough, he reproaches himself with 'the breach of my duty to God and my father' (*RC* 9). Then when the weather calms, there is 'little or no wind and a smooth sea, the sun shining upon it, the sight was, as I thought, the most delightful that ever I saw' (*RC* 9). After the second storm, Robinson cannot fathom his own obstinacy, saying that despite everything prompting him to return home, 'yet I had no power to do it'. He even speculates about fate, and some 'decreed unavoidable misery attending' (*RC* 13–14), which, he suggests, is the only possible explanation for his own obstinacy. On the next page, however, it is 'shame' and expectation of being 'laugh'd at among the neighbours', which deters him from returning home; then the 'evil influence' which first carried him away from home, 'the same Influence, whatever it was', makes him ship with a Guinea trader (*RC* 14–15). This is after his memory of danger and his desire for home both 'wore off' (just as we noted in our extract that 'a few days wore [it all] off' his father's advice). Then, and despite the doom-laden commentary, Robinson's first trading voyage is agreeable, beneficial, and profitable. It is the second voyage, not the first, that ends in slavery.

So, in the few pages following the father and son debate, the issues have seemingly changed shape and emphasis several times. God, 'Providence', or a perverse fate is now involved, alongside some naturalistic traits in Robinson's character, such as a young man's aversion to being laughed at. Every warning 'wore off'; and Robinson does not understand why he was obstinate. The point is that the theme – which began as an argument between adventurous ambition, and 'middle station' contentment, has changed its shape several times within these few pages, so that our ideas have to flex and adapt in order to cope: and this 'flexing' of the theme has altered the focus of the text, so that we feel we have moved on from the 'middle station'. Instead, we are now fascinated by that hard little core of risk-taking, obstinacy, and being as he puts it, 'the instruments of our own destruction' in Robinson's personality, and the interaction between this, and what increasingly seem to be chance events.

When we look at the few pages succeeding our extract from *Moll Flanders*, we find a similar overall effect taking place. There are numerous references to the initial theme, and the use of the term 'gentlewoman' or 'little gentlewoman' develops its ironic meanings amply. This said, Moll then finds that 'The fright of my Condition had made such an Impression upon me, that I did not want now to be a Gentlewoman, but was very willing to be a Servant, and that any kind of Servant they thought fit to have me be' (*MF* 54–5). Other topics then crowd in upon the narrative: vanity, debates about the marriage-market, and the elder brother's skill in snaring Moll's virtue. So, although Moll is emphatically not a born 'gentlewoman', and although this fact affects all aspects of her life, we find that the shape of the theme presented in our extract has flexed and changed. Our angles of view have become several and some of the original concerns have faded. It is hard to describe the effect, for the 'gentlewoman' theme does remain a recurrent element of *Moll Flanders*. However, its character does change: it is as if life moves on, ruled by succeeding events.

In the case of Roxana, her first husband's foolishness continues to dominate for about three pages until they are thoroughly ruined, when he disappears; then the emphasis of the text shifts to the consequences: poverty, the hostility, and meanness of his sisters; Roxana's desperation concerning her children; and Amy's and the old woman's solution, together with the humane behaviour of one sister's husband. So, just as Moll's common birth continues to be a crucial factor in her life, so Roxana's marriage is the cause of these distresses; but at the same time, the text seems to allow its first major theme to pale and fade away. We are soon reading a tale of starvation and distress, focused on a pitiless society, without reference to the marriage that caused such dire privations.

For the present, then, we can say that the three passages we have studied do 'set an agenda', in the sense that they announce themes which remain pivotal concerns for each protagonist: Robinson, Moll, and Roxana do struggle to interpret their lives in terms of these themes – the 'middle station', gentility, and marriage, respectively – throughout their lives. However, the relation between these 'mores' and behaviour, or true circumstances, is so loose as to be comically broken, or forgotten, virtually every time it is proposed – as happened when

Robinson's 'I was sincerely affected with this Discourse' 'wore... off'. At the same time, each story demonstrates that life goes on unpredictably: that life itself cannot be analysed or interpreted according to any set 'agenda'.

Conclusions

Conclusions are necessarily tentative at this early stage. Nonetheless, our thoughts may centre upon two major questions concerning Defoe's fictions:

1. We have considered the narrators as presenting or setting an 'agenda'; and we have suggested that the continuing story, developing the protagonist's experiences and bringing in unpredictable events, modifies or undercuts the narrator's attempt to regulate his or her life. In this context, then, how does Defoe present people, human life, and the experience of living? Crucially, is life-experience presented as orderly, or disordered; as making sense, or making absurdity?

   As a working answer for the present, we can suggest that the characters struggle to interpret their lives; and that the relation between people's ideas of life and its reality is at best comically unpredictable.
2. In *Robinson Crusoe*, the narrator places himself in a context he interprets as both moral and religious: it is his 'duty to God and my Father' that he ignores. Moll and Roxana, on the other hand, find themselves in pragmatic circumstances: being born to poverty and marrying a fool are practical, not moral issues; yet we know that both Moll's and Roxana's subsequent lives would be castigated for immorality and sin. What, then, are Defoe's suggestions regarding the moral and religious quandaries in which his narrators find themselves? Is anything recommended, and if so, what? If it is recommended, is it also a practical possibility?

   A working answer, for the present, suggests that Defoe's characters try to assemble and establish a morality relevant to their experiences. However, we can speculate that there is a relationship between the way these narrators are all, as it were, cast adrift or disconnected from conventional society and the apparently *ad hoc* nature of the moral and religious values they develop.

Both of these questions and answers point us towards areas to be studied in succeeding chapters. Questions concerning the morality, religion, and conscience of Defoe's narrators will be the particular focus of Chapter 2.

Methods of Analysis

We have studied three extracts, using a range of analytical techniques:

- We made a brief summary of the extract, paragraph-by-paragraph, then considered our summary in order to understand the structure of the narrative. This approach allowed us to appreciate, for example, the methodical structure of Robinson's account of the father/son debate in *Robinson Crusoe*, or the succession of different forms of dialogue in *Moll Flanders*.
- We focused on sentences, and used the technique of summarising their constituent sections to help us appreciate how they are constructed. Using this analysis as a basis for asking further leading questions has brought insights into the presentation of themes, and character as revealed by indirect speech. For example, we noticed how Robinson's father elaborates his proposition three times, or how he pivots his persuasion around a central flourish of carrot and stick; and we noticed how Roxana uses the final, throwaway section of a seemingly plain sentence, to tease the reader.
- We examined diction – the choice and use of words – and found this a particularly fruitful area of inquiry into our extracts. In particular, we noticed how richly Robinson's father is able to elaborate his argument, using an abundant variety of terms; how subtly Defoe shows variations of tone in the dialogue between Moll and her Nurse; and how superbly Roxana's blunt advice to 'Never, Ladies, marry a Fool' is set up by its surrounding clauses.
- We considered imagery – similes and metaphors – in our *Robinson Crusoe* extract, and found that Defoe makes easy and frequent

use of figures of speech, although the style is not metaphorically ornamented, nor do images provide an interpretative subtext.

- Finally, we turned our attention to the particular concern of this chapter, asking of each passage:
  - How far does this passage 'set an agenda' central to its novel?
  - What relationships between theme, narrator, and events are apparent in this passage?
- After analysing the extracts, we surveyed the three analyses we had carried out, and discussed some of the topics that had arisen, seeking to develop our ideas further in a **comparative discussion**. Again, this involved formulating the relevant leading question. So, we asked how far the topics announced in these extracts do turn out to be pivotal to their particular texts.

Suggested Work

Confirm, expand, and develop the work of this chapter, by carrying out detailed analysis of a second passage from the opening of each novel, as follows:

- *Robinson Crusoe*: See how the facts of danger and ease alter Robinson's mood, thoughts, and resolutions, and how Providence is introduced, on pages 8–10, from 'It was not till almost a year after this . . . ' to ' . . . to be such a one as the worst and most harden'd Wretch among us would confess both the danger and the mercy'.
- *Moll Flanders*: Study the narrative of Moll's visit to the Mayor's household, followed by the death of her benefactor, on pages 52–5, from 'At last one of the Ladies took so much Fancy to me . . . ' as far as ' . . . willing to be a Servant, and that any kind of Servant they thought fit to have me be.' In this extract, notice the development of the idea 'gentlewoman' and the flexing and flux of all social and economic parameters around Moll.
- *Roxana*: Look at the description of Roxana's circumstances after her husband leaves, on pages 47–9, from 'As I have said, I sent to his Relations, but they sent me short and surly Answers . . . ' as

far as '. . . capable to deliver me from any Part of the Load that lay upon me'. In this extract, you may consider how Defoe elaborates Roxana's circumstances when she is deserted.

Analysis of these extracts may contribute to our ideas concerning the casting adrift of narrators and the instability of values in the text.

2

Conscience and Repentance

In Chapter 1, we have noticed that Defoe fills his narratives with particularly unpredictable changes; and we have found that his themes are fluid, sometimes fading from the foreground, merging with a different theme, or subverted by irony. In this chapter we look at the moral and religious values encountered or expressed by Defoe's narrators: are they as hard to pin down as the 'agendas' we considered in Chapter 1?

Analysis: *Robinson Crusoe*, pp. 72–3

Our first extract is from *Robinson Crusoe*. Here, influenced by his illness, Robinson is inspired to pray for the first time since being cast away upon the island:

> It is true, when I got on shore first here, and found all my ship's crew drown'd, and my self spar'd, I was surpriz'd with a kind of exstasie, and some transports of soul, which, had the grace of God assisted, might have come up to true thankfulness; but it ended where it begun, in a meer common flight of joy, or as I may say, *being glad I was alive*, without the least reflection upon the distinguishing goodness of the hand which had preserv'd me, and had singled me out to be preserv'd, when all the rest were destroy'd; or an enquiry why Providence had been thus merciful to me; even just the same common sort of joy which seamen

generally have after they are got safe ashore from a shipwreck, which they drown all in the next bowl of punch, and forget almost as soon as it is over, and all the rest of my life was like it.

Even when I was afterwards, on due consideration, made sensible of my condition, how I was cast on this dreadful place, out of the reach of humane kind, out of all hope of relief, or prospect of redemption, as soon as I saw but a prospect of living, and that I should not starve and perish for hunger, all the sense of my affliction wore off, and I begun to be very easy, apply'd my self to the works proper for my preservation and supply, and was far enough from being afflicted at my condition, as a judgment from Heaven, or as the hand of God against me; these were thoughts which very seldom enter'd into my head.

The growing up of the corn, as is hinted in my Journal, had at first some little influence upon me, and began to affect me with seriousness, as long as I thought it had something miraculous in it; but as soon as ever that part of the thought was remov'd, all the impression which was rais'd from it, wore off also, as I have noted already.

Even the earthquake, tho' nothing could be more terrible in its nature, or more immediately directing to the invisible power which alone directs such things, yet no sooner was the first fright over, but the impression it had made went off also. I had no more sense of God or his judgments, much less of the present affliction of my circumstances being from his hand, than if I had been in the most prosperous condition of life.

But now when I began to be sick, and a leisurely view of the miseries of death came to place itself before me; when my spirits began to sink under the burthen of a strong distemper, and Nature was exhausted with the violence of the fever; conscience that had slept so long, begun to awake, and I began to reproach my self with my past life, in which I had so evidently, by uncommon wickedness, provok'd the justice of God to lay me under uncommon strokes, and to deal with me in so vindictive a manner.

These reflections oppress'd me for the second or third day of my distemper, and in the violence, as well of the fever; as of the dreadful reproaches of my conscience, extorted some words from me, like praying to God, tho' I cannot say they were either a prayer attended with desires or with hopes; it was rather the voice of meer fright and distress; my thoughts were confus'd, the convictions great upon my mind, and the horror of dying in such a miserable condition rais'd vapours into my head with the meer apprehensions; and in these hurries of my soul, I know not what my tongue might express: but it was rather exclamation, such as Lord! what a miserable creature am I? If I should be sick, I shall certainly die for want of help, and what will become of me! Then the tears burst out of my eyes, and I could say no more for a good while.

In this interval, the good advice of my father came to my mind, and presently his prediction which I mention'd at the beginning of this story, *viz. That if I did take this foolish step, God would not bless me, and I would have leisure hereafter to reflect upon having neglected his counsel, when there might be none to assist in my recovery.* Now, said I aloud, My dear father's words are come to pass: God's justice has overtaken me, and I have none to help or hear me: I rejected the voice of Providence, which had mercifully put me in a posture or station of life, wherein I might have been happy and easy; but I would neither see it my self, or learn to know the blessing of it from my parents; I left them to mourn over my folly, and now I am left to mourn under the consequences of it; I refus'd their help and assistance who wou'd have lifted me into the world, and wou'd have made every thing easy for me, and now I have difficulties to struggle with, too great even for Nature itself to support, and no assistance, no help, no comfort, no advice; then I cry'd out, *Lord be my help, for I am in great distress.*

This was the first prayer, if I may call it so, that I had made for many years. But I return to my Journal. (*RC* 72–3)

First, let us take an overview. The first four paragraphs of this extract all tell us that Robinson failed to make a connection between his own circumstances and any religious idea or belief. Then, at the word 'But . . . ' beginning the fifth paragraph, the narrative recounts his reaction to suffering from a fever, and tells us of the religious emotions and self-critical realisations his illness provokes. Finally Robinson cries out in prayer, and comments that this was his first prayer for a long time. So, this extract seems to tell us that Robinson was without religion for a long time (paragraphs 1–4), then fell sick, and found religion (paragraphs 5–8).

Let us start by analysing the sentences in the opening paragraphs of this extract, in order to remind ourselves of the care Defoe takes in constructing the state of his narrator's mind and the progress of his thoughts. The first paragraph/sentence seems to consist of four statements:

1. When I was first saved from the wreck I felt some stirrings of gratitude
2. But this was no more than mere happiness at being alive
3. Without any thought of God or Providence
4. But only a common joy at escaping danger, quickly forgotten

The first section of this sentence, then, leads via 'extasie' and 'transports of soul' towards the word 'thankfulness', clearly suggesting a religious experience. The three succeeding sections go in the opposite direction, however, first deriding Robinson's joy as a 'meer common' pleasure, then insisting that it lacked any religious dimension, and finally treating it with contempt as like the 'common' sensation sailors quickly drown in punch.

The next paragraph/sentence follows a similar pattern, again in four statements:

1. Even when I realised how lonely and cast away I was
2. As soon as I knew I could survive, I lost any sense of being punished
3. Instead, I worked to survive
4. Never thinking about God or Providence

The pattern, beginning with a move towards what Robinson now considers a proper spiritual feeling, is repeated. In the first paragraph, the proper feeling would have been 'thankfulness' for God saving his life; in this paragraph, the proper feeling would have been terror and a 'sense of affliction' at being punished by God. In both paragraphs, however, three of the four sections bring us down to earth: in the first, the comparison with a drunken sailor puts Robinson's joy at being alive on a vulgar level. In the second, Robinson tells us that he did not feel punished, because he was happy ('easy') that he could survive, and he hardly ever thought of God.

The next two paragraphs repeat this pattern: in four paragraphs, we read about Robinson's non-religious response to surviving the wreck, being cast away beyond hope of rescue, the surprise of the corn, and the earthquake. In each case, the majority of the text belittles Robinson's fledgling spiritual feeling and brings us down to earth. Robinson's mind clearly does not naturally deal in abstracts: he was 'without the least reflection' about God; such thoughts 'very seldom enter'd into my head'; once there was a practical explanation for the corn, his superstitious impression 'wore off'; the earthquake frightened him, but then it stopped and his fear also 'went off'. In short, these paragraphs are both cumulative and comic: cumulative because they pile example upon example of Robinson's extraordinarily pragmatic and literal cast of mind; and comic because each short-lived effort of his thoughts to approach a spiritual idea is quickly overwhelmed by his natural pragmatism, giving a bathetic effect. We should remember from our extract in Chapter 1, how his father's advice was briefly affecting, but then 'wore off'; and notice the use of 'wore off' twice more, as well as its variant 'went off', to describe how quickly abstract concepts seem to vacate Robinson's mind.

With regard to diction, Defoe uses the words 'meer' and 'common', and the figure of a sailor getting drunk as soon as he is ashore, to deride the incipient religious feelings; but we should notice the vocabulary Robinson employs for the proper beliefs he tells us he lacked. To describe these, he mentions 'the grace of God', 'true thankfulness', the 'goodness of the hand', and 'Providence had been thus merciful'; then, he talks of a 'judgment from Heaven' and the 'hand of God against me'. The corn suggests 'seriousness' and 'something miraculous', and the earthquake evokes 'invisible power', 'God or his judgments' and 'his hand'. These phrases all promote the idea that the events of life can be interpreted as acts of God or 'Providence'; and that such actions express either mercy or judgement. Such a series of suggestions about Providence is quite conventional for Defoe's time. It makes a believable strand in Robinson's not very energetic or connected spiritual life. On the other hand, we may already feel sceptical of these simple religious conventions: Defoe surely means us to notice that Robinson ascribes both mercy and judgement to Providence's treatment of himself. Is his being 'preserv'd' on the island a sign of God's mercy? Or is it a punishment? Robinson's religious ideas in paragraphs 1–4 are short-lived, of course; so the fact that he does not pursue the more complex questions raised never occurs to him. We now turn to the second half of our extract.

Having disposed of four events susceptible to supernatural interpretation, Robinson introduces the next paragraph with 'But . . . ', suggesting that we are about to meet a more enduring spirituality. The paragraph is a single sentence, again, and displays a clear and balanced structure. Four descriptions of Robinson's illness depend upon 'when . . . '. The sentence then hinges on its main clause, 'conscience . . . begun to awake', leading to another four descriptions (two of Robinson's guilt and two of God's consequent wrath), giving the consequences of the first half. Such a clear structure, with its logical framework of 'But when . . . then . . . ', creates an impression of inevitability that heavily underlines the asserted connection between cause and effect. This paragraph, then, seems to herald a significant change: it is fluent, logical, balanced, and clear; it lacks the dismissive contempt for Robinson's religious thoughts found up to now; and the opening word 'But . . . ' asserts a marked difference between what follows, and the four preceding events. On the other hand, if we look at the content dispassionately, we notice that there is nothing new here. Robinson is sick, Robinson is frightened: when frightened, Robinson imagines that God is punishing him, just as he did during the earthquake.

We turn to the next paragraph, Robinson's spiritual development still in the balance. Here again we meet a single sentence, but one of a very different kind from the clear logical structure we found in paragraph five. It will be helpful to analyse this sentence by summarising its sections, thus:

1. On the second or third day of my sickness, these reflections forced words like prayers from me.
2. But not real prayers, mere panic and fright speaking.
3. My head was confused and full of vapours from fear of death.
4. I did not know what I was saying.
5. I just exclaimed in self-pity.
6. Then I wept and could not speak.

This sentence clearly lacks the tight structure of the preceding paragraph. Rather, it moves from one statement to the next in a rambling manner which starts when Robinson corrects his 'like praying to God', by explaining that these were not real prayers after all. In terms of content, we are back with the 'meer' religious feelings dismissed in the first half of the extract. The difference is that this paragraph gives a more sympathetic description of his fear. This reminds us that his religious ideas are the product of strong emotions, however ephemeral they may prove to be. In the present case, Robinson reveals that the emotion driving him to utter a pseudo-prayer is self-pity.

The final long paragraph of this episode remembers the elder Mr Crusoe's advice, which we studied in Chapter 1. Robinson remembers this advice while he is sick, and reminds us of what his father said. Then, in a new sentence, he dwells on his own guilt in going against his father's wishes. We can again benefit from summarising Robinson's successive statements:

1. Father predicted this: God is punishing me, and I am alone.
2. I was providentially born to an easy life, but refused to learn of it from my parents.
3. I left them mourning over me, now I am mourning.
4. I refused their help to an easy life, now my life is too difficult to cope with and I have no help.
5. Lord help me, for I am in distress.

Statement 5 is, of course, the so-called 'prayer' that bursts from Robinson at the end of the paragraph. Our summary again helps to clarify the pattern of Robinson's ideas. Here, the first four statements are in two balancing parts, and in three of them the second part is a consequence of the first. So, Robinson left his parents who mourned his folly; consequently he now mourns his folly. He refused their help when it was offered; consequently he has no help now, when he needs it. Clearly, with this structure of phrasing and therefore thinking, Robinson is drumming home the lesson he claims to have learned: that it was wrong to reject his father's advice.

In this paragraph, again, Robinson claims some moral and spiritual progress: God apparently agrees with his father; and Robinson now interprets his life in terms of his own original error in leaving home. Again, however, Robinson's reasoning is suspect. We should remember our equivocal response to Mr Crusoe's advice: the language of 'smoothly' 'silently' 'sliding' hints at irony. Robinson retrospectively interprets his misfortunes as proof that his father was right; but there is no reason for us to accept such a connection uncritically. Additionally, Defoe frames the whole of this argument in ambivalence. The opening phrase of the paragraph, 'In this interval', confines Robinson's thoughts to his 'fit' of sickness, reminding us that he is usually most spurred to religious reflection by emotional stress; and the final paragraph casts doubt on his supposed 'first prayer', qualifying it by 'if I may call it so'.

We have now constructed a commentary, paragraph by paragraph, showing the development of moral and religious ideas in this passage. What we have found, however, does not encourage us to formulate interpretations of *Robinson Crusoe*. We have identified a series of occasions when Robinson speculates about Providential control of events on earth, showing intermittent interest in these ideas, contradicting himself, and then quickly forgetting them as they 'wore off'. Then, there is a more sympathetic presentation of his fear and self-pity; and a coherent judgement of his original error in leaving home. However, there is nothing in the extract which would allow us to make a positive statement: Robinson is open with us about his moral and religious speculations, and we can recognise the conventional beliefs Robinson has espoused by the time he writes his retrospective narrative. On the other hand, all his frights, events, and responses create a web of qualifying countercurrents, contradictions, and anti-climaxes, which prevent us from drawing conclusions about Defoe's position. Indeed, these countercurrents suggest an ironic distance between Robinson's simplistic beliefs, and the more complex and subtle insights of his author. One example shows plainly the distinction between Robinson's religious hindsight and his actual experience. We remember that he did not think of being marooned 'as the hand of God against me', which he clearly believes now. At the time, he began to feel 'very easy'. It is with hindsight that he calls it punishment; but we may still wonder how he could feel 'easy' while being punished.

The sample we have taken, then, is characteristically fluid: it dazzles with many elements but will not be pinned down. We can now consider the immediate context, which is the dream Robinson relates beforehand, and the finding of the Bible and development of his religion that succeed our extract. Then, we will think about this episode in relation to the novel as a whole.

The event initiating these moral reflections is Robinson's illness and dream: he imagines a fiery bright figure descending in a cloud, then landing on the earth and saying: 'Seeing all these things have not brought thee to repentance, now thou shalt die.' The figure then makes as if to kill him with a spear. Robinson felt 'Horrors of my Soul' and an 'Impression' remained upon his mind, from this dream. However, Defoe devotes the next several paragraphs to emphasising how irreligious Robinson was. He cannot remember having 'one thought' of God; he was like the most 'hardned, unthinking, wicked creature' or like a 'meer brute' following the 'dictates of common sense' (all from *RC* 71) and without thought of God; he lacked all religious sense for the 8 years between leaving home and falling sick on the island. This leads into the first half of our extract, where Robinson belittles his 'meer' sub-religious ideas.

The exact order of Robinson's experiences is not quite clear. The dream comes to him during his second sleep on 27 June; and following our extract, Robinson tells of being 'somewhat refresh'd' with this sleep on the morning of 28 June. On the other hand, he tells us during the extract that 'These reflections oppress'd me for the second or third day of my distemper'; but that it was 'In this interval' that he remembered his father and spoke 'the first prayer, if I may call it so' of many years. We are not sure, therefore, whether 'this interval' is, vaguely, the second or third day of his illness, or specifically, the second sleep of 27–28 June. Indeed, throughout this episode Robinson seems to offer two explanations of his religious and moral development: on the one hand, he suggests that a series of temporary emotions gradually led up to a realisation concerning his father's advice. According to this idea, he was 'oppress'd' with a growing series of 'reflections' for the first 2 or 3 days of his illness. On the other hand, Robinson seems equally eager to assure us that his preliminary states of mind were 'meer' reactions to stress, not properly religious at all. According to this narrative, Robinson suffered a sudden enlightenment from, first, the terror of his dream, and, second, regret over rejecting his father's advice; both of these mental events occurring during Robinson's second sleep on the morning of 28 June.

Whichever story we accept, the sequel tells us that Robinson began to develop some religious beliefs at around this time. He tells us of a typically divided state of mind the following day: for 'tho' the fright and terror of my dream was very great, yet I consider'd, that the fit of the ague wou'd return again the next day' (*RC* 73–4). His first actions are therefore directed by 'common sense', gathering water, rum, and food: clearly, Robinson sets aside his 'fright and terror' and defers settling the state of his soul until after he has done what he can to preserve his body. He eats and says a grace over his food for the first time, but it is only when he finds himself weak and has to sit down that he pursues religious reflections. In other words, Robinson develops his first religious ideas during a period of enforced physical inactivity. Abstracts do not naturally thrive in Robinson's head; they come to him when he cannot do anything else.

The substance of Robinson's enlightenment, at this stage, is twofold. First, he answers his question about the creation by saying 'It is God has made it all', and consequently reasons that God knows and controls everything. Secondly, his 'conscience' speaks to him in the style of a preacher lambasting his wicked flock, telling him that he is lucky to be alive, for he has deserved death several times: '*WRETCH! dost thou ask what thou hast done!* look back upon a dreadful mis-spent life, and ask thy self *what thou hast not done*?' (*RC* 75). We can hear the traditional hammering of heavy sarcasm, rhetorical questions, and repetitive, antithetical patterns of language ('ask what thou hast done . . . ask . . . what thou hast not done') as an accusing preacher berates miserable sinners.

Robinson's first religious meditation is followed by a further ambivalent passage: his 'thoughts were sadly disturb'd', but he finds practical occupations, lighting a lamp and looking for tobacco as medication. On going to a chest for tobacco, he finds 'a cure, both for soul and body' (*RC* 75), in the form of the tobacco he was looking for, and a Bible. The succeeding few pages chart Robinson's developing religious beliefs, beginning with a comic interlude when the fumes of rum and tobacco defeat conscience and the Bible for a while; then a further stage while Robinson focuses on being 'deliver'd' from his island, rather than understanding God's words 'and I will deliver' as having a wider application. Finally, Robinson tells us 'This was the first time that I could say, in the true Sense of the Words, that I pray'd in all my Life' (*RC* 77); because this time he prayed with 'a sense of my condition' and 'a true Scripture view of hope' from 'the word of God'. Robinson eventually comes to the view that God's promise refers to 'deliverance from sin' rather than 'deliverance from affliction'. This achievement brings Robinson to a state 'much easier in my mind' and gives him 'a great deal of Comfort within'. At the same time, he tells us, 'as my health and strength returned, I bestirr'd myself to furnish my self with every thing that I wanted' (*RC* 77–8). We then hear no more of religion until the anniversary of his arrival on the island, which Robinson sets aside for 'religious exercise' such as prostrating himself, confession, prayer, and fasting (*RC* 76).

What does the whole of this episode represent? We can make a variety of suggestions. First, Robinson explains how he found a comforting belief in God. Second, Defoe depicts floundering religious thoughts, a patchwork of conventions and hearsay, together with a style that satirises conventional preaching and exposes contradictory or *naïve* nostrums: a sort of inconsistent and intermittent *ad hoc* faith that Robinson cobbles together while he is on the island. Third, we are amused as Robinson, labouring against the tendency of all his thoughts to 'wear off' quickly, struggles to digest the abstract thought: that 'deliverance' may be from 'sin' rather than from the island. Fourth, we are saddened that Robinson should castigate his own wickedness, but remain uncritical of his father's negative philosophy. Fifth, we may wonder whether Defoe, the author, proposes any governing Providence or Deity at all; for Robinson cannot work out whether he has been mercifully or punitively treated; and, to the question 'Why is it *that thou wert not long ago destroy'd*?' (*RC* 75), there seems to be no logical answer. So, the episode we have studied here can provide us with several simultaneous narratives, ranging from a simple fable in which the protagonist wakes up to spiritual life and finds faith, to a complex ironic account of the protagonist attributing natural events to providence, from a sympathetic and indulgent author, to a further interpretation in which Defoe shows his character constructing beliefs that will consequently justify his own ambition.[1]

How does this episode relate to the novel as a whole? Can we see Robinson's illness as the start of a consistent process whereby his spiritual life and ideas develop? Up to a point, yes. On the second anniversary of his shipwreck, for example, Robinson declares himself 'much more happy' on the island than in his previous 'wicked, cursed, abominable life'; but he stops short of thanking God for being marooned, saying to himself 'how canst thou be such a hypocrite'; and only thanks God for 'opening my eyes' and enabling him to 'repent' (*RC* 90–1). A further stage seems to be reached with the conversion of Friday, when Crusoe brings him to be 'such a Christian, as I have known few equal to him in my life', despite relying on 'the bare reading the Scripture' and himself having no 'teacher or instructer; I mean, human' (*RC* 174).

On the other hand, on re-reading the final pages of *Robinson Crusoe*, we find no significant mention of religion or ethics: as soon as he has gathered together his wealth, the narrative is limited to physical facts, such as his marriage and children, how he supplied his islanders with women and cattle, and so forth. The only reflective element comes when he describes 'a life of fortune and adventure, a life of Providence's checquer-work, . . . Beginning foolishly, but closing much more happily than any part of it ever gave me leave so much as to hope for' (*RC* 239). This comment acknowledges that Providence has controlled Robinson's life; but does not offer an interpretation: life has been 'checquer-work' and 'variety', and no divine purpose is mentioned. We can recognise Robinson's typical habit of mind again: he goes as far as to conceive a 'Providence' and makes a reference to living 'foolishly' in youth, but further abstract reasoning is not in his nature, so with a sort of mental shrug he dismisses the subject with the vague term 'variety'. Conceptual thinking seems, yet again, to have 'worn off' from Robinson's mind.

Is inconsistency about spiritual and ethical matters a recurrent element in the novel, then? Can we find other examples of Robinson's ideas wearing 'off'; other episodes where religious convention is satirised as it is by the pastiche sermon on page 75? Clearly, yes. We need only glance at Robinson's worthy reflections about money ('O drug! . . . what art thou good for?') which are comically brief before 'upon second thoughts, I took it away' (both from *RC* 47); or remember his response to Friday's questions about religion ('at first I could not tell what to say, so I pretended not to hear him' – *RC* 172), to recognise that Robinson continues to struggle with theology. Watching Robinson cobble together his faith still leaves us uncertain of Defoe's position. Ironic complication allows us to read the text in different ways. As we have remarked, there is a story in which Robinson finds faith and repents his youthful disobedience as a failure of duty to his father and God, and this is the story which Robinson himself proposes; but, there are several other potential interpretations, all encouraged by reading the text ironically rather than taking Robinson's account as Defoe's, at face value.

If we think about the novel as a whole, however, we may be most struck by the fact that religion is not a consistent topic: that Robinson forgets about it for long periods of time, and so do we; and that it comes into Robinson's mind at times of stress, such as during his illness, or when he considers attacking the cannibals (see *RC* 155–9).

Analysis: *Moll Flanders*, pp. 364–6

We now turn to our extract from *Moll Flanders*, which finds Moll in Newgate prison, and being visited by a Minister:

> It was now that for the first time I felt any real signs of Repentance; I now began to look back upon my past Life with abhorrence, and having a kind of view into the other Side of time, the things of Life, as I believe they do with every Body at such a time, began to look with a different Aspect, and quite another Shape, than they did before; the greatest and best things, the views of felicity, the joy, the griefs of Life were quite other things; and I had nothing in my Thoughts, but what was so infinitely Superior to what I had known in Life, that it appear'd to me to be the greatest stupidity in Nature to lay any weight upon any thing tho' the most valuable in this World.
>
> The word Eternity represented itself with all its incomprehensible Additions, and I had such extended Notions of it, that I know not how to express them: Among the rest, how vile, how gross, how absurd did every pleasant thing look? I mean, that we had counted pleasant before; especially when I reflected that these sordid Trifles were the things for which we forfeited eternal Felicity.

With these Reflections came in, of meer Course, severe Reproaches of my own Mind for my wretched Behaviour in my past Life; that I had forfeited all hope of any Happiness in the Eternity that I was just going to enter into, and on the contrary was entitul'd to all that was miserable, or had been conceiv'd of Misery; and all this with the frightful Addition of its being also Eternal.

I am not capable of reading Lectures of Instruction to any Body, but I relate this in the very manner in which things then appear'd to me, as far as I am able; but infinitely short of the lively impressions which they made on my Soul at that time; indeed those Impressions are not to be explain'd by words, or if they are, I am not Mistress of Words enough to express them; It must be the Work of every sober Reader to make just Reflections on them, as their own Circumstances may direct; and without Question, this is what every one at sometime or other may feel something of; I mean a clearer Sight into things to come, than they had here, and a dark view of their own Concern in them.

But I go back to my own Case; the Minister press'd me to tell him, as far as I thought convenient, in what State I found myself as to the Sight I had of things beyond Life; he told me he did not come as Ordinary of the Place, whose business it is to extort Confessions from Prisoners, for private Ends, or for the farther detecting of other Offenders; that his business was to move me to such freedom of Discourse as might serve to disburthen my own Mind, and furnish him to administer Comfort to me as far as was in his Power; and assur'd me, that whatever I said to him should remain with him, and be as much a Secret as if it was known only to God and myself; and that he desir'd to know nothing of me, but as above, to qualifie him to apply proper Advice and Assistance to me, and to pray to God for me.

This honest friendly way of treating me unlock'd all the Sluices of my Passions: He broke into my very Soul by it; and I unravell'd all the Wickedness of my Life to him: In a word, I gave him an Abridgement of this whole History; I gave him the Picture of my Conduct for 50 Years in Miniature. (*MF* 364–6)

There are six paragraphs in this extract, each consisting of a single sentence. We can begin in our customary manner, by noticing how each of these units is structured. The first paragraph develops to the statement that all things looked different 'than they did before'. The semicolon then acts as a kind of fulcrum, and the second half of the paragraph elaborates the statement of the first half. Paragraph 2 follows a similar shape, making a statement up to the colon after 'them'; then illustrating the statement in the remainder of the sentence. Paragraph 3 hinges similarly, at the semicolon following 'Life'. Paragraphs 4 and 5, however, are more complex. In paragraph 4, Moll expresses some humility ('I am not capable of reading Lectures . . . ') and notes that she cannot express the strength of her feelings and ideas. It is following her apology for lacking 'Words enough to express them' that a semicolon signals a change of direction, and the remainder of the paragraph urges all of us to seek the 'clearer Sight into things to come' Moll claims to have achieved. This change of direction, making a transition from Moll's humility to lessons for the reader, reveals something of how her mind works. We can connect this with paragraph 5, in which the Minister's plea for Moll's confession alternates negative and positive elements: he says that he is not a snitch or informer, and he is on her side with God, twice. Paragraph 6 confirms that the minister's repetitive alternations have a powerful effect in unlocking Moll's emotions.

This extract tells us of the emotional and mental events which lead Moll to confess, and begins by elaborating three statements about her new perspective. First, she calls it 'a kind of view into the other Side of time'; then she tells us that 'the Word Eternity' appeared to her with 'all its incomprehensible Additions', and she had 'extended Notions' of it. Finally she says that the thought of Eternity made all her regrets more terrifying, because her misery had 'the frightful Addition of its being also Eternal'. These three points, neatly elaborated in three paragraphs, show how Moll experiences a sudden opening out, or reversal, of her point of view about everything. It feels like a revelation,, and she emphasises how new everything seems with 'different Aspect', 'quite another Shape', 'quite other things', all being so different from the ideas she was used to that she did not know 'how to express them'.

It is easy to understand how Moll arrives at this new state of mind. She is in Newgate, condemned to death, and she has sinned and committed numerous crimes: no wonder, if she subscribes to conventional beliefs, that her mind fills with forebodings of eternal punishment. Having established Moll's new perspective, Defoe then prepares her confession. First, paragraph 4 denotes a period of hesitation: Moll apologises, admitting that she is in no position to preach; then she apologises for her words, which fall short of conveying her 'lively impressions'. Then, however, her apologies are turned around to bear upon the reader: such spiritual experiences are 'not to be explain'd by words'; and it is the reader's responsibility to think about them. Finally, Moll imagines that everybody goes through at least 'something' of the same experience; and she spells out again that her religious awakening was to do with eternity and judgement: 'clearer Sight' of eternity, and a 'dark view', by which she seems to mean a partial understanding of the judgement she deserves.

In this paragraph, then, Moll has altered her circumstances. She has humbled herself, apologising twice; but then the entire topic of sin, repentance, and eternal punishment expands to include the reader. Notice that Moll claimed that she could not deliver 'Lectures of Instruction'; but then clearly does so when she intones that 'it must be the Work of every Sober Reader' to think about eternity and their own sins. There is even an element of threat in her use of 'things to come' and 'here' for death and this world, respectively; as well as in her reference to the 'Sober Reader's' sins as 'their own Concern in them'. By the end of this paragraph, Moll is no longer a solitary sinner facing death. Now, she and her Sober Reader share the threat of eternal punishment. This expansion of the subject, and change of focus, would be very comforting for Moll.

The minister offers to hear Moll's confession in absolute confidence, reassuring her that it will be 'as much a Secret as if it was known only to God and myself'; and at the same time he offers positive aid, mentioning 'to disburthen my own Mind' and 'administer Comfort'; and offering 'Advice and Assistance to me, and to pray to God for me'. The offer he makes, then, involves a change of focus: Moll has concentrated on her eternal punishment, and the dreadful things she has done; but now, the minister opens up the prospect of 'Comfort' and forgiveness. It is at this point that Moll's emotions, and therefore her confession, are set free. She uses a series of metaphors to convey the release she felt: it 'unlock'd all the Sluices of my Passions'; it 'broke into' her soul, and she 'unravell'd all the Wickedness of my Life' to him. The first two metaphors suggest a sudden and perhaps violent breaking: first of water set free through a sluice, then of breaking through some hard defence; while 'unravell'd' further suggests loosening or releasing from restraint. These images appropriately express the wild release involved in Moll's long-withheld confession; but they also have overtones of crime ('unlock'd' and 'broke into') loss ('unlock'd') and disorder, or chaos ('unravell'd'). Finally, Moll says that her confession was a 'Picture . . . in Miniature' of her career.

We can conclude, then, that certain processes had to be completed, before Moll would be able to confess; and in this extract Defoe shows us how the moment of release is prepared. Moll reduces the sting of her first shocks, about judgement and eternity, by connecting herself with others, and by turning herself from guilty object of sermons to a preacher in her own right; then, the minister introduces hope of redemption, and promises confidentiality. The metaphors, particularly the vivid 'unlock'd all the Sluices of my Passions', persuade us that the confession the minister caused to gush (as we may say) from Moll was sincere, and produced by powerful emotion. As readers, we respect the narrator's honesty about her experience in Newgate. Defoe, however, combines this sympathetic respect with strictly pragmatic elements. Specifically, Moll's confession depended upon the following three pre-conditions: first, the sentence of death, which terrified Moll and initiated her 'view into the other Side of time'; second, the assurance that she could speak in confidence – that is, without further incriminating herself; and third, that God's mercy could bring 'Comfort' to offset her terror of death and punishment. How do these elements fare as events proceed?

The ecstasy of sincere repentance reaches its climax two paragraphs after the end of our extract. Here, Moll again expresses the combination of her emotions: she is 'cover'd with Shame and Tears for things past, and yet had at the same time a secret surprizing Joy'. The 'impression' of these wild emotions ran 'so high' that Moll would have faced immediate execution 'without any uneasiness at all'. At this point, on the second day of the Minister's visiting, Moll appears to have achieved an absolute faith, and declares herself ready to cast her 'Soul entirely into the Arms of infinite Mercy' (all from *MF* 366). After that climax, Moll's faith gradually recedes. So, finding her name on the 'Dead Warrant' is a 'terrible blow . . . to my new Resolutions' and she faints. Clearly, the dominance of her faith in 'infinite Mercy' has been upset.

The following day she 'waited with great impatience, and under the greatest oppression of Spirits imaginable' (*MF* 367) before the Minister brings her news of the reprieve. Clearly, the intensity of her faith has waned during the 12 intervening days, and she is frightened of death. This is, of course, entirely natural; and Defoe does not imply that her repentance was insincere, or forgotten. He does, however, subject Moll's faith to the same ironic definition by time, change, and human nature, as is the consistent arbiter of his novels. We have no difficulty in understanding Moll's terror of execution; and we never expect her to confess all her crimes in court. On the other hand, her natural emotions and behaviour repeatedly fall away from any absolute religious or ethical standard.

The succeeding pages tell of a further episode of sincere thankfulness, which lasted 'all that Night' after hearing of the reprieve; and we read of Moll's fits of 'trembling' followed by 'crying involuntarily' as others are taken away to execution, after which she again feels a proper 'humble Penitent serious kind of Joy'. After another fortnight Moll is finally sentenced to Transportation, and she complains about being treated as 'an old Offender', whereas, strictly speaking, this was her first offence. Here Moll appeals to what the court knew about her, rather than the truth as we and God know it! She then declines to comment upon the sentence, saying that 'we shall all choose any thing rather than Death, especially when 'tis attended with an uncomfortable prospect beyond it, which was my Case' (all from *MF* 370–1). Moll's faith in divine Mercy, and the intensity of her repentance, has evidently diminished since the climax of her first sentence and reprieve.

What are we to make of Moll's repentance in jail? She herself discusses its place in relation to the rest of her story, as follows:

> This may be thought inconsistent in it self, and wide from the Business of this Book; Particularly, I reflect that many of those who may be pleas'd and diverted with the Relation of the wild and wicked part of my Story, may not relish this, which is really the best part of my Life, and most Advantageous to myself, and the most instructive to others; such however will I hope allow me the liberty to make my Story compleat: It would be a severe Satyr on such, to say they do not

> relish the Repentance as much as they do the Crime; and that they had rather the History were a compleat Tragedy, as it was very likely to have been. (*MF* 368–9)

Defoe is characteristically playful here. He clearly recognises that *Moll Flanders* will be popular for its sensational content; and apologises for preaching to the reader, saying that religion and ethics may be seen as 'wide from the Business of this Book'. At the same time, he hopes those who do not 'relish' Moll's repentance will at least read to the end of the story. It would be a cruel criticism of such readers to say they enjoy the crime more than the repentance (which is what he has just said of them), or to say that they want the story to end tragically. This paragraph, then, implies a particular kind of reader: one who takes lascivious pleasure in reading about wickedness, and is bored by religion and morality. At the same time, Defoe hints that it is just such readers who are cruel: they are the ones who want Moll's story to end on the scaffold. Next to this speculation is placed an unjudgeable reality: Moll's story has 'wild and wicked' parts, and this 'best part'; and as for a tragic ending, although that did not happen, it was 'very likely to have been'. In short, having played with speculations about the place of moral instruction in her story, Moll's narrative returns quickly to the bedrock of truth: human behaviour and what happened.

Throughout our analysis of Moll's experiences in Newgate, we have found that religion and ethics bear a curious relation to the continuing naturalism of the narrative. Concepts of faith and right and wrong are intermittently mentioned but seem to occupy another sphere from that inhabited by the characters, and by real quandaries or events. At the same time, such concepts are treated with respect, and attain reality at certain emotional – and physical – cruxes in the protagonist's life. We can regard Robinson's illness, and Moll's imminent execution, as equally 'physical' crises. It is difficult to describe this detached relation between religion and ethics on the one hand, and nature on the other. There are elements of cynicism, sympathy, amusement, and seriousness all at work at the same time, as any mention of spirituality is brought back down to earth by ensuing events and concerns. Before moving on to look at an extract from *Roxana*, we may quote Moll's reaction to discovering her own incest, as a perfect example of the insoluble we have been attempting to define:

> I was now the most unhappy of all Women in the World: O had the Story never been told me, all had been well; it had been no Crime to have lain with my Husband, since as to his being my Relation, I had known nothing of it. (*MF* 136)

Analysis: *Roxana*, pp. 104–5

Now let us turn to *Roxana*. In this extract, she discusses the morality or otherwise of her liaison with the Prince in Paris; and rejects the idea that she should seek guidance from Catholic priests:

> To finish the Felicity of this Part, I must not forget, that the Devil had play'd a new Game with me, and prevail'd with me to satisfie myself with this Amour, as a lawful thing; that a Prince of such Grandeur, and Majesty; so infinitely superior to me; and one who had made such an Introduction by an uparalell'd Bounty, I could not resist; and therefore, that it was very Lawful for me to do it, being at that time perfectly single, and uningag'd to any other Man; as I was, most certainly, by the unaccountable Absence of my first Husband, and the Murther of my Gentleman, who went for my second.
>
> It cannot be doubted but that I was the easier to perswade myself of the Truth of such a Doctrine as this, when it was so much for my Ease, and for the Repose of my Mind, to have it so.
>
> In Things we wish, 'tis easie to deceive;
> What we would have, we willingly believe.
>
> Besides, I had no Casuists to resolve this Doubt; the same Devil that put this into my Head, bade me go to any of the *Romish* Clergy, and under the Pretence of Confession, state the Case exactly, and I should see they would either resolve it to be no Sin at all, or absolve me upon the easiest Pennance: This I had a strong Inclination to try, but I know not what Scruple put me off of it, for I could never bring myself to like having to do with those Priests; and tho' it was strange that I, who had thus prostituted my Chastity, and given up all Sence of Virtue, in two such particular Cases, living a Life of open Adultery, should scruple any thing; yet so it was, I argued with myself, that I could not be a Cheat in

> any thing that was esteem'd Sacred; that I could not be of one Opinion, and then pretend myself to be of another; nor could I go to Confession, who knew nothing of the Manner of it, and should betray myself to the Priest, to be a Hugonot, and then might come into Trouble; but, in short, tho' I was a Whore, yet I was a Protestant Whore, and could not act as if I was Popish, upon any Account whatsoever.
>
> But, I say, I satisfy'd myself with the surprizing Occasion, that, as it was all irresistable, so it was all lawful; for that Heaven would not suffer us to be punish'd for that which it was not possible for us to avoid; and with these Absurdities I kept Conscience from giving me any considerable Disturbance in all this Matter; and I was as perfectly easie as to the Lawfulness of it, as if I had been Marry'd to the Prince, and had had no other Husband: So possible is it for us to roll ourselves up in Wickedness, till we grow invulnerable by Conscience; and that Centinel once doz'd, sleeps fast, not to be awaken'd while the Tide of Pleasure continues to flow, or till something dark and dreadful brings us to ourselves again.
>
> I have, I confess, wonder'd at the Stupidity that my intellectual part was under all that while; what Lethargick Fumes doz'd the Soul; and how it was possible that I, who in the Case before, where the Temptation was many ways more forcible, and the Arguments stronger, and more irrisistable, was yet under a continued Inquietude on account of the wicked Life I led, could now live in the most profound Tranquility, and with an uninterrupted Peace, nay, even rising up to Satisfaction, and Joy, and yet in a more palpable State of Adultery than before; for before, my Gentleman who call'd me Wife, had the Pretence of his Wife being parted from him, refusing to do the Duty of her Office as a Wife to him; as for me, my Circumstances were the same; but as for the Prince, as he had a fine and extraordinary Lady, or Princess, of his own; so he had had two or three Mistresses more besides me, and made no Scruple of it at all. (*R* 104–5)

In this passage, Roxana displays her understanding of rationalisation and picks apart the excuses that helped her to reconcile being the Prince's mistress, with her conscience. Each paragraph is a single sentence; and they show characteristic structural features. So, for example, the first paragraph begins by stating that Roxana believed her new liaison to be 'a lawful thing'; then, the sentence proceeds to demonstrate that statement in greater detail and in a balanced form. The prince's irresistible superiority, and her single status, sit either side of the rationale that 'I could not resist; and therefore, that it was very Lawful'. We have come across this structure before, where a statement is then elaborated in a more detailed re-statement. However, in the present case, subsequent paragraphs both add to, and pick apart, the same materials with which Roxana begins her account. So, for example, the first paragraph ends with her insistence that she was 'perfectly single, and uningag'd to any other Man'; but does not refer to the Prince's marital status. The final (fifth) paragraph ends on the same subject, but this time mentions the Prince's wife. It is as if the incomplete idea, expressed as 'very Lawful' in the first paragraph, is later completed by truths Roxana ignored at first. We could say that the sentence and paragraph structures imitate the rationalisation by which Roxana excuses her conduct. Her actual moral situation is revealed in stages, as she revisits each issue, adding something each time.

Amusingly, however, this effect of incremental elaboration happens in both directions: that is, Roxana simultaneously develops her moral insight, and elaborates her self-excusing arguments. So, for example, the argument that the Prince was 'so infinitely superior . . . I could not resist' and therefore submission was 'Lawful' is given an additional gloss in paragraph four: 'Heaven would not suffer us to be punish'd for that which it was not possible for us to avoid.' So, not only does this passage play upon retrospective narrative to reveal the insufficiency of her excuses, but, at the same time, we are given a taste of her mind's resourcefulness, building what she calls the devil's 'new Game' by inventing new reasons to bolster her self-excuse as she goes along. Here, the power of the Prince's superiority is suddenly given Heaven's seal of approval.

Roxana makes three clear statements about rationalisation. She found it 'easier to perswade myself' because it was 'for my Ease', and her tag couplet ends 'What we would have, we willingly believe'; then, she reflects 'So possible is it for us to roll ourselves up in Wickedness', before wondering at her own self-deceptions: 'the Stupidity that my intellectual Part was under all that while; what Lethargic Fumes doz'd the Soul', where the image ('Stupidity' meaning 'stupor' rather than the modern 'idiocy') is one of being drugged, so that the conscience sleeps. There is, then, no doubt about the moral judgement

Roxana retrospectively applies to her behaviour: she was sinful, she was a whore, and she was living in adultery; her moral state was worse than in her previous liaison, for she was now in 'a more palpable state of Adultery than before'. At the same time, however, we have seen how the structure of sentences and paragraphs plays, as it were, both sides against the middle, being fertile in arguments on each side, so that the overall effect is one of satiric amusement and excitement. The older Roxana's moralising, being only one ingredient, never renders the narrative solemn. To show how Defoe achieves such a feat, we will take a closer look at the third paragraph of our extract.

It will be helpful to summarise the sections of this sentence-paragraph, in our habitual manner:

1. I had no moral adviser
2. The devil suggested that Catholic confession would either excuse me or give easy absolution
3. I always felt unwilling to be involved with Catholic priests
4. I was a brazen adulteress, but I scrupled to cheat in sacred matters
5. I could not pretend a false opinion
6. Besides, I did not know how to behave at Catholic confession, the priest would notice, and I would get into trouble as a Huguenot
7. I was a protestant whore, and could not bring myself to act Catholic

What an insoluble moral quagmire Defoe has created here. Roxana is astonished at her own double standard – she calls herself a prostitute yet scruples to lie to a priest; but the remainder of her explanation provides parallel motives for her reluctance. To her credit, Roxana finds it uncongenial to pretend a hypocritical opinion; and she shies away from cheating the sacred. These, then, are the moral scruples that keep her from the priests. At the same time, Roxana does not know how to behave like a Catholic, and she has a very practical fear of getting into trouble if her Protestantism is discovered (in France, after the repeal of the edict of Nantes in 1685). As usual, then, Defoe provides equivalent moral and practical motives, and we must accept both; but there are also further elements in Roxana's brief flirtation with Catholicism. Why would she think of going to confession in the first place? She tells us: because a Catholic priest would probably 'resolve it [her prostitution & adultery] to be no Sin at all' or would give easy penance. In other words, she regards the 'Popish' church as corrupt and immoral. In that case, we may ask, what would be the point? How could a corrupt absolution ease her conscience? Here, Roxana seems to treat Catholicism as just another form of self-excuse. But then she tells us of her scruples: she did not like to lie about anything sacred. She seems unsure whether she would be lying to a priest, which might not matter, or to God, which would. Then comes her practical fear, the danger of government persecution; and finally, Roxana turns the entire question off with a joke which refers to a famous remark of Nell Gwynn, about being 'a Protestant Whore'.

The reader laughs, and we share Roxana's anti-Catholic prejudice as she shows her English Protestant pride and uses its vocabulary in 'Romish', 'those Priests' and 'Popish'. Simultaneously, we are entirely tangled in Defoe's moral web. There were both moral and practical reasons for avoiding confession: Roxana's frank nature recoils from it, and it could be dangerous. Then, confession would only reinforce her in sin, being corrupt; but at the same time, it is sacred. Finally, we remember from the start of the paragraph that it was 'the same Devil['s]' idea in the first place; and we notice that Roxana avoids seeking such religious advice; and that she has turned her whoredom into an entertaining joke by the end of the paragraph. The reader is manipulated by her frankness, her honesty, her humour, and by sharing her anti-Popish prejudice along the way, further complicating our moral judgement. Notice, finally, that the word 'Casuists', or the advice Roxana needs, has commonly two definitions. A casuist either uses 'specious or excessively subtle reasoning intended to rationalize or mislead', just as Roxana does herself throughout this episode, or he helps with 'the determination of right and wrong in questions of conduct or conscience'.[2] Does Roxana lack and need a 'casuist'? The answer, according to these definitions, is the same as all the other answers available in this moral quagmire: it depends.

The remainder of *Roxana* provides an equally unresolved moral context. At the end of the novel, we are fairly certain that Amy murders Susan, and rejoins Roxana when she comes over to Holland. The final sentence tells of dreadful calamities in Roxana's life, mentioning both 'the Blast of Heaven' and 'my Repentance'; yet in both cases the verb is 'seem'd'. Heaven's punishment 'seem'd to follow the Injury done the poor Girl', but we are not sure whether this is or only seems to be the work of Providence; then, Roxana's repentance 'seem'd to be only the Consequence of my Misery', ambiguously describing either true remorse or self-pity. The only certainty in this final paragraph is that Roxana's misery 'was' the consequence of her 'Crime'. However, describing these 'Calamities' as the 'very Reverse of our former Good Days' implies that her career as a courtesan is not the 'Crime' she repents. Only the murder of Susan causes her 'Misery'. This final sentence/paragraph, then, needs as careful reading as the paragraph we have analysed above. We need to consider all the elements, including reference to the 'former Good Days' the two uses of 'seem'd' which cut in opposite directions, and the circumscribed definite statement with which *Roxana* ends.

The extracts we have analysed in this chapter remind us that we are studying three distinct works. We have commented that Robinson's intellect does not naturally hold abstract or religious concepts for long, and neither does he analyse such ideas acutely. Then, we have found that Moll's emotional crisis plunges her into an episode of spiritual ecstasy and what appears to be a sincere experience of faith and repentance. Finally, Roxana demonstrates a complex analysis of her own rationalisations together with clear statements of moral rectitude; and yet at the same time she weaves a self-undercutting web in which moral and pragmatic motives, and human and religious values, all co-exist. In short, each of Defoe's narrators is an individual and unlike the other two. On the other hand, there are elements in common between the three treatments of morality and religion we are studying.

Concluding Discussion

First, let us acknowledge that Defoe is a master weaver of different and mutually counterbalancing moral threads. Then, we will propose a few general statements, and briefly discuss each one.

- When religion is mentioned, the narrator is always provided with a pragmatic motive as a co-existent foil to spiritual or theological ideas.

We have found this feature in most of our studies in the present chapter. In the case of *Roxana*, the narrator has a well-founded practical caution that dissuades her from going to confession: it could be dangerous to her as a Protestant in France. Roxana adds to this her conviction that Catholic absolution is corrupt, and her own reluctance to 'cheat' in any matter that is sacred. In *Moll Flanders*, we sympathise with, and respect, Moll's religious fervour, whipped up by the Minister's skilful counsel; and we believe that she would 'freely have gone out that Minute to Execution' while the mood lasted. On the other hand, any willingness to sacrifice her life is a temporary state in Moll; and she has the strongest possible pragmatic motive to repent. Even in constituent details, Defoe mixes the pragmatic with the spiritual: for example, Moll confesses in order to relieve her soul, but only after she has been assured of confidentiality. Nobody – least of all the reader – would expect her further to incriminate herself to the authorities. Then, the authorities have only limited knowledge of Moll's crimes, a fact she later uses as grounds for complaint about her sentence. In our analysis of *Robinson Crusoe*, we found slightly different characteristics: there, Robinson alternates regularly between pragmatic physical action and the intermittent development of his religion. This alternation often seems to be treated comically, such as when he befuddles himself with brandy and tobacco fumes while trying to read the Bible.

Elsewhere in *Robinson Crusoe*, however, there are many instances of the 'dual motive' characteristic we are discussing. See, for example, Robinson's internal debate about attacking the cannibals. He hesitates because 'this was not only a very desperate attempt, and might miscarry; but on the other hand, I had greatly scrupled the lawfulness of it to me; and my heart trembled at the thoughts of shedding so much blood, tho' it was for my deliverance' (*RC* 157). Robinson's hesitations in attacking the savages are canvassed over a number of pages. He is sometimes 'so fill'd with indignation at the sight' of cannibalism that he is in a 'murthering humour'. Then he thinks he would become 'no less a murtherer than they were' and 'perhaps much more so' should he then need to kill hundreds more of them (all from *RC* 145–6). Robinson's previous concerns about the 'lawfulness' of killing savages proceeded from his questions about how Providence can allow their existence. Robinson worries this problem on pages 129–39, through his theory of nations, reflections on the Spaniards, and definition of what is his own business. Robinson's mind is a welter of shock, horror at cannibalism, anger, disgust, and fear for himself. He finally comments that from this episode he learned to trust and follow his own intuition, something he calls a 'secret hint' that may even run counter to 'sense, our own inclination, and perhaps business' which 'call'd to go the other way, yet a strange impression upon the mind, from we know not what springs, and by we know not what power, shall over-rule us to go this way; and it shall afterwards appear, that had we gone that way which we should have gone, and even to our imagination ought to have gone, we should have been ruin'd and lost' (*RC* 139). It seems that Robinson ascribes to Providence as a 'secret hint', the instinct for caution and self-preservation that counsels him to avoid an open attack on the savages. Here, then, the pragmatic motive of self-preservation is re-interpreted by Robinson, who believes it to be a gift of Providence. To return upon our own argument, however, there are also ethical reasons for his restraint. In short, religious ideas and practical motives are thoroughly intermixed.

Robinson's self-restraint in this matter has an additional resonance for the history of the colonising era, because he refrains from imposing his European and Christian values upon the native population by force. In these pages, Robinson decides not to carry out the kind of genocide recorded, for example, by Bartolomé de Las Casas in his *Short Account of the Destruction of the Indies* (1552). Robinson cannot understand how Providence allows savages to live so differently from Europeans, but he wisely decides to leave dispensing justice to God. We may well wonder how different the history of the world might have been had all colonial powers followed Robinson's example.

- There are different forms of morality. 'Conventional' mores are thoroughly exposed for their hollowness in all three texts. Much comedy is made of these; and the characters live in an instrumental relation to convention.

We have met the comedy of Robinson's hindsight a number of times. We noted, for example, the parody of sermon-style in which he repents his 'uncommon wickedness', and the struggles of his intellect both to hold on to abstract concepts that repeatedly 'wore off' and to develop religious understanding in the first place. We have also been critical of his father's negative philosophy, which Robinson, with hindsight, holds up to us as a pattern of righteousness; and we will have reason to comment further on the 'middle station' ideal in our next chapter. In *Moll Flanders*, comedy is also present, as we recognise that repentance – however sincere it may be at the time – is part of the means by which she survives; and as we notice the natural erosion of her moods – even the best of them. For example, only a few lines after declaring her willingness to die repentant, Moll finds her name on the death warrant, and comments that 'a terrible blow this was to my new Resolutions'. Moll still feels remorse, but at the same time her spiritual ardour has abated, she is back to her more natural state, and hopes to stay alive. In *Roxana*, we find ourselves in the presence of a more analytical narrator, one who provides us with a critique of hypocrisy and self-deception, as well as a powerfully argued assault upon the institution of marriage (for discussion of which, see Chapter 4 below). *Roxana* provides much incidental satire and comedy, such as the paragraph concerning Catholic confession that we studied in this chapter. Overall, *Roxana* suggests a radical overhaul of conventional morality. It is a significant challenge to conventional ideas, for example, that Roxana believes her 'Crime' to be the murder of Susan, rather than her scandalous life as a courtesan.

To say that the characters live 'in an instrumental relation to conventional morality' is, on one level, self-evident of both Moll and Roxana: the former spends much of her life as bigamist, whore and thief; the latter makes her fortune as a courtesan. Both of these narrators seek an appearance of respectability, and make some effort to hide their peccadilloes. However, it is clear that the real misfortune, the real sin in the eyes of the world, is to be exposed. Both Moll and Roxana adopt different moral imperatives in private, from those society imposes in public. It is noticeable, for example, that both of them find themselves simultaneously married and single: Moll returns from America, her brother/husband still alive, and Roxana's first husband disappears. Neither narrator scruples to begin a new relationship, in Moll's case eventually marrying twice in quick succession. We have seen how Roxana calmed her conscience about her landlord's guilt, using the argument that his legal wife refused to fulfil her duty as a wife. When Moll decides to marry a fourth time, she is disturbed that 'this innocent Gentleman [is] going to be abus'd by me!' but resolves 'Well, if I must be his Wife, . . . I'll be a true Wife to him'; and further reflects that she will 'make him amends, if possible, by what he shall see, for the Cheats and Abuses I put upon him, which he does not see' (all from *MF* 244). Both Moll and Roxana, then, live according to a private morality, making decisions with which they can feel comfortable. They only square these with public mores in the sense of keeping up a respectable appearance where possible. In other words, as our statement suggests, both of these narrators live in an instrumental relation to convention.

In this regard, Robinson needs to be considered separately, simply because there is no social standard of morality or respectability upon his island. Robinson's relation to morality, therefore, is largely apparent from the early part of his story; and from his occasional meditations during his solitude. For the present, we can comment that Robinson is less perceptive about his own rationalisations than either of the two female narrators; and that his moral reflections are unsophisticated and inconsistent. Robinson also repeatedly returns to his natural level of thinking that Virginia Woolf calls the 'earthenware pot': unadorned practicality. However, it does appear towards the end of his island life that he acts by a personal morality which is filtered through practical self-interest. So, for example, he distinguishes between ringleaders and others when dealing with the mutineers to regain control of the ship; and uses a judicious blend of leniency and threat to control his citizens. It seems that unnecessary cruelty, or acts of revenge, is not part of Robinson's nature: to this extent there are signs of a standard of decent, humane behaviour. This renders Robinson sympathetic, and Moll's and Roxana's private moralities do the same for them.

- There is no unequivocal sight of spiritual experience: there are a series of rationalisations concerning guilt, providence, the devil and temptation, and so on, often short-lived. There are very rare moments which may appear truly 'spiritual' but even these are undercut by doubt.

Our studies of extracts in this chapter have demonstrated the relevance of this statement quite clearly. We remember, for example, Robinson's progressive assertions that one or another occasion may have been the first time he uttered a prayer 'in the true Sense of the Words'; and how practical demands alternate with fledgling religious ideas in his head. We also remember Moll's brief spiritual ecstasy, how quickly it abates, and Roxana's ability to tiptoe around questions of sin, confession, and guilt. Certainly, we have not found a consistent religious theme advanced by the author: Defoe covers his tracks assiduously, usually by constructing multiple motives for the protagonist.

So, both morality and religion seem to exist in a rather drifting, intermittent, and detached form in the novels. They are a part of each narrator's mental 'superstructure', by which we mean that each narrator has had particular moral and religious nostrums installed in their brains either during their upbringing or through the development of hindsight as they attempt, retrospectively, to make coherent sense of their lives. Consequently, they refer to these mores; but they have surprisingly little connection to or influence upon behaviour or events.

- Speculatively, we can suggest that the narrators exist within an area bereft of moral/religious values, so that they have room for amoral manoeuvre to exercise their method of living. Their way of approaching and dealing with life is a combination of self-help, together with some qualities such as affection, loyalty, pity, and the humane treatment of others – qualities we have discussed as a sort of 'private morality'. Only occasionally do they meet a social boundary, and even then such boundaries flow and change position. The narrators' ethical position could be thought of, metaphorically, as the moral equivalent of early colonialism because they are settling, clearing, and building their own morality.

For the present, this suggestion is no more than a metaphor. However, we can remark for the present that all three of our texts treat protagonists who are in innovatory circumstances, and who challenge conventional society from the outside. As Roxana attempts to carve out a successful life for a woman, outside marriage; as Moll lives as bigamist, mistress, and thief in the unseen spaces between other members of society; and as Robinson has to carve out his solitary existence on the island, we can think of all three having to discover, test, and implement morality afresh.

- Finally, we may ask why these narratives exhibit such uncertainty and instability in religious or spiritual ideas? One possible reply is that the three narrators are human, and Defoe depicts them as such. Consequently, their motives and sentiments will always contain an admixture of personal pragmatism; and will always be subject to change, just as people must adapt to changing circumstances. It would be irrational to expect Defoe's narrators to behave as divinities, since they are not such; and as they are faced by unstable circumstances in the world, they cannot maintain any single principle inviolate.

We must thus draw a strict distinction between the mores and religious beliefs of Defoe's narrators and the author's own religious faith. Our point is not that Defoe lacked faith: it is only that nothing unequivocally identifiable as faith can be reliably found in his protagonists. Instead, his narrators' all-too-human ideas of religion are visible.

Methods of Analysis

1. We have again used the approaches described in Chapter 1. In particular, we have again found it useful to summarise the constituent parts of sentences and paragraphs, in order to appreciate their different structures, and the pattern of ideas brought together in each one. For example, we found the structure of Robinson's paragraph on self-pity, revealingly, to ramble in a manner different from that of the more tightly knit sentences leading up to it; and we found psychological processes subtly reflected in, for example, Moll's generalisation of her repentance as a common human condition; and in Roxana's turning off the confession question with her joke about being a 'Protestant Whore'.

2. Summarising a paragraph as a series of short statements also helps us to discern the combination of pragmatic and ethical/religious motives commonly co-existent in Defoe's narratives. This technique can be taken a stage further, by trying to label each statement as expressing either a pragmatic sentiment or a moral/religious one. Not all statements will fit one of these labels; but we can see how two kinds of motives are mixed, from those that do. Here is Roxana's 'confession' paragraph, analysed using this technique:
    - I had no moral adviser **[pragmatic]**
    - The devil suggested that Catholic confession would either excuse me or give easy absolution
    - I always felt unwilling to be involved with Catholic priests
    - I was a brazen adulteress, but I scrupled to cheat in sacred matters **[moral/religious]**
    - I could not pretend a false opinion **[moral/religious]**
    - Besides, I did not know how to behave at Catholic confession, the priest would notice, and I would get into trouble as a Huguenot **[pragmatic]**
    - I was a protestant whore, and could not bring myself to act Catholic
3. In this chapter we have also expanded our study, looking more widely in the texts. We have done this by thinking of the conclusions arrived at during close analysis of extracts, in relation to our knowledge of the text, to identify further passages to study, relevant to the theme in which we are interested. In *Robinson Crusoe*, for instance, this led us to look at the immediate context of his illness: the dream before our extract and his developing religious ideas afterwards. Then, thinking about places where Robinson has Providence in his thoughts led us to his internal debates about attacking cannibals. Similarly, thinking about Moll's relation to sin led us to revisit her discovery that she was married to her brother.

Suggested Work

To enlarge upon this chapter's focus on the ethical and religious development of Defoe's narratives, and develop your insight into these themes, study further relevant episodes, such as:

In ***Robinson Crusoe***: Look at pages 182–3, where Crusoe meditates the morality and righteousness of killing cannibals, then leaves such a difficult subject up to God to decide. Apply our techniques of analysis, in particular, to the paragraph beginning 'While I was making this March ... ' and ending ' ... I would not meddle with them': do this, first, by summarising the units and sections of the paragraph, statement by statement; then, by ascribing as many statements as will bear the labels, to either **pragmatic** or **ethical/religious** sentiments on Robinson's part.

In ***Moll Flanders***: On pages 232–5 Moll considers what to do with the child she has from her brief marriage to the highwayman, hears her 'governess's' opinion, and reflects upon the dependence and upbringing of children. The dilemma is, of course, how to get rid of the child. Moll's mental and emotional states and strategies are fascinating to study throughout this episode; but it may be particularly interesting to apply our analytical techniques to the paragraph on p. 163, beginning 'It is manifest to all that understand any thing of children ... '

In ***Roxana***: Look at pages 170–2, when Roxana is urged to set herself up in luxury, by *Amy*; and she reflects upon the differences between the lives of whores and wives. The two paragraphs that make up the bulk of page 171, and which describe wives and whores, respectively, will reward close study. In particular, it will be revealing to study summaries of these two paragraphs and relate your findings to Roxana's conventionally moral diction.

Each of these extracts will provide comedy, insight, contradiction, and moral puzzles enough – as have the extracts analysed in this chapter.

3

Society and Economics

This chapter considers how far Defoe can be regarded as a spokesman for or critic of the developing mercantile society about which he writes. There is much about colonial economics, merchants, and trade, in all three books. Robinson is a merchant at least three times, and his eventual fortune is earned from a Brazilian plantation; Moll becomes a Virginia planter twice; and Roxana's Dutch husband is a merchant. Additionally, Roxana and Moll both examine the roles of money, rank, and corruption in the old societies of England and Europe, as well as offer a revealing tour of the economics of sex and marriage. Defoe's views are difficult to locate, because of what Ellen Pollak calls the 'kaleidoscopic' effect of his narratives. We have noticed narrators with ambivalent motives, facing rapid changes in circumstances, what we might call the 'instability' of Defoe's fictional worlds. We attempt the question nonetheless, and begin by looking at an extract from each novel.

Analysis: *Robinson Crusoe*, pp. 31–3

Robinson begins to grow rich on his plantation in the Brasils, after surviving a North Sea shipwreck, enslavement to a Turk, and wild beasts on the shores of Africa. However, he is tempted to undertake a new adventure:

But as abus'd prosperity is oftentimes made the very means of our greatest adversity, so was it with me. I went on the next year with great success in my plantation: I raised fifty great rolls of tobacco on my own ground, more than I had disposed of for necessaries among my neighbours; and these fifty rolls being each of above a 100 Wt. were well cur'd and laid by against the return of the fleet from *Lisbon*: and now increasing in business and in wealth, my head began to be full of projects and undertakings beyond my reach; such as are indeed often the ruin of the best heads in business.

Had I continued in the station I was now in, I had room for all the happy things to have yet befallen me, for which my father so earnestly recommended a quiet retired life, and of which he had so sensibly describ'd the middle station of life to be full of; but other things attended me, and I was still to be the wilful agent of all my own miseries; and particularly to encrease my fault and double the reflection upon my self, which in my future sorrows I should have leisure to make; all these miscarriages were procured by my apparent obstinate adhering to my foolish inclination of wandring abroad and pursuing that inclination, in contradiction to the clearest views of doing my self good in a fair and plain pursuit of those prospects and those measures of life, which Nature and Providence concurred to present me with, and to make my duty.

As I had once done thus in my breaking away from my parents, so I could not be content now, but I must go and leave the happy view I had of being a rich and thriving man in my new plantation, only to pursue a rash and immoderate desire of rising faster than the nature of the thing admitted; and thus I cast my self down again into the deepest gulph of human misery that ever man fell into, or perhaps could be consistent with life and a state of health in the world.

To come then by the just degrees, to the particulars of this part of my story; you may suppose, that having now lived almost four years in the *Brasils*, and beginning to thrive and prosper very well upon my plantation; I had not only learn'd the language, but had contracted acquaintances and friendship among my fellow-planters, as well as among the merchants at St. *Salvadore*, which was our port; and that in my discourses among them, I had frequently given them an account of my two voyages to the coast of *Guinea*, the manner of trading with the *Negroes* there, and how easy it was to purchase upon the coast, for trifles, such as beads, toys, knives, scissars, hatchets, bits of glass, and the like; not only gold dust, *Guinea* grains, elephants teeth, &c. but *Negroes* for the service of the *Brasils*, in great numbers.

> They listened always very attentively to my discourses on these heads, but especially to that part which related to the buying *Negroes*, which was a trade at that time not only not far entred into, but as far as it was, had been carried on by the Assiento's, or permission of the Kings of *Spain* and *Portugal*, and engross'd in the publick, so that few *Negroes* were brought, and those excessive dear.
>
> It happen'd, being in company with some merchants and planters of my acquaintance, and talking of those things very earnestly, three of them came to me the next morning, and told me they had been musing very much upon what I had discoursed with them of, the last night, and they came to make a secret proposal to me; and after enjoining me secrecy, they told me, that they had a mind to fit out a ship to go to *Guinea*, that they had all plantations as well as I, and were straiten'd for nothing so much as servants; that as it was a trade that could not be carried on, because they could not publickly sell the *Negroes* when they came home, so they desired to make but one voyage, to bring the *Negroes* on shoar privately, and divide them among their own plantations; and in a word, the question was, whether I would go their super-cargo in the ship to manage the trading part upon the coast of *Guinea*? And they offer'd me that I should have my equal share of the *Negroes* without providing any part of the stock.
>
> This was a fair proposal it must be confess'd, had it been made to any one that had not had a settlement and plantation of his own to look after, which was in a fair way of coming to be very considerable, and with a good stock upon it. But for me that was thus entered and established, and had nothing to do but go on as I had begun for three or four years more, and to have sent for the other hundred Pound from *England*, and who in that time, and with that little addition, could scarce ha' fail'd of being worth three or four thousand Pounds Sterling, and that encreasing too; for me to think of such a voyage, was the most preposterous thing that ever man in such circumstances could be guilty of. (*RC* 31–3)

We immediately notice that Robinson laces his narrative with self-critical hindsight; and that we learn much about colonial economics, including the planters' scheme for a slaving voyage. To gain an overview, however, we will benefit from summarising Robinson's seven paragraphs, thus:

1. I prospered, but my head was still full of foolish projects.
2. If I had remained on the plantation, I could have lived a happy life in the middle station; but I left, which led me to misery.
3. As when I ran away from home, like an idiot I left my prosperity, which led me to misery.
4. I had made friends, and often told them about my Guinea voyages, and how cheaply one could buy Negro slaves.
5. My friends listened, particularly about the slaves. Slave dealers needed a royal licence then, which made slaves very expensive.
6. Three planters proposed a secret voyage to buy slaves, and asked me to manage the trading in return for a share of the slaves.
7. This was a good offer for a man without a plantation; but for me to leave on such a voyage was madness.

This summary highlights considerable repetition of ideas: Robinson castigates his own restless nature in paragraphs 1, 2, 3, and 7, for example; and he refers to his quarrel with his parents in both paragraphs 2 and 3. As for the story, we discover events in a disorderly manner. Only paragraphs 4 and 6 provide narrative of the time before Robinson left the Brasils: we learn that he told other planters about his African voyages, whereupon they proposed their scheme. Otherwise, this passage reveals nothing more than that Robinson prospered. On the other hand, we learn something about later events: that he became the author of his own 'miseries', and fell into 'the deepest gulph of human misery that ever man fell into'; and there are hints about how this would come to pass, for 'projects and undertakings beyond my reach' are often the 'ruin of the best heads in business'. We know that Robinson will accept the planters' offer: his self-castigations lead to the statement that for him to accept would be 'the most preposterous thing', and we are therefore sure that he will do just that. In summary, then, this passage is heavily weighted with Robinson's morality of hindsight, but only one event is partly narrated, while forewarnings about the future and references to the past are incorporated.

Robinson seems to use two vocabularies: there is one kind of diction for the course he believes he should have followed, and another, disapproving language for the course he (foolishly) chose. We notice the words 'fair', 'good', 'happy', and 'increase' are repeated, and bolstered by various uses of 'prosperity', 'rich and thriving', and a number of terms that sound judicious, almost as if put down in a legal document, such as 'in a fair way', 'considerable', 'entered and established', and 'content'. All of this language is connected together by the reference to Robinson's father, who had 'so earnestly recommended a quiet retired life, and of which he had so sensibly describ'd the middle station of life to be full of'. This vein of approval, couched in moderate terms, provides a strong and consistent thread of persuasion throughout our extract: Robinson is persuading us that he was wrong to leave his plantation.

The other vocabulary – that of excess, impetuousness, and so on – imposes a further pressure of persuasion upon us. Robinson's decision is called 'abus'd prosperity'; and his plans are twice described as unrealistic, being 'projects and undertakings beyond my reach', and 'desire of rising faster than the nature of the thing admitted'. These ideas were like an intoxication: his 'head began to be full of' them; he was 'wilful', 'obstinate', 'could not' be content but 'must' be 'rash and immoderate'. When, finally, he calls his own action 'preposterous', Robinson has laid the groundwork by describing his restlessness as a kind of mental illness. The claims made by Robinson's persuasive hindsight are, ironically, equally extreme. The prosperity Robinson abandons when he leaves is a gift 'which Nature and Providence concurred to present me with'. In other words, the moderate route to wealth is God's will: so, not only are Robinson's dreams impetuous and unrealistic because 'beyond my reach' and too fast for 'nature', but also they are contrary to God's will. Robinson is attempting to persuade us, in fact, that he flew in the face of Providence: he rejected his father's advice for a second time, but also, he rejected God's gift of prosperity. It is for this reason that Robinson believes he abandoned his 'duty'.

We should notice, in passing, that he shows no qualms about the morality of slavery or slaving. The merchants who came to him made 'a fair proposal it must be confess'd', and he would have been right to accept were he not already a prosperous planter.

We have remarked that this extract subjects the reader to considerable persuasive pressure; and that Defoe skilfully draws in events from both past and future of the narrative in order to interpret Robinson's departure from the Brasils. So, what is the final effect of our narrator's effort? We are subjected to persuasion: but are we persuaded? Let us examine Robinson's claims.

First, Robinson returns to the beginning of his story, and remembers his father's advice, even going so far as to remind us of the phrases 'the middle station of life' and a 'quiet retired life'. There are two problems with this reference. First, as we have previously noticed, Mr Crusoe senior described his 'middle station' in a negative manner – lacking 'disasters' and 'vicissitudes', yes, but also lacking all activity – and in potentially self-satiric language, going 'silently and smoothly' through the world and 'comfortably' out of it (all from *RC* 6). So, as readers we respond ambivalently to the elder Crusoe's philosophy. Secondly, how does this reference apply to Robinson? We will discuss the economics of the colonising age in a moment; for now, it is enough to remark that Robinson's 'prosperity' and 'increase' leading him to become 'rich and thriving' and quickly worth 'three or four thousand': in other words, the prosperity he expects in the Brasils, has nothing to do with the 'middle station' and a 'quiet retired life'. Rather, they suggest a man whose aim is to become rich; and they are the fruit of Robinson's disobedience. Far from a 'quiet retired' life, he embraced a seafaring adventure. This led him into slavery, escape, and some hardships, but it is also the reason why he is becoming rich on the other side of the world, rather than trying to be as lifeless as possible in an English backwater. So, calling his father into evidence may only arouse our suspicions: is our narrator's opinion sound, or is it a lot of nonsense?

Robinson's second claim is that he grasped 'beyond my reach' and tried to accelerate too fast for 'nature'. In other words, he asks us to believe that the very fabric of reality is tied to a moderate pace that cannot be speeded up. Does this claim hold water? There are two possible answers. First, hindsight tells Robinson and us that the slaving voyage was a disaster. The ship was wrecked, Robinson was marooned, and he spent 28 years on his island. That is what happened, so perhaps the decision to set sail was foolish. The second answer is quite different, however. If we consider Robinson's decision at the time when he made it, it seems less foolish. He had already undertaken two slaving voyages to the Guinea coast, one of which was extremely profitable. The planters' offer 'was a fair proposal it must be confess'd': Robinson stood to gain slaves at no cost; and as 'they all had plantations as well as I, and were straiten'd for nothing so much as servants', we can argue that the voyage was a sensible way to ensure his future prosperity. Sooner or later Robinson would need labourers: why not fetch them now?

These two answers are diametrically opposed: was it a foolish decision (as it turned out), or was it a good idea that (by chance) went wrong? What these two answers actually do is to raise radical questions concerning Robinson's hindsight and concerning Providence itself: is the world an expression of some divine or providential purpose; or, do events happen by chance? Of course, it is equally possible to believe that Providence exists, but is beyond Robinson's understanding. Defoe presents us with these questions and possibilities, but leaves us without a definitive answer.

Does the story suggest that Providence ruled Robinson's life? The answer seems to be no. He experienced both successes and disasters following his first leaving home; and as readers, we are not convinced by Crusoe senior's idea that the only way to avoid the brickbats of fate is to keep your head down. Finally, we notice that Robinson becomes prosperous again, after he has committed the 'ORIGINAL SIN' of rejecting his father's advice and his duty to Providence. In short, events do not consistently support the idea of providential punishment; they are merely illogical. It is Robinson who is struggling to make sense out of his existence. So, the persuasive pressure we feel is always ambivalent in its effect. It attempts to sustain a superstructure of belief. Its flaws highlight the role of chance in the story, and convey to us the urgency of Robinson's desire to have an explanation for his existence.

So far, we have focused upon Robinson's invocation of Providence in relation to his construction of a personal belief-system. We should now turn to what this extract tells us of economics. The first paragraph is filled with information: Robinson tells us that he set aside 50 hundredweight rolls of tobacco to sell to Europe that year. This success, we know, is due to the fact that he quadrupled his money by selling the cargo sent from England; and that he bought a Negro slave, another servant, and took the bondman brought for him by the Captain. In other words, he now had three men working for him on his plantation and prospered accordingly. He had invested £100 in goods, and spent 220 pieces of eight on land. The £100 was half Robinson's saved profit from his first slaving voyage, which was, in its turn, the product of £40 probably (but indirectly) provided by his mother; while the pieces of eight were his profit from selling the boat and other goods he took from his Turkish master, the animal skins from Africa, and the boy Xury. Robinson decided to invest in a plantation, from 'seeing how well the planters liv'd, and how they grew rich suddenly' (*RC* 29). Our first paragraph, then, shows the investment beginning to pay off.

As we have noted, Robinson makes a persistent effort to connect the prospects of the plantation with the elder Mr Crusoe's philosophy and advice; and we have remarked that this is a flawed argument, because Robinson never aimed at the 'middle station', but on the contrary wished to copy those who 'grew rich suddenly'. The new economic information in the remainder of our extract concerns the slaving project itself. This consists of several characteristic elements. First, there is the opportunity to turn an enormous profit: Robinson explains how you can exchange worthless 'trifles, such as beads, toys, knives, scissars', for gold, ivory, and slaves. Secondly, there is a shortage: the planters are 'straiten'd for nothing so much as servants'. Thirdly, there is official control in the form of the Kings' 'assiento's' holding a monopoly, which serves further to inflate the price of Negroes. Finally, there is what we can call the consortium: the group of three planters who decide to solve their labour problem through self-help. This is the economic context within which Robinson and his fellow planters live. Immense profits running to thousands of per cents; regulation that artificially inflates prices and is easily circumvented; and a shortage. What more could a capitalist want?

Robinson's experience teaches him of a world consistent with these circumstances. He profited enormously from a slaving voyage; he has just enjoyed quadrupling another investment; he even managed to make a good profit from selling the boat and the boy he stole (admittedly while escaping slavery); and his conscience about selling the loyal Xury was calmed by the Captain's promise to set him free: after 10 years, and provided he turns Christian. None of the events in Robinson's life so far have attracted his criticism, except for his decision to 'act the rebel to their [his parents'] authority' and leave home. Equally, now, Robinson is comfortable with an illegal project: it is simply a matter of being able to 'bring the *Negroes* on shoar privately'; and his conscience is not troubled about buying or owning slaves. The only equalising element in Robinson's history so far is the fact that he has been a slave himself. Of course, these details sound like the worst excesses of capitalist/imperialist colonialism: pure exploitation without conscience; and we will have to consider how we, as modern readers, respond to such a text. Before we do so, however, there is more to say about Robinson's own apparent opinion.

Robinson's retrospective narrative accepts his father's philosophy of the 'middle station' and urges moderation in desire and action. However, in Robinson's world people become rich 'suddenly', opportunities for huge profits abound, everything – including human life – has a price, and laws count for little because people help themselves. What, then, has happened between the elder Crusoe's time and Robinson's? The answer is exploration, colonising, and settlement of the New World. The elder Crusoe inherited his philosophy from the past economic environments of Bremen and then England, European locations where business offered moderate opportunities and rewards. The 'middle station' philosophy is also reminiscent of medieval attitudes: the word 'Authority' and the concepts of Providence and Duty (to parents and to God) as well as exhortations to moderation (the medieval virtue of 'temperaunce') would echo of an earlier age to Defoe's readers.[1] The new situation, with its monstrous opportunities and amoral lawlessness, was ready for the younger generation to exploit and was becoming a source of undreamed-of wealth for the nations of Europe. In fact, Robinson's persuasive hindsight attempts to apply an outdated code to a new and fluid situation. That Robinson, the new man of the colonising era, believes in his father's nostrums is thus one of the most cutting ironies of the novel's social critique.

In this way, *Robinson Crusoe* has a powerful effect, provoking us to question many social and economic mores, but hardly ever expressed in words. The effect is produced by juxtaposition, that is, by placing ill-matched elements next to each other. In the extract we have been studying, satire is produced by the inappropriate juxtaposition of the elder Crusoe's philosophy of moderation, next to the lawless, opportunistic exploitation of the colonising era. These two are a bad fit; and as Robinson increasingly strives to impose his father's views retrospectively onto a world that resists them, so the mores of the narrative become increasingly uncertain.

We have studied an extract in which Robinson argues his father's opinion, and which plays upon the economics of adventure, trade, and colonies: the new commercial context of a growing wider world. This has raised issues regarding the international 'society' of mercantile exploitation, the new colonial class to which Robinson belongs. We should remember, however, that Robinson spends his final three island years in the company of Friday, which creates a sort of emblematic society of two; and Robinson's account of these years explores some of the most vexed questions of colonial history.

Analysis: *Robinson Crusoe*, pp. 165–6

We will begin by remarking the more personal aspects of Robinson's relationship with Friday. We read that Friday is 'a comely handsome fellow, perfectly well made' and, among other compliments on his appearance, Robinson includes 'something very manly in his face', the 'sweetness and softness' of his smile, 'a great vivacity and sparkling sharpness in his eyes', and that his skin colour has 'something very agreeable' in it (all from *RC* 162). The gushing lists of Friday's virtues – which foreground such qualities as 'affection' and 'fidelity' – suggest Robinson's strong response to the native's charm, and as we shall see, counterbalance his religious meditations. The value of this relationship is fully expressed when Robinson remarks how Friday is always 'so merry, so constantly diligent, and so pleas'd . . . that it was very pleasant to me to talk to him; and now my life began to be so easy, that I began to say to my self, that could I but have been safe from more savages, I cared not, if I was never to remove from the place while I lived' (*RC* 166).

This is Robinson's primary relationship in the novel; and creates a society in which he finds contentment. We are justified in commenting that he responds to 'manly' beauty and a homosocial friendship. Some critics have gone farther and suggested that *Robinson Crusoe* reveals homosexual feelings. However, we must also remember that Robinson has been alone for 24 years, so that the mere presence of another man is enough to transform his life. Think of the poignancy of Robinson's remark: 'I began now to have some use for my tongue again, which indeed I had very little occasion for before': together with Friday's humble and cheerful character, this is enough to justify Robinson's 'I began really to love the creature' (both from *RC* 168), without attributing sexual feelings to this particularly asexual narrator. Our final comment may be that Robinson represents a conventional male of the time, whose most intimate relationships will be with men, and who relegates women to a negative existence where they may avoid giving 'dissatisfaction' or being a 'disadvantage' to men (*RC* 240).[2]

Having remarked the enthusiastic description of Friday and this idyllic society of two, we turn to Robinson's troubled meditations. We will briefly study the two paragraphs following the ringing declaration that 'never Man had a more faithful, loving, sincere Servant, than *Friday* was to me':

> This frequently gave me occasion to observe, and that with wonder, that however it had pleas'd God, in his Providence, and in the government of the works of his hands, to take from so great a part of the world of his creatures, the best uses to which their faculties, and the powers of their souls are adapted; yet that he has bestow'd upon them the same powers, the same reason, the same affections, the same sentiments of kindness and obligation, the same passions and resentments of wrongs; the same sense of gratitude, sincerity, fidelity, and all the capacities of doing good, and receiving good, that he has given to us; and that when he pleases to offer to them occasions of exerting these, they are as ready, nay, more ready to apply them to the right uses for which they were bestow'd, than we are. And this made me very melancholy sometimes, in reflecting as the several occasions presented, how mean a use we make of all these, even though we have these powers enlighten'd by the great lamp of instruction, the spirit of God, and by the knowledge of his Word, added to our understanding; and why it has pleas'd God to hide the like saving knowledge from so many millions of souls, who if I might judge by this poor savage, would make a much better use of it than we did.
>
> From hence, I sometimes was led too far to invade the sovereignty of *Providence*, and as it were arraign the justice of so arbitrary a disposition of things, that should hide that light from some, and reveal it to others, and yet expect a like duty from both: But I shut it up, and check'd my thoughts with this conclusion, (1st) that we did not know by what light and law these should be condemn'd; but that as God was

> necessarily, and by the nature of his being, infinitely holy and just, so it could not be, but that if these creatures were all sentenc'd to absence from himself, it was on account of sinning against that light which, as the Scripture says, was a law to themselves, and by such rules as their consciences would acknowledge to be just, tho' the foundation was not discover'd to us: And (2d) that still as we are all the clay in the hand of the potter, no vessel could say to him, Why hast thou form'd me thus? (*RC* 165–6)

Robinson refers to the corruption of the old world obliquely, suggesting that ignorant savages could 'make a much better use' of religion than decadent Europeans, and deploring the 'mean' use Europeans make of the Word of God. However, the most telling part of the first paragraph is its gushing list of natural human qualities, including 'reason . . . affections . . . sentiments of kindness and obligation . . . passions and resentments of wrongs . . . gratitude, sincerity, fidelity . . . capacities of doing good, and receiving good'. This is an enthusiastic list and follows from another admiring list in the preceding paragraph, so that the virtues of innocent savages figure far more prominently than European corruption. Consequently, the force of Robinson's question is enhanced: why does God deny salvation, where he bestows so much natural goodness? God's contradictory action seems to make no sense. Observing that the savages are 'as ready, nay, more ready' to do good than 'we are', Robinson becomes 'very melancholy'.

The second paragraph proposes a solution. Robinson so questions Providence that he is 'sometimes led too far' and even dares 'arraign the justice of so arbitrary a disposition of things'; but he finally settles his disquiet with two references to the Bible. First, he refers to Romans, Chapter 2:

> 12. For as many as have sinned without law shall also perish without law: and as many as have sinned in the law shall be judged by the law;
> 13. (For not the hearers of the law are just before God, but the doers of the law shall be justified.

14. For when the Gentiles, which have not the law, do by nature the things contained in the law, these, having not the law, are a law unto themselves:
15. Which shew the work of the law written in their hearts, their conscience also bearing witness, and their thoughts the mean while accusing or else excusing one another;)[3]

Robinson proposes that there is a 'light' which can guide even the ignorant so they can be 'a law to themselves'. This 'light' even provides them with 'rules' and 'consciences': as the scripture says, it is 'the law written in their hearts'. Robinson then adds the observation that God is 'holy and just', and from these two remarks, he concludes that all pagans must have done something wrong: they must have been sentenced 'on account of sinning against that light'. We do not know what dreadful sin they have committed, because 'the foundation was not discover'd to us', but Robinson's second biblical reference reminds us that we cannot expect to understand, and indeed should not ask. The reference is to Jeremiah and Isaiah, both of whom use the image of God as the potter and the individual as clay.[4]

Robinson's second 'conclusion' about the potter and the clay abandons the inquiry: it tells the questioning mind to accept a senseless world. It echoes Robinson's feeling that his questions went 'too far' and which led him to 'shut it up' when he 'check'd my thoughts': the short verbs 'shut' and 'check'd' have a hard, even cruel sound, almost as if Robinson mentally slaps himself. These harsh verbs contrast with the flowing lists of virtues and the gentle 'melancholy' that dominated the preceding paragraph.

Robinson's first 'conclusion' is more complex, for it proposes a standard of ethical behaviour that is natural to all human beings: a standard Scripture calls 'the law written in their hearts' even for those ignorant of the law. It is for some unknown sin against this internal, natural 'law' and its attendant 'conscience' that millions of savages the world over have been banished from salvation. Furthermore, the savages' 'consciences' would acknowledge their punishment to be 'just', presumably if they knew how they had sinned.

As we are coming to expect from Defoe, an impenetrable ethical tangle faces us. Are these savages naturally good, or not? Are they punished for their ancestors' sins, or their own? Does God's mercy not extend to them? What about the virtues Robinson discerns in Friday, the assertion that he is more inclined to goodness than a European? Then, the supposed 'law': is one culture more moral than another? Is there any such thing as a universal standard of human behaviour? All of these questions are raised, and none answered. At the same time, we remember Robinson's reflections on cannibalism, and the questions that bothered him in his murderous rage against the savages. Then, he did not propose any universal human morality, but recognised the gulf between different cultures. Robinson's meditations are typically muddled, here as elsewhere; and his reference to the Scriptural potter and clay is a mere surrender. Robinson's theological ideas, because confused, fade into the background. Instead, Friday's engaging virtues enumerated in that admiring list; and Robinson's disquiet about Christianity, together with the way he 'shut . . . up' his criticism of God: these two elements stand out and stay with us. Defoe, then, raises many of the thorniest issues that have bedevilled the era of colonialism and imperialism. He does not provide answers, but paints a thoroughly human picture of his protagonist, who also fails to solve the riddles with which he is confronted.

We are left, then, with a vivid impression of Friday's virtues as well as a sympathetic view of Robinson's natural, but balked, sense of justice. Cynically, we should also remark that Robinson's praise of Friday is weighted with overtones of their master and servant relation: Friday is 'faithful', 'oblig'd', his affection 'ty'd' to Robinson who evokes a father/child relationship between them (*RC* 165). More generally, he includes 'obligation', 'gratitude', and 'fidelity' among the qualities shown by savages. Robinson clearly assumes, without question, that he is the master.[5] In this respect, Defoe shows him to be the colonial man of his time.

There remains the question of how we, with our twenty-first century tenderness, respond to Robinson's obtuse relationship with early colonial mores. Is it bad taste to find comedy in Robinson's struggles? Crucially, what is our relationship, as readers, with Defoe? Must we look askance at much of what this book tells us? Do we make allowances because Defoe was born into a less enlightened time? Such questions concern readers' personal responses, and may provoke different individual answers. It is also true to say that such questions arise with virtually all texts written. There are some remarks it is possible to make, however.

First, we should beware of patronising the author. We may be equipped with the post-colonial perspective of the twenty-first century, sensitive to issues of gender-equality, racial equality, cultural difference, and so on. This 'full set' of moral instincts will be aroused by Robinson's exploitations both in the Brasils, as a slaver on the coast of Guinea, and eventually also on his island. We must beware of feeling superior, however: on the contrary, our feelings need to be educated with an admixture of humility. Defoe is presenting us with an image of the world in 1659. I am aware, in the present, of horrific exploitations of the third world; and little is being done to rectify these. Furthermore, I do not think about this deeply, or often. Only a few days before writing this paragraph, I noticed a news item about a gang who kill people, then sell their fat to the cosmetics industry. Clearly, we should not think ourselves superior to Defoe. Rather, we should regard Defoe as a writer of great intelligence, who speaks to us *across time.*

Secondly, we should not 'make allowances' for Defoe. We must confront what happens in his narratives, and take what we can from the text, not sweep the unwelcome under the carpet. The example of Xury underlines this point:

> . . . he offer'd me also 80 Pieces of Eight more for my boy *Xury*, which I was loath to take, not that I was not willing to let the Captain have him, but I was very loath to sell the poor boy's liberty, who had assisted me so faithfully in procuring my own. However when I let him know my reason, he own'd it to be just, and offer'd me this medium, that he would give the boy an obligation to set him free in ten years, if he turn'd Christian; upon this, and *Xury* saying he was willing to go to him, I let the Captain have him. (*RC* 28–9)

Robinson expresses the sense of fairness we might feel when he says he was 'loath' to sell Xury. However, upon limiting his enslavement to 10 years, and imposing Christianity upon him, Robinson is happy to compromise. This does not show Defoe's limited outlook: on the contrary, Defoe shows himself to be as alive as we are to the moral issue, and he treats it with the comic technique of bathos. Robinson's acquisitive nature easily overcomes his conscience, and he sells Xury with no further qualms, while we recognise that his conscience has its price. So, far from making allowances for Defoe, and reading him with any special care of our attitudes, we should enter into the game he makes of the attitudes and practices of his time, wholeheartedly; and in the case of Robinson and Xury, we can take from the irony a comment on how human nature reasons when tempted by profit that is partly cynical, and partly understanding.

Analysis: *Moll Flanders*, pp. 180–2

We now turn to *Moll Flanders*. The following extract comes from one of those occasions when Moll does her accounts:

> I now began to cast up my Accounts; I had by many Letters, and much Importunity, and with the Intercession of my Mother too, had a second return of some Goods from my Brother, *as I now call him*, in *Virginia*, to make up the Damage of the Cargo I brought away with me, and this too was upon the Condition of my sealing a general Release to him, and to send it him by his Correspondent at *Bristol*, which though I thought hard, yet I was oblig'd to promise to do: However, I manag'd so well in this case, that I got my Goods away before the Release was sign'd, and then I always found something or other to say to evade the thing, and to put off the signing it at all; till *at length* I pretended I must write to my Brother, and have his Answer, before I could do it.
>
> Including this Recruit, and before I got the last 50 *l*. I found my strength to amount, put all together, to about 400 *l*. so that with that I had above 450 *l*. I had sav'd above 100 *l*. more, but I met with a Disaster with that, which was this; that a Goldsmith in whose Hands I had trusted it, broke, so I lost 70 *l*. of my Money, the Man's Composition not making above 30 *l*. out of his 100 *l*. I had a little Plate, but not much, and was well enough stock'd with Cloaths and Linnen.
>
> With this Stock I had the World to begin again; but you are to consider, that I was not now the same Woman as when I liv'd at *Redriff*; for first of all I was near 20 Years older, and did not look the better for my Age, nor for my Rambles to *Virginia* and back again; and tho' I omitted nothing that might set me out to Advantage, except Painting, for that

I never stoop'd to, and had Pride enough to think I did not want it, yet there would always be some difference seen between Five and Twenty, and Two and Forty.

I cast about innumerable ways for my future State of Life and began to consider very seriously what I should do, *but nothing offer'd*; I took care to make the World take me for something more than I was, and had it given out that I was a Fortune, and that my Estate was in my own Hands, the last of which was very true, the first of it was as above: I had no Acquaintance, which was one of my worst Misfortunes, and the Consequence of that was, I had no adviser, at least who cou'd advise and assist together; and above all, I had no Body to whom I could in confidence commit the Secret of my Circumstances to, and could depend upon for their Secresie and Fidelity; and I found by experience, that to be Friendless is the worst Condition, next to being in want, that a Woman can be reduc'd to; *I say a Woman*, because 'tis evident Men can be their own Advisers, and their own Directors, and know how to work themselves out of Difficulties and into Business better than Women; but if a Woman has no Friend to Communicate her Affairs to, and to advise and assist her, 'tis ten to one but she is undone; nay, and the more Money she has, the more Danger she is in of being wrong'd and deceiv'd; and this was my Case in the Affair of the Hundred Pound which I left in the Hand of the Goldsmith, *as above*, whose Credit, it seems, was upon the Ebb before but I that had no knowledge of things, and no Body to consult with, knew nothing of it, and so lost my Money.

In the next place, when a Woman is thus left desolate and void of Council, she is just like a Bag of Money, or a Jewel dropt on the Highway, which is a Prey to the next Comer; if a Man of Virtue and upright Principles happens to find it, he will have it cried, and the Owner may come to hear of it again; but how many times shall such a thing fall into Hands that will make no scruple of seizing it for their own, to once that it shall come into good Hands.

This was evidently my Case, for I was now a loose unguided Creature, and had no Help, no Assistance, no Guide for my Conduct: I knew what I aim'd at, and what I wanted, but knew nothing how to pursue the End by direct means; I wanted to be plac'd in a settled State of Living, and had I happen'd to meet with a sober good Husband, I should have been as faithful and true a Wife to him as Virtue it self could have form'd: If I had been otherwise, the Vice came in always at the Door of Necessity, not at the Door of Inclination; and I understood too well, by the want of it, what the value of a settl'd Life was, to do any thing to

> forfeit the felicity of it; nay, I should have made the better Wife for all the Difficulties I had pass'd thro', by a great deal; nor did I in any of the Time that I had been a Wife, give my Husbands the least uneasiness on account of my Behaviour.
>
> But all this was nothing; I found no encouraging Prospect; I waited, I liv'd regularly, and with as much frugality as became my Circumstances, but nothing offer'd; nothing presented, and the main Stock wasted apace; what to do I knew not, the Terror of approaching Poverty lay hard upon my Spirits: I had some Money, but where to place it I knew not, nor would the Interest of it maintain me, at least not in *London*. (*MF* 180–2)

This extract focuses on a different aspect of economics: Moll visits Virginia twice, and there are passages that discuss the economics of plantations, the status of transports, and other colonial matters. This extract, however, deals with the home economy, and particularly with the disadvantages attending a single woman. We will begin by taking an overview, summarising each of the seven paragraphs as succinctly as possible:

1. I received more from my brother and avoided signing a release for him.
2. I had 480 *l*. in all. I lost 70 *l*. through the bankruptcy of a Goldsmith.
3. I had to begin life anew. I was still good-looking, but nearly 20 years older.
4. I gave out that I was rich, but my disadvantage was I had no adviser, which is terrible for a woman, because men can look after themselves, but women need advice, which is shown by my mistake about the Goldsmith.
5. A woman alone is prey. She is more likely to fall into unscrupulous than principled hands.
6. I was alone and therefore defenceless. I wanted to be settled as a wife, and when married I always was a good wife, taught by my experience of insecurity.
7. However, no opportunities appeared, and I was frightened of poverty.

This extract, then, mingles Moll's finances with comments on marriage, the disadvantages of being a woman, concerns about her age and looks, and an assertion of her virtue. With the exception of paragraph 2 which gives us the figures, each paragraph is punctuated as a single sentence. How does Moll navigate between these different aspects of her situation?

The first two paragraphs purport to tell us Moll's wealth: she begins the first 'I now began to cast up my Accounts', and the second 'Including this Recruit . . . I found my strength to amount . . . ': in both cases using a factual tone. However, each of these paragraphs digresses to tell us a different story. In the first Moll recounts her success in having 'manag'd so well' as to obtain the goods and avoid signing a general release – a document that would have left her brother free from any further obligation towards her. The second paragraph tells of a failure: Moll trusted £100 to a Goldsmith, and when he went bankrupt he could only pay his creditors – including Moll – 30 per cent. The effect of the two anecdotes is to convey fragility. First, Moll is a canny businesswoman; then, she is a victim. Meanwhile, she never quite finishes the project with which she began – that of casting up her accounts – never arriving at the final figure of £480. On the other hand, Moll shows familiarity with commercial diction: she mentions 'sealing a general Release to him' as glibly as any lawyer; and her use of the term 'Composition' shows her knowledge of bankruptcy proceedings. Clearly, these two paragraphs indicate the instability of economic life for Moll, and one effect is to suggest that you cannot measure your wealth: the total changes so fast that it is never a sure figure.

The third paragraph begins, again, with Moll's familiar forthright voice: 'With this Stock I had the World to begin again'. The subject-matter then slips sideways to discuss Moll's other kind of 'Stock': her sexual attractiveness. She begins this digression with the fact that she is 20 years older, saying that this is 'first' among the differences that make her 'not now the same Woman'. She never tells us the others: instead, she builds reasons on each side, until we have a troubled assessment of her gradually declining looks. On the one hand, she has undergone 20 years, strenuous voyages, and life in a colony; on the other hand, Moll sets herself out to advantage, and has enough natural beauty to need no 'painting'. By arguing in her own mind, Moll manages to mitigate the ravages of time, concluding minimally that there would 'always be some difference seen' now that she is 42 years old. We can sympathise with the emotional importance Moll attaches to keeping her looks; and we recognise her potential for self-deception on this matter. However, we remember that this paragraph is also part of casting up Moll's 'Accounts'. Here she values her 'Stock': she estimates her value as a woman, in the economics of sex.

The structure of Defoe's sentence, in this paragraph, is psychologically revealing. Moll begins with her statement about having 'the World to begin again', then the remainder of the paragraph should be negative, being governed by the conjunction 'but'. However, when Moll introduces 'and tho' I omitted nothing', she encloses a positive argument within the negative, and allows herself to add three subclauses to boost her ego, before returning to the fact of her age after 'yet'. In this paragraph, then, Moll's reassurance to herself is doubly enclosed, but seems to swell, threatening to break out of its restricted grammatical space.

Something similar is noticeable in the fourth, and longest, paragraph. When Moll says one of her 'worst Misfortunes' was her lack of 'Acquaintance', she then pretends to tell us the 'Consequence'. What happens, however, is that we enter a repetitive complaint lasting seven further phrases, full of Moll's need for an 'adviser' who could share a 'Secret' and offer 'Secresie' and 'Fidelity'. The structure of this plaint advertises 'Consequence', then 'above all' and 'I found by experience', but the whole does no more than elaborate on her lack of 'Acquaintance', and the manner in which her complaint swells again stretches the structure within which it is supposedly contained. Men take the foreground next, as ''tis evident' that men can look after their own affairs (three clauses), before Moll returns to her complaint, repeating that a woman with no 'Friend . . . to advise and assist her' faces disaster described in three terms as being 'undone', 'wrong'd', and 'deceiv'd'. Clearly, Defoe here shows Moll's anxiety, and her complaint at the injustice of a society in which women are victimised, swelling to dominate the paragraph.

The next paragraph continues the theme that women are defenceless 'Prey', unable to avoid becoming victims of unscrupulous men.

Moll uses an extended simile in order to underline what she is saying. Moll does not use imagery often: in this passage, aside from paragraph 5, there are only two ordinary figures of speech: that the Goldsmith's credit was 'upon the Ebb', and the mention of two doors of 'Necessity' and 'Inclination'; otherwise Moll's narrative remains literal. Here, the simile compares a single woman to a 'Bag of Money, or a Jewel' left on the road, ready to be picked up by any man who passes. This is an effective image to express Moll's meaning, and in addition, the simile enables Moll to describe a woman as an object – 'which', 'it', 'it', 'it', 'such a thing', 'it', and 'it' – throughout the paragraph, thus emphasising the crude mingling of sex and commerce that is a major theme of the novel.

The final two paragraphs express further modulations of Moll's mood. In paragraph 6, she wishes to assure us that, if only society would give her a chance, she would be virtuous. Paragraph 7 expresses her terror of poverty, the fear she first experienced as a little orphan girl. Up to this point, Moll has led up to her complaint: that women do not have a chance, in her experience of English society. The fourth paragraph conveys a bitter complaint about her helpless isolation; and the simile of the 'Bag of Money' is an angry image – it expresses resentment against society for treating women as objects of commerce. In paragraph 6, by contrast, Moll's diction returns within the fold: she seeks a 'settled' life, and piles together the terms 'sober', 'good', 'faithful', 'true', and 'Virtue'. Furthermore, she claims that 'the want of' such a life has taught her its value, and she would be 'the better Wife for all the Difficulties I had pass'd thro', by a great deal'. Moll, then, surrenders: she is eager to obey the rules. In society's hard school, she has learned the consequences of trying to flout convention: she is now frightened enough to submit; and the suffering she has endured, together with her 'Terror of approaching Poverty', will keep her virtuous and obedient.

Thus, we are brought into sympathetic contact with Moll as she struggles to shape her course, hoping to find both a viable identity, and a stable form of living within her society. It is clear that the economic context is unstable; women are mistreated; and the commerce in female sexuality is a cause of both misery and resentment; but Moll, in particular, has suffered enough, and has no intention of rebelling against society's rules again.

If we ask: is this the sum of what we learn from the extract? The answer is, not quite. Defoe demands to be read in close detail, and his narrators give up their complexity to careful scrutiny. In our extract, there are perhaps two moments when Moll is less than honest, or less than fair. First, when she argues that men have an absolute advantage over women, this comes in the same sentence she began by saying that she 'had it given out that I was a Fortune' and pretended to be 'something more than I was': this being the deception which catches her next husband. Second, Moll denies that vice was ever her 'Inclination'; yet we know that, in bed with her Bath Gentleman, 'the first Breach was not on his part' but that 'I found my Weakness, the Inclination was not to be resisted' (*MF* 171–2). In short, it is true that Moll has been forced and moulded by fear of poverty, and by her society, so that she will be virtuous and obedient; however, it is also true that sex, love, and affection remain enjoyable. So, even a chastened Moll has to fight temptation, or lie to us and herself about her pleasures. Defoe implies that there will always be a contradiction between human nature and society's mores – people and convention will never be a happy fit, even if, like Moll, the people have been battered into submission.

The passage we have examined from *Moll Flanders* was initiated by her attempt to add up her accounts, an effort she makes again and again, until we come to recognise the constantly changing sums as a symptom of anxieties not only in Moll, but also in the society the text presents. This passage shows such instability in finance that the constant summing ups are drained of meaning. How can you assess your wealth, when it may double, or disappear, in a flash? We have also noticed that Moll has strong grounds of resentment, and makes a powerful case to show that gender-prejudices persecuted women, treating them as objects of sexual commerce. At the same time, not all of Moll's behaviour and attitudes follow this single line: she is a complex person to whom we respond with sympathy, but also noticing the humour of Defoe's creation. As with *Robinson Crusoe*, we could say that much of the satirical humour in *Moll Flanders* is produced when ideas are misapplied to passing, or changeable, facts.

Analysis: *Roxana*, pp. 210–11 and 212–13

Let us now turn to *Roxana*. We will study the narrative at a moment when Roxana rejects matrimony in favour of continuing her career as a whore:

> However, Sir *Robert* came seriously to me one Day, and told me, he had an Offer of Matrimony to make to me, that was beyond all that he had heard had offer'd themselves, and this was a Merchant; Sir *Robert* and I agreed exactly in our Notions of a Merchant; Sir *Robert* said, and I found it to be true, that a true-bred Merchant is the best Gentleman in the Nation; that in Knowledge, in Manners, in Judgment of things, the Merchant out-did many of the Nobility; that having once master'd the World, and being above the Demand of Business, tho' no real Estate, they were then superior to most Gentlemen, even in Estate; that a Merchant in flush Business, and a capital Stock, is able to spend more Money than a Gentleman of 5000 *l*. a Year Estate; that while a Merchant spent, he only spent what he got, and not that; and that he laid up great Sums every Year.
>
> That an Estate is a Pond; but that a Trade was a Spring; that if the first is once mortgag'd, it seldom gets clear, but embarrass'd the Person for ever; but the Merchant had his Estate continually flowing; and upon this, he nam'd me Merchants who liv'd in more real Splendor, and spent more Money than most of the Noblemen in *England* cou'd singly expend, and that they still grew immensely rich.
>
> He went on to tell me, that even the Tradesmen in *London*, speaking of the better sort of Trades, cou'd spend more Money in their Families, and yet give better fortunes to their Children, than, generally speaking, the Gentry of *England* from a 1000 *l*. a Year downward, cou'd do, and yet grow rich too.
>
> The Upshot of all this was, to recommend to me, rather the bestowing my Fortune upon some eminent Merchant, who liv'd already in the first Figure of a Merchant, and who not being in Want or Scarcity of Money, but having a flourishing Business, and a flowing Cash, wou'd at the first word, settle all my Fortune on myself and Children, and maintain me like a Queen. (*R* 210–11)

Roxana explains to Sir Robert that she has no desire or need to try matrimony again. The narrative then continues:

But to go on with my Story as to my way of living; I found, as above, that my living as I did, wou'd not answer; that it only brought the *Fortune-Hunters* and Bites about me, as I have said before, to make a Prey of me and my Money; and in short, I was harrass'd with Lovers, *Beaus*, and *Fops* of Quality, in abundance; but it wou'd not do, I aim'd at other things, and was possess'd with so vain an Opinion of my own Beauty, that nothing less than the KING himself was in my Eye; and this Vanity was rais'd by some Words *let fall* by a Person I convers'd with, who was, perhaps, likely enough to have brought such a thing to pass, had it been sooner; *but that Game began to be pretty well over at Court*: However, he having mention'd such a thing, it seems, a little too publickly, it brought abundance of People about me, upon a wicked Account too.

And now I began to act in a new Sphere; the Court was exceeding gay and fine, tho' fuller of Men than of Women, the Queen not affecting to be very much in publick; on the other hand, it is no Slander upon the Courtiers, *to say*, they were as wicked as any-body in reason cou'd desire them: the KING had several Mistresses, who were prodigious fine, and there was a glorious Show on that Side indeed: If the Sovereign gave himself a Loose, it cou'd not be expected the rest of the Court shou'd be all Saints; so far was it from that, tho' I wou'd not make it worse than it was, that a Woman that had any-thing agreeable in her Appearance, cou'd never want Followers.

I soon found myself throng'd with Admirers, and I receiv'd Visits from some Persons of very great Figure, who always introduc'd themselves by the help of an old Lady or two, who were now become my Intimates; and one of them, I understood afterwards, was set to-work on purpose to get into my Favour, in order to introduce what follow'd.

The Conversation we had, was generally courtly, but civil; at length, some Gentlemen propos'd to Play, and made, what they call'd, a Party; this it seems, was a Contrivance of one of my Female hangers-on, *for, as I said, I had two of them*, who thought this was the way to introduce People as often as she pleas'd, and so indeed, it was: They play'd high, and stay'd late, but begg'd my Pardon, only ask'd Leave to make an Appointment for the next Night; I was as gay, and as well pleas'd as any of them, and one Night told one of the Gentlemen, my Lord –, that seeing they were doing me the Honour of diverting themselves at my Apartment, and desir'd to be there sometimes, I did not keep a Gaming-Table, but I wou'd give them a little Ball the next Day, if they pleas'd; which they accepted very willingly. (*R* 212–13)

The famous dance in Turkish costume follows this final paragraph, and leads to Roxana's 3-year royal affair. So, this extract tells us that Roxana pursues the career of a courtesan or whore, when honourable and luxury marriage was offered to her. With her narrator's hindsight, she remarks 'had I taken his [Sir *Robert's*] Advice, I had been really happy' (*R* 211). Roxana does not dwell upon any regrets, however. The main content of these two passages is a description of two different strata in the society of the time. In the first, Sir Robert Clayton[6] describes a successful merchant, in contrast to landed Gentry, and Roxana thinks him 'certainly right' (*R* 211). In the second, Roxana tells us of her progress as she begins to make contact with the Court. We can study these two descriptions for the insights they offer into the society and economics of the time.

The first passage consists of four paragraphs, each punctuated as a single sentence. We can summarise them as follows:

1. Successful merchants are wiser and can spend more than many of the nobility, and make large profits at the same time.
2. Land produces only limited profit, mortgaged land is never cleared; the potential of trade is unlimited. Successful merchants spend more than the nobility and make large profits at the same time.
3. Even tradesmen do better than many of the landed gentry and make large profits at the same time.
4. So I should marry a merchant who would settle my fortune on me and keep me in luxury.

The repetition and reinforcement stand out: paragraphs 1 and 2 overlap a great deal, while the assertion that merchants and tradesmen are growing richer and richer all the time, despite also spending, leads on to the statement in paragraph 4 that Roxana could keep her own fortune *and* be kept like a Queen. Clearly, the idea of a win-win offer, or of simultaneous double gain, is prominent throughout Sir Robert's advocacy of merchants. Repetition also applies to some phrases and constructions. So, for example, we read that a merchant 'is able to spend more Money' in paragraph 1, 'spent more Money' in paragraph 2, and tradesmen 'cou'd spend more Money' in paragraph 3. Then, each of the four paragraphs ends with a clause introduced by 'and' which adds 'great Sums', 'immensely rich', 'grow rich', and 'maintain me like a Queen'. These short final phrases, which add, as it were, profit to profit, act as if to 'double' the paragraphs to which they belong.

So, Sir Robert hammers home his point about the profits of merchants and tradesmen, returning to the themes of spending and growth as if repeating a refrain. Notice, however, that the opening paragraph includes some non-financial comment. So, at the start of his encomium, Sir Robert points out that he is talking about a 'true-bred' merchant who has 'master'd the World, and being above the Demand of Business' is 'in flush Business, and a capital Stock'. In other words, he is talking of a merchant who is already rich. Then, such a merchant is the 'best Gentleman in the Nation', superior to the Nobility in 'Knowledge, in Manners, in Judgment'. The concept of 'a true-bred Merchant', by which Defoe seems to mean a man of refined education and culture, but not a born gentleman, is ambitious for Roxana's time.

This question may echo in our minds; and we may also question Sir Robert's meaning when he mentions 'Knowledge' and 'Manners': is a merchant's 'Knowledge' more useful than an obsolete Classical education? Are a merchant's 'Manners' less offensive, because more sober, than those of the decadent courtiers Roxana describes? Certainly, these terms suggest attitudes towards social rank to which we will return. What is equally noticeable, however, is that all personal qualities vanish with the phrase 'tho' no real Estate', half-way through paragraph one. The character of a merchant is not mentioned again: money is the only topic of the three-and-a-half paragraphs that remain.

What Sir Robert tells us about money is straightforward, and expressed as a simile: 'an Estate is a Pond; ... a Trade was a Spring'. The meaning is clear that a landed estate is limited: it will never produce more than it does each year; while merchandise is like a 'Spring' because it goes on producing more and more. This contrast is then hammered home by Sir Robert's diction. First, the estate is associated with fixed sums starting with 5000 *l.* a year, then diminishing to 1000 *l.* a year; then its limit is emphasised by a mortgage being 'for ever'. In contrast, the merchant's wealth conjures flowing water in the 'Spring' image amplified by 'flush', 'flowing', 'flourishing', and 'flowing', all reminiscent of running water and onomatopoeic with watery 'f' and sibilant sounds. This intensive impression is supported by the 'doubling' at the end of each paragraph that we have already mentioned, and by 'grew' and 'grow'.

This picture of merchants may strike us as overstated: to have your wealthy cake, eat it, and have it grow as well, while an unlimited flow of new wealth-cakes continues to bubble up, may strike us as a magical rather than a realistic belief. On the other hand, merchants were making huge fortunes at that time: remember Robinson's tenfold profit from his first Guinea voyage. Even if Sir Robert overstates his case, however, the case itself is revealing; for Sir Robert – and by endorsing his view on Roxana as well – comes down firmly in favour of capitalism, and consigns the medieval order of land and lordship to the past. Sir Robert approves the merchant-adventurer, and the urban tradesman, both at the expense of the landed class – aristocrats and gentry. Defoe was writing at a time when the old and new forms of wealth, and simultaneously old and new criteria in hierarchies of power and social rank, were in a melting pot: society was in an uncertain form and in flux. Sir Robert makes no bones about his position in this argument; but we should now keep the old/new, feudal/bourgeois, and land/trade arguments in mind while we study our second extract from *Roxana*.

Here is a summary of the four paragraphs:

1. I was surrounded by admirers and fortune-hunters, but I was aiming at becoming a royal mistress, but I was too late.
2. I became known to the Court, which was luxurious and wicked and followed the King's example of promiscuity.
3. I had many admirers and two old ladies who were social 'fixers'.
4. Some gentlemen gambled at my apartments, and wanted to do the same the next night. I offered to give a ball the next day.

Although not as repetitive as Sir Robert's extract, there are two references to Roxana's admirers. However, the main point we notice from this summary is that the paragraphs do not follow each other as a smooth narrative.

In the phrase '*But that Game began to be pretty well over at Court*', Roxana appears to shelve her ambition of becoming a royal mistress, suggesting that she arrived after the heyday of the King's promiscuity.

The next three paragraphs seem to contradict this idea. The King sets an example of promiscuity that his courtiers emulate, and Roxana prepares to display herself before royalty, planning her celebrated dance in Turkish costume. Similarly, the reader may feel thrown about by Roxana's judgements at this point. We have absorbed Sir Robert's opinions of gentry and merchants, and Roxana agrees. Now, when we meet the Court – that is, the landed nobility and gentry – we find it to be depraved and wicked. Roxana complains that she is surrounded by parasites: they are '*Fortune-Hunters*' and 'Bites', '*Beaux*', and '*Fops*', and she is their 'Prey'. When her royal ambition is rumoured, people gather around Roxana 'upon a wicked Account too', and she says that the Court 'were as wicked as any-body in reason cou'd desire them', and that they were not 'all Saints'. Roxana is now 'throng'd with Admirers' and has 'an old Lady or two' – probably little better than society bawds – helping to arrange her social progress: one of them 'was set to-work on purpose to get into my Favour', while gaming 'was a Contrivance of one of my Female hangers-on'. All of this suggests that Roxana is sinking into a pit of sinful plots and corruption, unaware of her danger. Indeed, the remark that she had 'so vain an Opinion of my own Beauty' that she aimed at the King suggests that we will witness our heroine's hubristic downfall. In a more conventional story, the wicked Roxana would reap the rewards of her vanity and would be ruined and cast out to die in poverty.

Not so in Defoe's version, however. Roxana can manage her wicked entourage for her own benefit: we are told that she is 'as gay, and as well pleas'd as any of them', whereupon she sets up the occasion for her Turkish dance. We should notice that Roxana, when conversing with one of the 'wicked' throng who use her apartment as a casino, speaks humbly, saying that 'they were doing me the Honour of diverting themselves at my Apartment'. Clearly, Roxana can manipulate the situation, and is familiar with the ceremonious humility – the bowing and scraping – required by the Court, with its emphasis on hierarchy based on noble birth.

In this extract, then, Defoe provides us with a moral fable describing two aspects of contemporary society. The sector of society that is concerned with commercial activity is characterised by natural growth, health, wealth, and virtue; while in contrast, the traditional ruling class, which is concerned with depraved and licentious luxury, is shown as wicked, parasitic, and dangerous. The irony of Defoe's fable, however, is that it turns upon the equivocal intelligence and ethical originality of his heroine Roxana. She does not play the expected role of ruined victim; neither does she marry a merchant. Instead, she manipulates the sinful world of the court so successfully that she obtains the top job in her chosen profession: that of royal mistress.

Between the two extracts we have studied, Roxana explains her aversion to marriage, and admits that she was 'yet a Whore', planning to increase her fortune. Sir Robert allows some justice in Roxana's '*Amazonian*' reasoning when she determined to be a '*Man-Woman*; for as I was born free, I wou'd die so' (both from *R* 212); but his reaction is indulgent amusement: he 'smil'd' and 'laugh'd heartily at me'. Roxana's analysis of gender-stereotyping is studied in the next chapter. The point at present is that Defoe provides us with a moral fable concerning the divided and rapidly changing society of his time; then he undermines our expectations by recounting Roxana's success; finally, he casts doubt upon our moral assumptions as well, by means of his heroine's reasoning.

Comparative Discussion

We have considered an extract from each of our texts in detail; and we have learned a certain amount about Defoe's treatment of society and economics. Our extracts have highlighted three areas of these themes in particular that are explored.

First, in *Robinson Crusoe* and *Roxana*, we have met a social and economic system in the midst of radical change: both texts hint at wealth, power, and influence shifting away from what can be called an older hierarchy and economic dominance, towards a new one. We have suggested that this change is nothing less than the transition from a medieval world view and the concomitant land-based economy and feudal hierarchy, to a modern world view founded on bourgeois-capitalism and mercantile enterprise. Our two texts present different aspects of this change, however: in *Robinson Crusoe*, the two world views are represented by his father's 'middle station' philosophy in contrast with greed, profits, and lawless opportunism. Ironically, Robinson approves of the old but adheres to the new. In *Roxana*, by contrast, the new economic power – presented in the person of a successful merchant – is described with approval, while the decadent aristocracy is treated as wicked, sinful, and parasitic. Again, the narrator's loyalty is ironic: Roxana thoroughly approves of merchants, but adheres to the decadent court. If we think of the novel's dark outcome, a further irony appears when she ultimately marries her merchant. Ironically, Roxana's period as a decadent courtesan is profitable and successful; while her eventual marriage to the merchant is a doomed enterprise.

The economic and social upheavals that occurred as the mediaeval world, with its feudal society and land-economy, gradually gave way to a modern world, with its nostrums of democracy, opportunity, and its capital-based economy, were of course multiple and far-reaching. We have found that Defoe presents different aspects of such fundamental changes at different times in his novels. So there are elements of this theme in *Moll Flanders* also. For example, Moll's mother explains how little value attaches to criminal stigma from the old world, once in the colonies (see *MF* 134–5): some who were petty criminals in England become magistrates and other dignitaries in the New World; and she blames Newgate for creating 'more Thieves and Rogues' than all other places put together. Moll's mother, then, suggests that the colonies provide an honest route to prosperity; while the old country encourages crime. We may also notice that Moll's eventual respectability is built upon colonial prosperity. This could suggest that Defoe advocates the new colonial society for bringing new freedoms and opportunities. On the other hand, Moll's colonial prosperity is itself the fruit of crime and incest. Typically, Defoe has constructed these ironies to cut counter to each other.

Secondly, our extracts have all contained a strong element of insecurity or instability. *Robinson Crusoe* subjected us to relentless persuasion from hindsight, arguing that any undertaking involves a terrible risk; and emphasising the 'deepest gulph of human misery that ever man fell into' as the outcome. So unstable are all events, indeed, that Robinson recommends his father's philosophy of frightened inactivity (although his own nature never allows him to adhere to this). In *Moll Flanders*, we found instability in her unfinished attempt to total her possessions, as well as in the terror of poverty that is fundamental in her character. We should also notice her brother's attempt to impose a legalistic control, by demanding a 'general Release' in his favour. This attempt to control events by contract fails, as do many other contractual and legalistic attempts to safeguard the characters' interests in Defoe's novels. See, for example, Robinson's attempts at protecting his interests with the Spaniards, and later with the Captain. Ironically, matters of contract and legality are so unpredictable in these novels that agreements are sometimes surprisingly successful (see, e.g. Robinson's Portuguese Captain; or Roxana's quaker). Contracts and laws, in themselves, are ineffective: everything depends on the trustworthiness of the people involved. As Moll remarks of a jewel, 'how many times shall such a thing fall into Hands that will make no scruple of seizing it for their own, to once that it shall come into good Hands.' In short, Defoe presents a world in which events, wealth, possession, activity, people, and legal or contractual agreements are utterly unpredictable. Whatever your circumstances today, you cannot predict what they will be tomorrow.

Thirdly, two of our extracts have highlighted issues of gender and the topic of sexual commerce. In *Moll Flanders* we found the narrator expressing a sort of desperate submission, seeking the solution to her financial insecurity in the institution of marriage. Roxana boldly pursues her fortune outside marriage, in the profession of a courtesan or whore; and argues trenchantly against marriage as disastrous for women. This topic will be the particular focus of the next chapter. For the moment, we can merely comment that the issues raised clearly contribute to the sense that established structures and values are crumbling, or are changing; and that social and moral attitudes are also fluid.

We will now go one stage further: having studied one extract from each novel, we will use our insights as a basis for thinking about each text as a whole, hoping to add further detail to our ideas about society and economics.

In *Robinson Crusoe*, the years of his isolated existence on the island provide a continuous commentary on society and economics by the simple virtue of their absence. We have already met Robinson's amusing ambivalence regarding money – that he despises it as ''Twas to me as the dirt under my feet' (*RC* 152–3), but takes and keeps it – and in Chapter 2, we suggested that the development of Robinson's religious beliefs can be thought of as a satire upon convention, whereby he tailors his interpretation of events to suit his concept of Providence. However, it is when Robinson begins to become a part of a society again that civilisation comes under the spotlight. Suddenly, a series of demands and thorny issues invade Robinson's life, which has been free from such contacts for almost 30 years. One of many examples where Defoe exploits this situation occurs when Robinson proposes to rescue the Spaniards.

All the uncertainties of society appear, for 'I fear'd mostly their treachery and ill usage of me' because 'gratitude was no inherent virtue in the nature of man': on the contrary, people are often influenced by 'advantages they expected' rather than 'obligations they had receiv'd'. Robinson then declares that cannibals are to be preferred to the 'merciless claws of the priests . . . the *Inquisition*' (all from *RC* 192). Clearly, Robinson is terrified of people, and all his self-reliance is undermined. He reflects on how unreliable other human beings are, and remembers how often you meet treachery and vice rather than trust and virtue. It is amusing to note that, in the middle of this panic, Robinson's suspicions of Spaniards and Catholics, unused for 28 years, re-surface.

Robinson's problem is that faced by all three of Defoe's protagonists: how can you control your circumstances in an unstable world? How can your fear of disaster be reduced and your hope for security be bolstered in order to reduce anxiety and render life tolerable? The solution offered by the Spanish sailor is contractual or legalistic: he offers that the Spaniards will swear loyalty 'upon the Holy Sacraments and the Gospel', and that he 'would bring a contract from them under their hands for that purpose' (*RC* 193). Robinson accepts, finding some reassurance in formality. However, we notice that circumstances have not changed: there will be only one of him to fifteen of them, should they prove treacherous, as human beings so often are. Defoe clearly achieves a signal effect in this and other similar episodes in this part of the story: after the long narrative of self-reliance, and the down-to-earth practicality of the period on the island, the sudden resurgence of anxiety, instability, and paranoia is startling.

Needless to say, it coincides with the reappearance of society and economics.

A slightly different effect is achieved simultaneously by Robinson's reflections about being 'like a king' and 'very rich in subjects'. He uses the terms of society, such as 'peopled', 'dominion', 'king', 'property', 'absolute lord and lawgiver', and so on. Suddenly, the language is filled with conventional social terminology. This cluster of terms bursting in upon the isolated island, with its population of four souls, has a satirical effect. The absurdity of lordship, hierarchy, dominion, and the other social concepts called into action here is highlighted by juxtaposition with Robinson's marooned existence.

We found Moll Flanders casting up her accounts on one of the several occasions when she has 'the World to begin again'; and our analysis emphasised her helplessness as a woman, and the financial uncertainty facing her. In Chapter 1, we met Moll as a small girl terrified of poverty, as well as confusedly aspiring to becoming a 'Gentlewoman'. The *naïve* pretentiousness of the child, who does not understand society, becomes a more serious disadvantage when Moll chooses her second husband. She is preoccupied by the appearances that belong to different social strata, and is particularly exercised in distinguishing a 'gentleman' from a 'tradesman'. Moll's mistake is to look for an equally pretentious and misleading man: a tradesman who can look like a gentleman: 'at last I found this amphibious Creature, this *Land-water-thing*, call'd, *a Gentleman-Tradesman*, and as a just Plague upon my Folly, I was catch'd in the very Snare, which *as I might say*, I laid for my self' (*MF* 104). The impossible '*Gentleman-Tradesman*' creature may remind us of the merchant/aristocrat contrast we studied in *Roxana*. If we think about the rest of Moll's story, it is clear that this is a recurrent theme: Moll continues to indulge in social pretensions herself, acting up to the rank of 'gentlewoman', exaggerating her fortune, and so forth; then, she is deceived by the very man she traps with her deceit. Moll, then, has a desire for security that is expressed as a longing for financial ease, but that is also manifested as a yearning for social status, the respectability she aspires to but does not fully understand. Further thought about the social and economic themes developed in *Moll Flanders* would lead us to study the role of Moll's 'Governess', her thriving business in whores' babies, and as a fence. It can be argued that Moll's 'Governess' exemplifies much of the decadence of the old country, contributing to the contrast between England and Virginia that is worked into Defoe's text in manifold ways.

We have found that society in *Roxana* is in a fluid state, changing from a hierarchy where aristocrats and royals demand ceremonial lordship and are treated as belonging to a superior species, to a modern mercantile society dominated by a capitalist bourgeoisie. Thinking about the text as a whole, however, we should also remember the opening scenes when Roxana and her five children are in 'inexpressible distress' (*R* 49), and where her husband's relations are cruel and selfish: 'I receiv'd not one Farthing of Assistance from any-body, was hardly ask'd to sit down at the two Sisters' Houses, nor offer'd to Eat or Drink at two more near Relations' (*R* 48). Defoe paints a detailed picture of the suffering and misery Roxana experiences after her husband's disappearance (see, e.g. page 50); and this account underpins many details of jewellery, plate, riches, and luxury described in later scenes.

Conclusions

We have noticed that the world described in Defoe's novels is dominated by uncertainty and change. As a consequence, important themes, such as society, or economics, appear in a wide variety of guises and in widely differing contexts. Analysing selected passages can only be a start to the study of such a theme.

This chapter has barely scratched the surface of social and economic themes as they are explored in Defoe's fictions. Put simply, on every page the scene changes so radically, as the protagonist stumbles or steps from one episode to another, from one setting to another, that new and different material is constantly introduced. We have studied an extract from each text, and begun building onto our insights in the **comparative discussion** above, but our work remains incomplete. This said, we can suggest some interim conclusions, as follows:

- In all three novels, Defoe presents a society that is changing. The changes depicted are contributory elements of the big, long-term transformation of English society that was taking place. Broadly speaking, society was being transformed from a mediaeval feudal structure founded on aristocratic and royal lordship, and on land ownership; into a modern mercantile and commercial society founded on capitalist enterprise, greater democracy, and opportunity. In this chapter in particular, we have met Robinson as the new colonial man, ironically attempting to apply his father's old-fashioned philosophy to new circumstances; Moll engaged in a quest for security and respectability, and an impossible search for a '*Tradesman-Gentleman*'; and Roxana contrasting the stereotypes of merchant and courtier, to the shame of the latter. This sense of society in flux between the old and the new in every aspect of life is perhaps the most consistent element in Defoe's exploration of these themes.

- All three novels describe people as unpredictable. There seems no rule at all that would enable you to tell the honest from the dishonest, the trustworthy from the corrupt; but both exist (when we think of the crime and corruption of Moll's London and Roxana's Paris and London, we must not forget Crusoe's widow, his Portuguese Captain, or his planting partner; Moll's fourth husband; or Roxana's Sir Robert, her quaker, and her Dutch merchant).
- All three novels describe events as unpredictable: people fall sick, die, reform, lose their wealth, change their minds, and betray; ships sink, lose their cargoes to pirates, and arrive safely; criminals are hanged, escape, grow rich, are killed; and so on.
- There are several encomiums on the comfort and virtues of the middle class, but all three protagonists avoid such an outcome: Robinson restlessly undertakes another voyage; Moll seeks a '*Tradesman-Gentleman*', then an Irish squire; and Roxana chooses depravity and royalty over a merchant of the bourgeoisie.
- Moll's banker and Roxana's merchant are more respectable choices; but the outcomes are not more secure.
- All three narrators are preoccupied with earning and saving, and with a mercantile assessment of their circumstances, their goods, and their consequent value.
- However, economic activity seems to involve immorality – as if the profit motive cannot be combined with virtue.[7] This is evident from Moll's career as a thief, and Roxana's as a whore. In *Robinson Crusoe*,

profits are not as obviously the result of immorality, although theft, slavery, and illegal projects are clearly part of the norm.

- A society is depicted where anything not bolted to the floor will be stolen – by the rich as much as by the poor. In all three novels the narrators strive against human untrustworthiness by legalistic efforts (see e.g. Crusoe's proposed contract with the Spanish castaways; the Landlord's contract with Roxana, and the Dutch merchant's marriage offers). However, events often bypass such legalistic attempts.
- Are the narrators free or are their lives determined? We have commented that all three struggle to make sense of their place, both socially and economically; and that they all chase the hope that they will be able to control their destiny. However, the forces that render life so unpredictable and unstable come from both within and outside the protagonists, and the abiding impression is of people at the mercy of sudden and repeated surprises.
- We have headed this list of conclusions with the idea that society was in the midst of changing from a mediaeval to a modern world view, and we have glossed this in the broadest terms as a feudal society changing to bourgeois-capitalism. There are specific events that focus social and political change even more tightly onto Defoe's lifetime, however. First, we must remember that the English Civil War ended in 1651, and Charles II was restored to the throne in 1660 – the year of Defoe's birth. By the time Defoe was writing his novels (1720–5), the Glorious Revolution had taken place and Britain had become a constitutional monarchy ruled by parliament. The number and extent of the political changes that occurred during Defoe's life cannot be over-estimated, and is hard to imagine. Secondly, between 1660 and 1731, Britain became the strongest maritime and commercial power in Europe, out-competing Spain, Portugal, Holland, and France in colonial exploitation and trade. Two possible further ways of thinking about Defoe's socio-economic theme may therefore occur.

1) How far does Defoe depict a consistent contrast between old European societies and the new colonies? Thus, we may see Europe as creating and fostering corruption, crime, poverty, and suffering (as, e.g. Moll's mother describes the influence of Newgate; or as Roxana is driven into her first prostitution by want); while the colonies, by contrast, provide a new start, an absence of the outdated hierarchy and enough opportunity so that there is no need to resort to crime.

2) How far can we see Defoe describing a society in the process of being formed but still in a state of fluidity, whether in old Europe or in the colonies – so the protagonists are, as it were, colonists in a new world, caught up in the process of making and defining a new, future society, trying out its limits and boundaries for themselves?

- Both of these ways of considering Defoe's socio-economic theme are valid and enlightening and the two are not mutually exclusive. Indeed, we can think about all the characteristics and the malaise we have noted as peculiar to the colonising period in which European nations were involved at the time, as well as characteristic of the transformation from mediaeval and feudal on the one hand, to bourgeois-capitalism on the other, and the rapid changes in political structures that were coterminous.

Methods of Analysis

As in previous chapters, we have continued to consider:

- A paragraph-by-paragraph summary, in order to gain an overview of how the narrative unfolds;
- Diction, in the sense that we notice both the kinds of vocabulary and terminologies used, and the 'tone of voice';
- Features of sentence-structure, such as numbers of interjected clauses, or inverted arguments;
- In addition, we have thought about each text as a whole, in relation to the particular theme of this chapter. In each case, we then chose another part of the text to look at in order to broaden insight and render our study more complete.

Defoe treats his themes in so many different and varied contexts, and subjects his protagonists to such a high level of instability, that our method still results in a notably incomplete study of the theme. You are recommended to repeat the fourth process described above several times. Look for and study further wider examples of the theme in context until you have achieved a more comprehensive understanding.

Suggested Work

Look at the following three extracts and make a detailed study of how social class and its attendant attitudes are portrayed. Is there any evidence that a person can be liberated from a class attitude?

Robinson Crusoe: pages 199–200, from 'It was just at the Top of High-Water . . . ' as far as ' . . . Can we serve you? – What is your Case?' See how Robinson depicts the behaviour and conversation of the sailors, the Captain, and himself – remembering that they meet unexpectedly on a desert island!

Moll Flanders: pages 294–6, Moll reflects on the effect of alcohol on her gentleman-victim, from 'These are the Men of whom *Solomon says*, . . . ' as far as ' . . . every time a Glass of Wine got into his Head.' See in this extract, the manner of Moll's description of the man; and her Governess's reaction to the story.

Roxana: pages 98–9, when Roxana entertains the Prince, from 'When he sent away his Gentleman, . . . ' as far as ' . . . and value myself infinitely upon the Honour of *his Highness's* Visit'. Here, notice the juxtaposition of admiring compliment against the coarseness of the events.

4

Women and Patriarchy

This chapter considers a question that has been controversial throughout the history of Defoe criticism: how successful are his female narrators – and how far does Defoe provide a critique of the gender-stereotypes of his time? Clearly most discussion will focus on Moll and Roxana. In *Robinson Crusoe*, we will glance at the four occasions when women appear, rather than studying a single passage.

Analysis: *Robinson Crusoe*, His Mother, His Wife, the Widow, and Women

There is one surprising occasion when Robinson sees nine naked dancing savages, but 'whether they were men or women, that I could not distinguish' (*RC* 145). This seems to suggest something androgynous about Robinson's eyesight, rather than the presence of women. Otherwise, only male savages ever visit the island; and there is no mention of women during Robinson's sojourn in the Brasils. The brief mentions of women that do occur reveal that Robinson has stereotypical attitudes. In Chapter 1, we noted how he appealed to his mother rather than his father: 'I took my mother, at a time when I thought her a little pleasanter than ordinary' (*RC* 7). Robinson clearly hopes to exploit feminine soft-heartedness. Defoe shows something quite different: Robinson's arguments – which are really threats laced with emotional blackmail – are a satire on male self-centredness. The utter failure of his approach and the steadfast reply of his mother demonstrate how deluded Robinson's expectations were. In Mrs. Crusoe, Defoe contradicts the stereotype, and shows us a clear-minded personality. Robinson's delusion about female pliability may also account for his belief that the 40 *l*. he raises from relations, actually came from his mother (see *RC* 16).

Robinson lodges his savings with his Captain's widow. She is said to be 'very just to me' (*RC* 16), she sends the Portuguese Captain a handsome present 'out of her own pocket' (*RC* 31) and is found to be fallen into poverty, and is widowed a second time, when Robinson returns. He helps her 'in gratitude to her former care and faithfulness to me' (*RC* 219). When wealthy and settled, Robinson calls her his 'true Friend' because she 'earnestly diswaded' him from returning to sea (*RC* 219). Apparently this widow can influence Robinson, for her arguments 'so far prevail'd' as to keep him ashore (*RC* 239). On the other hand, during this time Robinson also marries and has three children; and it is when his wife dies that he goes to sea again. Presumably the widow continues her 'earnest' dissuasions, but this time she is ignored.

Robinson's marriage marks the third and penultimate appearance of a woman. The narrative treats his wife even more dismissively than his mother or the widow. He tells us 'I marry'd', the forthright verb implying that his bride's role was to acquiesce. Of his marriage, Robinson tells us that it was 'not either to my disadvantage or dissatisfaction' (*RC* 240). We notice also that the act of marrying, which is Robinson's masculine activity, is an event described by an indicative verb. His wife's death, on the other hand, is mentioned with the participle 'my wife dying' (*RC* 240), and only as one of the reasons for his leaving England again. The event – her death – is accorded a feminine passivity of language. Notice that her achievement – avoiding 'disadvantage or dissatisfaction' – is also negative.

The fourth and final mention of women occurs on the final page of the novel. Here, the narrator tells us of 'five women' native Prisoners; 'seven women, being such as I found proper for service, or for wives to such as would take them', provided by Robinson from the Brasils; and 'some women from *England*' who were sent to the island later, to mate with the English men. The five natives account for the fact that there are 20 children on the island when Robinson arrives there. As for the other women, he clearly regards them as breeding stock, and equates marriage with 'service'. It is revealing that Robinson sends women to the island together with 'five cows, three of them being big with calf, some sheep, and some hogs'; and sends women from England 'with a good cargoe of necessaries' (all from *RC* 240).

There has been some controversy concerning the near-total absence of women from *Robinson Crusoe*, and critics have commented adversely on the narrative's dismissive treatment of women when they do appear. However, it would be *naïve* to identify Defoe with Robinson, when the protagonist is so frequently presented ironically. We are already critical of Robinson's late adoption of his father's 'middle station' philosophy; and we respond to his religious experiences with ambivalence. Here, we have travelled from noticing how ill-conceived is Robinson's attempt to manipulate his mother, to the suggestion of women as livestock on the final page. Although gender stereotypes are a marginal issue in *Robinson Crusoe*, they are critically satirised by the author. The subtle detail of Defoe's satire should also be appreciated. For example, notice the contrast between active (masculine) and passive (feminine) verbs that we found in Robinson's description of married life.

From *Robinson Crusoe* we turn to our other two novels, both of which feature female narrators, and in both of which women and patriarchy are central concerns.

Analysis: *Moll Flanders*, pp. 97–100

We will study relevant extracts from each of our two female narrators, beginning with the painful passage in which Moll learns about masculine power:

> He came back to me, and took me in his Arms and kiss'd me very Tenderly; but told me, he had a long Discourse to hold with me, and it was now come to that Crisis, that I should make my self Happy or Miserable, as long as I Liv'd: That the Thing was now gone so far, that if I could not comply with his Desire, we should be both Ruin'd: Then

he told me the whole Story between *Robin*, as he call'd him, and his Mother and Sisters and himself; as it is above: And now dear Child, *says he*, consider what it will be to Marry a Gentleman of good Family, in good Circumstances, and with the Consent of the whole House, and to enjoy all that the World can give you: And what on the other Hand, to be sunk into the dark Circumstances of a Woman who has lost her Reputation; and that tho' I shall be a private Friend to you while I live, yet as I shall be suspected always, so you will be afraid to see me, and I shall be afraid to own you.

He gave me no time to Reply, but went on with me thus: What has happened between us Child, so long as we both agree to do so, may be buried and forgotten: I shall always be your sincere Friend, without any Inclination to nearer Intimacy, when you become my Sister; and we shall have all the honest part of Conversation without any Reproaches between us of having done amiss: I beg of you to consider it, and do not stand in the way of your own Safety and Prosperity; and to satisfie you that I am Sincere, *added he*; I here offer you 500*l*. in Money, to make you some Amends for the Freedoms I have taken with you, which we shall look upon as some of the Follies of our Lives, which 'tis hop'd we may Repent of.

He spoke this in so much more moving Terms than it is possible for me to Express, and with so much greater force of Argument than I can repeat, that I only recommend it to those who Read the Story, to suppose, that as he held me above an Hour and a Half in that Discourse, so he answer'd all my Objections, and fortified his Discourse with all the Arguments, that human Wit and Art could Devise.

I cannot say however, that any thing he said, made Impression enough upon me, so as to give me any thought of the Matter; till he told me at last very plainly, that if I refus'd, he was sorry to add, that he could never go on with me in that Station as we stood before; that tho' he Lov'd me as well as ever, and that I was as agreeable to him, as ever; yet, Sense of Virtue had not so far forsaken him, as to suffer him to lye with a Woman, that his Brother Courted to make his Wife; and if he took his leave of me, with a denial in this Affair; whatever he might do for me in the Point of support, grounded on his first Engagement of maintaining me, yet he would not have me be surpriz'd, that he was oblig'd to tell me, he could not allow himself to see me any more; and that indeed I could not expect it of him.

I receiv'd this last part with some tokens of Surprize and Disorder, and had much a do, to avoid sinking down, for indeed I lov'd him to

> an Extravagance not easie to imagine; but he perceiv'd my Disorder, he entreated me to consider seriously of it, assur'd me that it was the only way to Preserve our mutual Affection, that in this Station we might love as Friends, with the utmost Passion, and with a love of Relation untainted, free from our just Reproaches, and free from other Peoples Suspicions; that he should ever acknowledge his happiness owing to me; that he would be Debtor to me as long as he liv'd, and would be paying that Debt as long as he had Breath; Thus he wrought me up, in short, to a kind of Hesitation in the Matter; having the Dangers on one Side represented in lively Figures, and indeed heighten'd by my Imagination of being turn'd out to the wide World, a mere cast off Whore, *for it was no less*, and perhaps expos'd as such; with little to provide for myself; with no Friend, no Acquaintance in the whole World; *out of that Town*, and there I could not pretend to Stay; all this terrify'd me to the last Degree, and he took care upon all Occasions to lay it home to me, in the worst Colours that it could be possible to be drawn in; on the other Hand, he fail'd not to set forth the easy prosperous Life which I was going to live.
>
> He answer'd all that I could object from Affection, and from former Engagements, with telling me the Necessity that was before us of taking other Measures now; and as to his Promises of Marriage, the nature of things *he said*, had put an End to that, by the probability of my being his Brothers Wife, before the time to which his Promises all referr'd.
>
> Thus in a Word, I may say, he Reason'd me out of my Reason; he conquer'd all my Arguments, and I began to see a Danger that I was in, which I had not consider'd of before, and that was of being drop'd by both of them, and left alone in the World to shift for myself. (*MF* 97–100)

This passage describes Moll's encounter with the reality of her situation as the elder son's mistress. She has prepared us by criticising her own vanity and foolishness when seduced: 'Thus I gave up myself to a readiness of being ruined without the least concern, and am a fair *Memento* to all young Women, whose Vanity prevails over their Virtue: Nothing was ever so stupid . . . ' (*MF* 64). It will help us to appreciate the young man's tactics, if we make our usual paragraph-by-paragraph summary of his discourse:

1. He told me I must now decide between being happy (the wife of a gentleman) and miserable (a woman who has lost her reputation).
2. Without letting me reply, he told me we should forget our love affair, be friends, and he offered me 500 *l*.
3. He spoke for 1 1/2 hours using all possible cleverness and cunning in his arguments.
4. I was not very affected until he told me he would no longer see me as he was too virtuous to continue seeing his brother's future wife.
5. I nearly fainted, but he told me we could continue to love as friends, and he would always be grateful to me; I became terrified of being exposed a whore, and left friendless; but he reminded me that an alternative easy prosperous life was offered.
6. He said his promises of marriage had been overtaken by events, his brother proposing before he himself had reached his estate.
7. I was frightened of being dropped by both of them, and left alone with nothing.

Re-reading this summary, we are struck by how the young man's arguments progressively encircle Moll so that she has less and less room for objection or manoeuvre, until she is left with a stark choice between the younger brother, and scandalous poverty: in other words, no choice at all. We are also struck by the gross injustice of what he says.

Which are the most offensive arguments marshalled by the young man? The answer to this question is likely to vary between readers. It is hard to choose between the coarse insulting offer of 500 *l*., which treats Moll as a whore; the breathtaking insouciance with which he invokes his own 'Sense of Virtue' in dropping her; or the hypocrisy with which he dismisses his promises of marriage, which (he says) were always conditional on him having his estate, and are now therefore irrelevant. We recognise these as examples of flagrant hypocrisy, but how are they narrated?

He offers the money for two reasons, he says: first, 'to satisfie you that I am Sincere'; then, 'to make you some Amends for the Freedoms I have taken with you'. It is obvious to us that neither of these reasons is adequate. The money to compensate for 'Freedoms' is to pay for Moll's virginity, of course. We know, however, that more is involved, because she loves him. By offering money as proof of his sincerity, he shows that he has no understanding of Moll's emotions, or of his own. Is he only sincere when he pays for something? Then, anything he can obtain for free is valueless. He is thus an early example of utterly Commercial Man.

When we turn to his 'Sense of Virtue', we notice that this argument is urged as part of an undeniable nature. It is not that he has decided to drop Moll, he says: rather that he 'could never go on with me'. This is all laid at the door of his 'Sense of Virtue' which has 'not so far forsaken him' and therefore would not 'suffer him' to carry on with her for he 'could not allow himself' to do so. This 'Sense of Virtue' he invokes is presented as such a natural and normal item that she should not be 'surpriz'd', and indeed she 'could not expect it of him' to see her any more. This argument, then, is urged in such a way as to present him as passive, unable to choose but carried along by the overwhelming power of a supposedly universal 'Sense of Virtue'.

We recognise the young man's self-excusing hypocrisy: that is obvious. What is equally powerful, however, is the strategy that silences reproach. This paragraph issues a challenge to Moll: if she dares to object, she will be objecting to the conventional sexual morality of that time. His pretence of having superior morals invites her to define herself: if she also has a 'Sense of Virtue', she cannot be 'surpriz'd' at his, or 'expect' to continue their affair. If, on the other hand, she objects to being dropped, she defines herself as lacking any 'Sense of Virtue'; she must be an incontinent whore. We realise that the young man chooses when to have a 'Sense of Virtue' and when to forget it; but we should also appreciate his strategy, because of the challenge it issues to Moll, and the tyrannical power it exerts over her response. This pressure of public morality the young man applies to Moll appears elsewhere in his discourse as well. For example, he mentions being friends 'without any Reproaches between us, of having done amiss', at another moment talks of a 'Relation untainted, free from our just Reproaches', and refers to their affair as 'some of the Follies of our Lives, which 'tis hop'd we may Repent of'. All of these comments invite Moll to share his and society's moral attitudes and are founded on that same bullying but unchallengeable assumption: that only a wicked whore could disagree.

When he disavows his promises of marriage, we are not surprised, but we recognise his habitual irresponsibility. The lame excuse that his promises of marriage referred to an undefined future date, and are irrelevant now that his brother has made an offer in the present, is one of those 'Arguments, that human Wit and Art could Devise', that is at the same time both an insult to Moll's intelligence, and an unanswerable retraction of the promise. Clearly, she can forget about his promise of marriage.

The young man does show anxiety about being discovered, when he mentions the danger that 'we should be both Ruin'd'; and comments that 'I shall be suspected always' or mentions being 'free from other Peoples Suspicions'. However, he is in danger from a temporary scandal while Moll would be 'a mere cast off Whore' and her life ruined. Furthermore, he warns her that he might 'be afraid to own you' and he 'could not allow himself to see you any more', a plain warning that he will drop her if necessary. So, in this faint motif of his fear of scandal, we can understand the difference between his and her situations. He can, and will, deny any accusation she might bring; he can, and will, drop her; he can, and will, survive any temporary unpleasantness. She, on the other hand, has no such assurance. Her reputation, once tarnished, will never recover, and she will be cast off into poverty and friendlessness.

We have looked at the young man's persuasions, and anatomised his arguments. How does Moll react? We may think of her as a helpless and *naïve* girl, and with regard to the former – her helplessness – this would be correct; but she is not *naïve*. Moll is shocked by the contrast between his earlier promises, and his barefaced retractions now. She can see his 'Arguments' for what they are, and comments that they are devised by 'Wit and Art' so that in the end 'he Reason'd me out of my Reason'. Moll is far from being a fool, then, and understands his hypocrisy. At the same time, she provides no counter-argument. The narrative simply reports his 'Discourse' in full, while Moll limits herself to her general comments in paragraphs 3 and 7.

Moll understands him with her intellect, then; but her feelings remain relatively untouched until he threatens to stop seeing her: she cannot say that his words 'made Impression enough upon me' until this point. Then she records two stages of emotion. First, she 'had much a do, to avoid sinking down, for indeed I lov'd him to an Extravagance, not easie to imagine'; that is, she almost faints from the prospect of being parted from her love. She quickly begins to be aware of a new emotion, however, which is fear. The danger of being abandoned without reputation is 'heightn'd by my Imagination', which 'terrify'd me to the last Degree'. This is the dominant emotion at the end of the scene: Moll sees 'a Danger that I was in' of being dropped by both brothers, and left alone to 'shift for myself'.

Defoe has charted Moll's experience of this scene very clearly: we can follow both her intellectual and her emotional reactions closely; and we notice the time lag between the two. From the point of view of gender issues, we can share both of Moll's reactions: her recognition of the sophistry of his arguments, first; then, her personal suffering from being abandoned by her lover, and her terror of the consequences that may be visited upon her, while he risks no equivalent hardship. Our ability to share Moll's reactions is enhanced by the absence of any counter-arguments from her, and the absence therefore of an explicit critique of the young man's appalling attitude. As readers, we face his reported speech, so that our own outrage is directly inspired by him, and we hear him just as Moll does. Our other abiding impression from the scene is that of terror, despair, and submission. At the end of his discourse, Moll is 'terrify'd' and has been left with no choice.

The scene we have studied records a significant moment in Moll's gender training: it impresses upon her the man's power, and the woman's vulnerability, and represents a stage on her journey from her childish incomprehension of the word 'gentlewoman', to such acceptance of the ascribed female role as Moll acknowledges much later, when she says 'I wanted to be plac'd in a settled State of Living', whereupon she would become 'as faithful and true a Wife... as Virtue it self could have form'd' (*MF* 182). What this scene underlines for us is the self-interested battering and bullying from a patriarchal world that bashes Moll into her compliant shape; and the pain and fear she experiences during the process of gender-socialisation.

Analysis: *Roxana*, pp. 61–3

We will discuss *Moll Flanders* further, later in this chapter. For the present, the study of one extract has been richly rewarding, and we must now turn to *Roxana*. In the following scene, Amy and Roxana discuss the Landlord's offer of support, and disagree about his motives:

> When he was gone, *Amy* chang'd her Countenance indeed, and look'd as merry as ever she did in her Life; Dear Madam! *says she*, what does this Gentleman mean? Nay, *Amy, said I*, he means to do us Good, you see, don't he? I know no other Meaning he can have, for he can get nothing by me: I warrant you Madam, *says she*, he'll ask you a Favour by and by: No, no, you are mistaken, *Amy*, I dare say, *said I*; you heard what he said, didn't you? Ay, says *Amy*, it's no matter for that, you shall see what he will do after Dinner: Well, well, *Amy, says I*, you have hard Thoughts of him, I cannot be of your Opinion; I don't see any thing in him yet that looks like it: As to that, Madam, *says Amy*, I don't see any thing of it yet neither; but what should move a Gentleman to take Pity of us, as he does? Nay, *says I*, that's a hard thing too, that we should judge a Man to be wicked because he's charitable; and vicious because he's kind: O Madam, *says Amy*, there's abundance of Charity begins in that Vice, and he is not so unacquainted with things, as not to know, that Poverty is the strongest Incentive; a Temptation, against which no Virtue is powerful enough to stand out; he knows your Condition as well as you do: Well, and what then? Why then he knows too that you are young and handsome, and he has the surest Bait in the World to take you with.
>
> Well, *Amy, said I*, but he may find himself mistaken too in such a thing as that: Why, Madam, *says Amy*, I hope you won't deny him, if he should offer it.
>
> What d'ye mean by that, *Hussy, said I?* No, I'd starve first.
>
> I hope not, Madam, I hope you would be wiser; I'm sure if he will set you up, as he talks of, you ought to deny him nothing; and you will starve if you do not consent, that's certain.
>
> What, consent to lye with him for Bread? *Amy, said I*, How can you talk so?
>
> Nay, Madam, *says Amy*, I don't think you wou'd for any thing else; it would not be Lawful for any thing else, but for Bread, Madam; why nobody can starve, there's no bearing that, I'm sure.

> Ay, *says I*, but if he would give me an Estate to live on, he should not lye with me, I assure you.
>
> Why look you, Madam, if he would but give you enough to live easie upon, he should lye with me for it with all my Heart.
>
> That's a Token, *Amy*, of inimitable Kindness to me, *said I*, and I know how to value it; but there's more Friendship than Honesty in it, *Amy*.
>
> O Madam, says *Amy*, I'd do any thing to get you out of this sad Condition; as to Honesty, I think Honesty is out of the Question, when Starving is the Case; are not we almost starv'd to Death?
>
> I am indeed, *said I*, and thou art for my sake; but to be a Whore, *Amy*! and there I stopt.
>
> Dear Madam, says *Amy*, if I will starve for your sake, I will be a Whore, or any thing, for your sake; why I would die for you, if I were put to it.
>
> Why that's an Excess of Affection, *Amy*, said I, I never met with before; I wish I may be ever in Condition to make you some Returns suitable: But however, *Amy*, you shall not be a Whore to him, to oblige him to be kind to me; no, *Amy*, nor I won't be a Whore to him, if he would give me much more than he is able to give me, or do for me.
>
> Why Madam, says *Amy*, I don't say I will go and ask him; but I say, if he should promise to do so and so for you, and the Condition was such, that he would not serve you unless I would let him lye with me, he should lye with me as often as he would, rather than you should not have his Assistance; but this is but Talk, Madam, I don't see any need of such Discourse, and you are of Opinion that there will be no need of it.
>
> Indeed so I am, *Amy*; but, *said I*, if there was, I tell you again, I'd die before I would consent, or before you should consent for my sake.
>
> Hitherto I had not only preserv'd the Virtue itself, but the virtuous Inclination and Resolution; and had I kept myself there, I had been happy, tho' I had perish'd of meer Hunger, for, without question, a Woman ought rather to die, than to prostitute her Virtue and Honour, let the Temptation be what it will. (*R* 61–3)

This dialogue between Amy and Roxana is ironic within the plot, of course: we know that Roxana does become her landlord's mistress, and that this is the first occasion when she receives material goods in return for sex. Even those new to *Roxana* will expect Amy's opinion to be vindicated: they are reading a novel called *The Fortunate Mistress*, and they expect the 'mistress' part to begin at any moment. So, there is an element of light-hearted cynicism in the way we read this extract.

This said, the argument is far from merely comic: on the contrary, it is a serious matter that becomes a major and increasingly complex concern of the text. The current situation is straightforward: Roxana and Amy have run out of money, goods which can be exchanged for money, and food and drink. They are completely destitute, and already stare starvation in the face. Their debate asks: in the context of starvation, is it admissible to compromise one's sexual mores in order to survive? It is obvious and is part of the immediate satire that in this extract Amy opines 'I think Honesty is out of the Question, when Starving is the Case'; and we find, some 15 pages later as the seduction reaches its conclusion, Roxana's comment that 'the dreadful Argument of wanting Bread . . . master'd all my Resolution' (*R* 78). So, the cynical truth is seen to overwhelm Roxana's scruples in the short term as the amused reader expects. In the longer term, however, we find the same questions being posed in increasingly complicated circumstances. Should Roxana avoid starvation by living with this gentleman? The question is mitigated by their mutual status as deserted spouses, and their vow to live as if man and wife, as well as by his belief that they are doing no wrong. Then: should Roxana accept wealth and precious goods in return for offering her favours to the Prince, in Paris? Those are different circumstances, where she seems to be motivated by gratitude, admiration of his rank, a little greed, and a little anxiety over her safety in a foreign land; but the argument she expresses that it is 'lawful' because 'irresistable' (*R* 105) is remarkably similar to the excuse of starvation. Then: should Roxana follow her inclination and lie with the Dutch merchant, this time giving her sex for free, but still refusing wedlock? Next: should Roxana sell herself in marriage to a merchant, as Sir Robert advises; or sell herself as a royal mistress?

It is clear that these supposedly 'moral' questions repeatedly lead us into circumstances so extreme that the question becomes absurd. For example, it is plain that Roxana's affair with the Dutch merchant has nothing to do with the sexual mores of her time; and that her career as a royal, then aristocratic, mistress is equally a matter for hellfire and sinful wickedness: so it is plain that in these circumstances the moral 'question' is so far outdistanced as to be absurd. Absurd in the context of the mores of Defoe's time, yes; but in the context of the experiences and arguments related in *Roxana*? In that astonishingly adventurous and unconventional context, it is perhaps not absurd. The affair with the Dutch merchant was Roxana's healthiest adventure, being the only time she exchanges sex for no gain. Then, her royal affair merely represents the top of her profession. Since society prescribes that her only means of survival is by selling sex, either as a wife or as a mistress, why should she not be ambitious and aim for the highest reward?

We have considered our extract's immediate satirical context and some of its relevance to issues explored later in the text. Now we should return to look at this scene in closer detail.

Amy's first move is to distinguish between words and actions, and she does this in two stages: first by questioning 'what does this Gentleman mean?' when as Roxana points out he has explained that he means 'to do us good' in clear language; then, by dismissing 'what he said' because 'you shall see what he will do'. So far, Amy has argued the old adage that actions speak louder than words; but in her second move, Amy goes farther. There is an interlude when they agree that he has not yet offered any rude behaviour; but then Amy asks her cynical question: 'what should move a Gentleman to take Pity of us, as he does?' Clearly, in her view, only a selfish drive – greed or lust or something of that kind – motivates a man, even to generosity.

This is a crucial point in the dispute, for Roxana raises the ultimate objection that it is cruel to 'judge a Man to be wicked because he's charitable; and vicious because he's kind'. At this point, the debate becomes a dispute between optimistic and pessimistic accounts of human nature, and for a moment it rests there; but with Amy's next contribution the complicated nature of reality barges in: 'there's abundance of Charity begins in that Vice' she says, which begs the question: if the outcome is good, does the motive also have to be pure? Thus, Amy casts moral argument down from a high pedestal of absolutes, into the compromises, complications, and debates between means and ends that are the stuff of actual dilemmas in life.

The next, or fourth development of Amy's views, is her belief that Roxana will be powerless to resist. She states that 'Poverty is the strongest Incentive; a Temptation, against which no Virtue is powerful enough to stand out.' So, not only does Amy believe the gentleman must be motivated by some selfish end; she also believes that no woman – including Roxana – can hold out against the threat of poverty. We remember this statement in 15 pages time, when Roxana bears out its truth. We may also remember our extract from *Moll Flanders*, where it is the threat of destitution that finally terrifies her into submission.

The next part of the debate is, of course, merely a consequence of the two women's dispute between absolute and relative moralities. Roxana protests shock, and that she would 'starve first' rather than give up her virtue; and Amy declares her belief that Roxana 'ought to deny him nothing' in gratitude for saving their lives. At this point, Amy draws a clear moral line: there can only be one reason for submitting to him: 'it would not be Lawful for any thing else, but for Bread, Madam.' This statement introduces a new idea, which we can call Amy's fifth move: here, she suggests that people can make their own laws, from their own sense of morality, and that such an individual compromise can be called 'Lawful'. The driving force behind Amy's judgement of the 'Lawful' is then made clear: it is physical necessity, because 'nobody can starve, there's no bearing that'.

The final stage of Amy's argument is her declaration that she will lie with the gentleman, if it will help Roxana. In this context, Amy asserts that 'Honesty is out of the Question, when Starving is the Case.' The dialogue then leads to an exchange of statements, where Roxana declares that she will not be 'a Whore to him', and Amy declares that 'he should lye with me as often as he would', so Roxana says 'I'd die before I would consent' for either of them, and we arrive at the final paragraph of our extract, a most equivocal interjection in this part of the story.

In this short paragraph, Roxana voices the conventional morality of her time: the morality voiced and promoted by society's establishment, by all the religious sects whether Catholic, Anglican, or dissenting; and supported by the legal system and the authority of the state. She tells us that she would have been 'happy' had she resisted the gentleman's advances. In Defoe's time 'happy' retained some of its archaic meaning of 'lucky' (from 'happenstance' meaning 'chance'); but it also frequently connoted salvation, because 'eternally happy'. With these overtones, however, Defoe also uses 'happy' in the familiar sense of 'contented'. How do these meanings play within the context of this paragraph? 'Contented' or 'feeling happy' is very odd when applied to one who has starved to death. 'Lucky' also seems peculiar: lucky to have starved to death? Or, even, 'lucky' to have saved her Virtue? Surely not: we call a woman virtuous, not lucky, if she dies virtuous. No: Defoe has placed the word 'happy' in an extremely questionable context. All we can say is that it seems impossible to decode or is absurd. This very absurdity, in its turn, highlights the absurdity of the whole moral position: why should 'happy' apply to a choice between death and dishonour? That very choice shows a corrupt and cruel society. The absurdity of applying the word 'happy' to starvation from poverty shows up the entire moral pose as a piece of pompous humbug.

Very well; but, as we have found to be typical of Defoe, this extract provokes multiple perspectives, and to respond to Roxana's pat retrospective moralising by calling it 'pompous humbug' is only one of the reactions the text may call forth. We have followed the debate between idealism and cynicism, and between moral absolutes and moral compromise, within this extract. At the same time, however, the heroine's situation brings to mind many issues of sex-economics and gender-politics: how being female or male affected the facts of money and power and determined your existence. We should therefore consider Roxana's declaration that she would have been 'happy' to have died then, in relation to these issues as well.

Amy's cynicism, as we have noticed, wins the debate: the gentleman does have a lustful motive, and Roxana does submit. This debate and its outcome, then, is part of Defoe's satire on sexual morality and, as such, can be read as amusingly bathetic. On the other hand, the victory of Amy's opinion is a philosophical tragedy. It is the victory of pessimism over optimism, for the man is self-interested; Amy underlines the absence of choice in 'you will starve if you do not consent, that's certain'; and the conclusion is that compromise is necessary. Amy's principle is that it is 'Lawful' to 'lye with him for Bread', but not for anything else, and this clearly relates to Roxana's circumstances. There is a far wider application of Amy's conclusion, however; for behind Roxana's specific situation, we recognise the universal situation of women in that society. A woman had only one way to survive, by selling herself to a man; otherwise she would starve. Having recognised this truth, there only remained a choice between two forms of barter. She could sell herself into wedlock, and become her husband's property; or she could sell herself as a whore. Roxana cannot choose convention, of course, because her husband is alive. For much of the novel after her seduction by this gentleman, however, Roxana argues against marriage, and deliberately chooses the other form of barter as offering the better bargain.[1]

The immediate consequence of this extract, then, may be some cynical comedy; but the longer-term consequence is the story of Roxana's challenge to the gender-politics and sex-economy of her time. In the latter more thoughtful context, Defoe's word 'happy' raises the question, whether it is worth living as a woman in such a world, or whether it would be less painful just to give up and starve at the outset. Certainly, that is seen to be the only way to be 'happy' in the sense of eternal salvation. Amy puts the argument that deadly sin is so necessary to survival that in her view it is 'Lawful'.

We have now studied an extract from each novel. We found that Robinson has a consistently dismissive attitude towards women, which Defoe treats as a mild satire on the masculine outlook, going as far as to show Robinson treating women as livestock on the final page. We have then found both of our female narrators providing a clear analysis of the economic and social circumstances of women, damning to the society of Defoe's time. Both of the extracts we have studied show the female narrator in an appealing context: we feel for and with Moll, as she is encircled by argument, unable to challenge the masculine power of her first lover; and we sympathise with Roxana's *naïveté*, perhaps wishing it were realistic, even as we anticipate her comic submission. However, as we find repeatedly, Defoe's works consist of a continuous series of surprises, changes, and alterations of perspective. Women and patriarchy are constantly present and constantly changing topics in both *Moll Flanders* and *Roxana*. We will therefore consider these two texts more widely.

Comparative Discussion

Our extracts from *Moll Flanders* and *Roxana* both feature the narrators as victims of sexual exploitation because they are women. We have noted Moll's suffering and helplessness as she is bullied by the hypocritical masculine reasoning that oppresses her. Elsewhere, she has likened a woman without friends to a jewel 'dropt on the Highway' (*MF* 182), left for any unscrupulous man to pick up. However, we see Moll in different circumstances at different times. Let us look at the episode of the drunken gentleman Moll robs, and who is then inveigled into maintaining her for about a year.

Moll and the Drunken Gentleman

First, during her account of the evening, Moll tells us that she went into a house with him 'in Hopes to make something of it at last' and that 'as for the Bed, &c. I was not much concern'd about that Part' (*MF* 293). Such hardened comments introduce for the first time a level of unmitigated whoring to which Moll does not descend at any other time: she beds her drunken John, and then robs him. Within another page, however, Moll adopts a different tone. Now she deplores the fact that whores 'value not the Pleasure . . . the passive Jade thinks of no Pleasure but the Money' and seems horrified at the thought that an illness might be transferred to 'his Modest and Virtuous Wife, and thereby sowing the Contagion in the Life-blood of his Posterity?'. Indeed, for most of pages 294–6 Moll preaches what is hardly less than a sermon against male drunkenness. She repeatedly contrasts the gentleman, who is 'a good sort', a 'man of Sense', 'fine', 'comely', 'handsome', 'sober solid', 'charming', and 'agreeable'; and his family who are 'honest virtuous', 'innocent', and 'Modest', against the 'whore' from 'the worst of all Holes' full of 'Dirt' and 'Filth' and with danger of 'Pox' or 'a Dart . . . through his Liver' (all *MF* 294–6). In the course of her apparent sermon, Moll quotes Proverbs, and decries the horrors of syphilis, while the whole passage is a diatribe against the madness of drunkenness. The man is portrayed as a victim of the drink, for there is 'nothing so absurd, so surfeiting, so ridiculous as a Man heated by Wine in his Head' (*MF* 294), and is pitied for the 'shame and regret' he will feel when he comes to himself.

While this sermon lasts, Moll emphasises the contrast between a virtuous world of genteel marriage and family life, and the 'Filth of all the

Town' – the world of thieves, whores, drunkenness and debauchery, closely associated with syphilis. Notice that the lower world carries a threat of 'Contagion' to the gentleman's 'Posterity': this remark implies the purpose of that virtuous marriage-world – to produce a healthy heir to inherit the property. In her neo-sermon, Moll seems to decry drunkenness because it threatens to breach the border between virtuous and wicked worlds and so let 'Contagion' in.

We said 'While this sermon lasts': as we now expect from Defoe, there succeed a series of perplexing changes which complicate the mix. First, Moll tells us an amusing anecdote, about a whore who could pick a man's pocket during intercourse; then we are told of her Governess's mixed feelings: close to tears that a gentleman can be so much at risk from alcohol, but 'pleas'd . . . wonderfully' at the profitable outcome. A new scene opens as the Governess negotiates with the victim. Moll is pragmatic and blunt when she compares the two ways of making a living that are open to her, and hopes to be kept as his mistress: 'and tho' it was a Life wicked enough, yet it was not so full of Danger as this I was engag'd in' (*MF* 304); but within a page her moralising reflections obtrude: 'Thus you see having committed a Crime once, is a sad Handle to the committing of it again, whereas all the Regret, and Reflections wear off when the Temptation renews itself' (*MF* 306). At the same time she is alert enough to point out to him that she has not robbed him, and when he asks how she lives, she lies about working at her needle, a fiction that no doubt satisfies the feminine stereotype in which he believes; but which we remember caused hilarity when Moll proposed it as an 8-year-old child.

From looking at this episode, we do not discover any single development of the theme of gender in *Moll Flanders*. Rather, Defoe's critique of inequalities, stereotyping, gender-economics, and politics remains as trenchant as it has always been. The development is rather that Moll, our female narrator, responds in such a fluid and *ad hoc* manner, veering between learned morality on the one hand and learned cynical pragmatism on the other. Compared to the young girl she was when bullied by her first lover, Moll is now a much more complicated person. The many different standards of morality and honesty she applies to herself and to others change with circumstances, and she responds to situations as they occur. Several parallel strands of thought can occupy her mind simultaneously, and she can switch from moral reflection to amusing anecdote to coy euphemism to harsh cynicism, because several modes of thought are always in play. In short, Moll does not clarify a 'gender-theme' by developing her understanding, as we might expect from a conventional character. Instead, she has to live it day in and day out, improvising, and thinking on her feet, for sexual stereotyping never leaves her in peace. Moll changes from being a *naïve* young girl, to being a real woman trying to navigate her way through a confusing press of changing circumstances.

As we have seen from this further discussion, Moll is sometimes preacher, sometimes whore, sometimes the exploiter, profiting from the economics of sex, and sometimes victim. At different times she acts up to a feminine stereotype, or finds herself deserted, or grabs the main chance. Through all these changes, the novel tells Defoe's critical and penetrating story about the gender inequalities of the time. At the end of the novel, we may think of Moll as having arrived at a peaceful haven at last. She manages her husband successfully, organising their lives while he had 'his Gun to divert him . . . which he greatly delighted in'; and on the final page they are 'both in good Heart and Health', wealthy on the proceeds from their plantation. However, *Moll Flanders* is not a story of female empowerment – her roles are limited to wife, whore, and thief; and her actions and understanding are a matter of partial confusion and partial insight, always led by a great deal of improvisation and often the outcome of severe suffering. It is noticeable that Moll flatters her final husband's vanity by treating him to a 'fine Saddle with Holsters and Pistoles very handsome', 'two good long Wigs', and a 'Scarlet Cloak' (*MF* 424), and only reveals their wealth to him in increments. Defoe may be indulging his sense of humour here, having Moll dress up her colonial gentleman as a dashing highwayman; but there can be no doubt that she is playing the role of wife by indirectly managing their business and his ego.

Roxana contains as bewildering and complex a series of scenes, in relation to our theme, as are found in *Moll Flanders*. We will look at one further episode from *Roxana*, rather to add to our appreciation of the theme, than in any pretence that we can achieve a thorough understanding.

Roxana and the Debate on Marriage

On pages 181–94 there is an extended debate between Roxana and her Dutch merchant, on the subject of matrimony, because he has proposed and she rejects him.

At the start, Roxana rejects his proposals on account of her financial independence. She knows that 'if I shou'd be a Wife, all I had then, was given up to the Husband, and I was thenceforth to be under his Authority only.' Because she is independently wealthy, she sees herself having to 'give him twenty Thousand Pound to marry me', which would be stupid. Furthermore, she is in profit, because he gave her a thousand pistoles and paid other expenses for her in Paris, in the hope of marrying her. Now that they are lovers, he can hardly ask her to return the money. However, in their arguments on the subject, Roxana tells him that she 'could not give him a Reason for' not marrying, but that 'I had an Aversion to it, and desir'd he wou'd not insist upon it' (quotations are from *R* 183 and 185). The merchant then removes Roxana's objection by offering to settle all her fortune on herself and leave it in her hands. This ends the first stage of their dispute, and she is temporarily lost for an argument. Defoe trenchantly points out the difficulty: to marry him now would confess that her previous refusal was mere miserliness, 'which, tho' it was true, yet was really too gross for me to acknowledge' (*R* 186).

Roxana finds herself 'oblig'd to give a new Turn to it, and talk upon a kind of an elevated Strain, which really was not in my Thoughts at first, at-all', and so we enter the second stage of dispute. Roxana begins by pleading for a woman's freedom:

> That the very Nature of the Marriage-Contract was, in short, nothing but giving up Liberty, Estate, Authority, and every-thing, to the Man, and the Woman was indeed, a meer Woman ever after, that is to say, a Slave. (*R* 187)

This is a radical view, and the merchant is not slow to put forward the man's traditional counter-argument: Roxana is right 'in some Respects', he says, but in return the man has 'all the Care of things', the 'Weight of Business', and the 'Toil of Life' upon his shoulders, together with 'Labour' and 'Anxiety'; while the woman has only to be 'waited on, and made much of; be serv'd, and lov'd, and made easie'. There are weaknesses in the merchant's case, most particularly that the woman's advantages in married life depend upon the husband's behaviour: she will be 'easie; *especially if the Husband acted as became him*', and Roxana renews her attack by re-iterating her case: why should a woman who is free and therefore 'Masculine in her politick Capacity' or 'a Man in her separated Capacity' give away 'that Power'? A woman who does so, Roxana says, is a 'Fool' and deserves to be 'miserable' (quotations are from *R* 187–8).

The merchant pleads that a 'mutual Love' between husband and wife would rule out any 'Bondage' and mean their interests are 'one Interest; one Aim; one Design' shared between them. Roxana, however, claims that such unity in marriage does not mean equality. What he has described 'takes from a Woman every thing that can be call'd *herself*; she is to have no Interest; no Aim; no View; but all is the Interest, Aim, and View, of the Husband'. Returning to his picture of a wife living at ease and waited on, she re-casts this vision of a wife as a 'passive Creature' in 'perfect Indolence' and putting her faith in her husband, the outcome depending 'as he is either Fool or wise Man'. In the remainder of this part of her argument, Roxana re-visits the hardships she endured following her first husband's disappearance. She conjures a picture where 'she sees her Children starve; herself miserable; breaks her Heart; and cries herself to Death' (quotations are from *R* 189).

The next exchange is initiated by the merchant offering that she can have the authority in their marriage: he will allow her to manage their lives and all their money. He uses the image of their marriage as a ship that she 'should steer'. In reply, she re-casts the image, pointing out that the sailor on the helm does not direct the ship: he obeys the pilot's orders; and she urges her analysis of marriage again, in such a way as to dispose of all he has offered:

> It is not you, *says I*, that I suspect, but the Laws of Matrimony puts the Power into your Hands; bids you do it, commands you to command; and binds me, forsooth, to obey; you, that are now upon even Terms with me, and I with you, *says I*, are the next Hour set up upon

> the Throne, and the humble Wife plac'd at your Footstool; all the rest, all that you call Oneness of Interest, Mutual Affection, *and the like*, is Curtesie and Kindness then, and a Woman is indeed, infinitely oblig'd where she meets with it; but can't help herself where it fails. (*R* 190–1)

This is a damning indictment of the wife's powerlessness; and Roxana has dealt with his arguments effectively, by pointing out that she would not only have no power to enforce her comforts, but also would have to be grateful for them.

In this reverse, the merchant initiates the final phase of the debate, by invoking both religious and legal authority on the side of marriage. Matrimony was 'decreed by Heaven' for happiness and for 'establishing a legal Posterity'; and he mentions 'Inheritance', 'Scandal and Illegitimacy'. In other words, the merchant now urges all the weight of religious, social, economic, and legal pressures that bore down upon a woman of that time to force her into marriage. Roxana admits that he speaks well on this topic, but in her reply she casts him in the role of her seducer, and pleads her weakness in having submitted to his advances. This is a role he cannot in courtesy deny, whereupon Roxana follows up her advantage. They agree that he had expected her to marry him after lying with him, but Roxana points out how wrong she would have been to do so. She argues that a couple who have committed a folly can forget it if they then part; but will always be 'preserving the Crime in Memory' if they marry; and she describes a lifetime of guilt and reproaches, with children who 'do their Mother the Justice to hate her' for her immorality, and a husband who 'sometime or other upbraids' his wife. Only if the couple part is there 'an End of the Crime' and 'Time wears out the Memory of it' (quotations are from *R* 191–2).

The merchant says that Roxana has 'started a new thing in the World'; but he gives up the argument and makes ready to leave. Now for the second time Roxana is stuck for words, for 'I had no-mind to let him go neither' but 'I was in a kind of suspence, irresolute, and doubtful what Course to take' (*R* 193). Subsequently, she becomes pregnant, continues to reject marriage, and goes to England. For now, let us turn back to their debate on marriage: what have we learned about the theme we are studying, from these exchanges?

Firstly, and most prominently, Roxana has provided us with a definitive critique of marriage as an institution from a woman's point of view. The quotations we have cited could not be more powerfully or succinctly put, and they argue the point Roxana returns to again and again: that the wife is dependent because the law favours the husband. She must give up 'Liberty, Estate, Authority, and every-thing' to become her husband's slave; and marriage 'takes from a Woman every thing that can be call'd *herself*'. Furthermore, the man's traditional arguments – that he works and cares for his wife; that she need have no worries; and that mutual love unites them anyway – are effectively countered by Roxana's surprisingly modern interpretation. She denigrates the 'Indolence' expected of a wife, criticises the fact that a wife has to feel grateful for her husband's courtesy, and returns to the point that his 'Oneness' destroys her identity, or 'every thing that can be call'd *herself*'. Roxana maintains her argument – that matrimonial law is unjust – even in the face of his most generous offers: that she can direct their lives and their money, for example.

Secondly, Roxana does not reply directly when he urges the authority of religion and law. Instead, she manipulates her sexual surrender, using this trick to put him out of countenance. Perhaps the combined weight of religion and the law is too immovable to challenge head-on. Roxana therefore restricts herself to asserting her right to live an unconventional life, from choice; and uses her resourceful wiles to sidestep the full weight of convention. It is a measure of the realism and therefore the complexity of *Roxana* that we are left with a trenchant, unassailed critique of matrimonial law; and at the same time an appreciation that its power cannot be challenged.

Thirdly, Roxana develops her penetrating critique within a comic context. She is twice comically stuck for words, and once has to resort to what can be called 'feminine wiles' to sidestep his arguments. It is typical of Defoe that such a debate should be cast within a complicating context, within a comedy that can both strengthen and undercut each proposition. Look, for example, at Roxana's avoidance when the merchant urges religious and legal authority. At this point, she falls back upon a feminine stereotype, exploiting his guilt for having seduced her. This can undercut Roxana, as she uses 'feminine' manipulation to support a 'feminist' critique. On the other hand, it can heighten the poignancy of her argument, as it underlines how unequal is the struggle between one woman, and the whole massed weight of the patriarchal Church, State, system of property and inheritance, and society. So, Defoe maintains an ironic context that constantly cuts both ways. The theme comes to life, as there are always difficulties, improvisations, and compromises involved in the interaction between the theme and people in complex circumstances.

Fourthly and lastly, Roxana reminds us of the trauma behind her actions: the memory of the destitute state in which her 'Fool' husband left her is still vivid. This memory fuels the picture she paints, but the merchant 'did not know how feelingly I spoke this' (*R* 190). The connection with her past is clear. In addition, however, we may wonder how the fear of being reproached by a husband, and hated by her children, relates to Roxana's future. In short, Defoe is continuously sensitive to his character's inner life; and we can feel Roxana deriving her ideas from emotion and experience, throughout the debate. We should also notice the realistic delineation of the merchant's character. He is most generous and accommodating, so much so that he almost succeeds in disarming Roxana. However, he is a man, and his views are patriarchal; so, for example, he says that for a woman to manage her estates, 'was in some Sence, right, if the Women were able to carry it on so, but that in general, the Sex were not capable of it; their Heads were not turn'd for it' (*R* 193).

The sum of these observations is that Defoe sets his theme within an insistently complicated context. It is clear that a devastating critique of patriarchy and the sex-economy is presented in both Moll's and Roxana's texts; but this is carried through within a context of comedy, manipulation, sensitive characterisation, and the changing pressures of real circumstances. The result is that we are both impressed by the trenchant pursuit of the theme, and always reminded of how that theme is experienced by a real person in unstable circumstances.

Conclusions

There can be no doubt that Defoe is highly critical of the social and commercial conventions governing gender, sexuality, and marriage.

- Defoe's male characters are perceptively portrayed. Crusoe is suitably oblivious of the whole matter, dismissive of his mother, his wife, and the widow, and delivers women as breeding stock; Moll's first lover is a cruel and selfish hypocrite, a man who preys on women, and Jemy is a boy; Roxana's merchant subscribes to gender stereotypes – as do all men, it seems – but is more civilised, and prepared to indulge Roxana until she convinces him that she is serious. Sir Robert is also amused by Roxana's independence.
- Moll learns and suffers and eventually manages to find some security in old age; however, she is buffeted and thrown about by surprises, change and events, and relies on improvisation. Moll repeatedly tries for a settled married life, and eventually achieves this goal in old age, when she controls the marriage in stereotypical manner, by anticipating and satisfying her husband's boyish pleasures. We have described Moll as being bullied into acquiescence by the gender-system of her time. We could equally say, with the critic Miriam Lerenbaum, that she is 'a woman on her own account' because of her 'involuntary involvement in the feminine role' which is 'part of a lifelong pattern'.[2]
- Roxana makes a bolder attempt – she seeks to exploit sexual economy in defiance of society's prescriptions. Roxana ends tragically. Her story can be interpreted in terms of a tragic hubris, and whether the outcome represents a commentary on gender or on Roxana's pride, or is simply part of that unstable pattern of chance and fate that is always present in Defoe's works, remains an open question.[3]
- There is a great deal of material critical of gender-stereotypes, gender politics, and the economics of gender. Defoe provides a powerful critique. He particularly emphasises the legal authority a husband has over his wife and her possessions; and that only three ways to survive are open to a woman: as a wife, as a whore, or as a thief.
- Marriage is treated to extensive discussion and debate in *Roxana*. She is the narrator most openly defiant of convention, who consciously chooses the second means of survival.
- Both female narrators, however, express a rich and natural emotional life, often at odds with their apparent purposes. Moll often seems to act contrary to her own best interest, or is taken up by events and recognises her errors with hindsight. She is repeatedly a

victim as a woman. Roxana is more decisive, and through much of the narrative she adopts the contradictory role of exploited-exploiter.

- Defoe always provides a complicated profusion of the 'down-to-earth', what Virginia Woolf (referring to Crusoe) calls the 'large earthenware pot', and of the chance surprises of fate. These pragmatic elements are in such an anarchic relation to the theme that we experience it in a complex form rather than as simplified nostrums.
- In short, Defoe's novels partake of the quality of ordinary life: they resist purpose and shaping, they remain stubbornly unpredictable, anarchic, and 'real'. At the same time, the themes of women and patriarchy are explored thoroughly and perceptively by both of the female narrators.

Methods of Analysis

Generally this chapter has followed approaches already demonstrated in previous chapters. Two particular developments of method are worth mentioning, however.

1. We have allowed ourselves to take some short-cuts: for example, we have paid less attention to punctuation or sentence-structures. We have been able to do this because we think about the nature of the extract and the purpose of analysis first, and take an approach that seems likely to achieve that purpose.

   a. In this chapter our interest was in issues of women and patriarchy. Thinking about Robinson Crusoe, our common sense tells us that there is no relevant extract suitable for close analysis. We therefore decided to summarise the relevant material there is. Robinson is the only male narrator, so we focused on his attitudes towards women.
   b. We approached the *Moll Flanders* extract knowing that the young man is selfish and Moll is hurt. Our interest was in gender issues, and the extract describes a conflict in which the woman is victim. It made sense, therefore, to focus on defining the man's

strategy, and the woman's reaction. This helped us to show how adroitly he invites her to join the moral majority.

c. Our extract from *Roxana* is a debate concerning the gentleman's intentions. It is in the form of exchanges between Roxana and Amy, much of it in direct speech. There was therefore little point in summarising paragraphs where the speakers exchange contradictory arguments. As we were dealing with two opposed opinions, it made sense to build a full picture of each, noting how each supports and develops her argument. This helped us to realise how Amy builds her point of view in stages, by adding subsidiary statements.

2. We have been aware for some time that Defoe's texts are unusually rich in changes: in the instability of events (bringing constant surprises) and the uncertainty and changeableness of people. This feature has led us to sense that analysing one extract gives a particularly incomplete taste of any theme. In this chapter, we therefore allowed ourselves to look at another part of the text in order to fill out our view of the theme. When studying another text, it would often be helpful to select an insight found from one extract, and look elsewhere in the text for corroboration, or additional detail. When studying a Defoe novel, such an approach is possible, but it is often more rewarding to look for episodes where the theme appears under different circumstances. This method helps us gain an oversight of the variety of the theme within Defoe's unusually changeable and fluid narratives.

   a. So, in *Moll Flanders*, our extract showed Moll as a victim. In the concluding discussion, we therefore chose to look at an episode where Moll is the exploiter when she seduces and robs the drunken gentleman. She is, of course, sexually used; but at least this episode shows her in very different circumstances because in control.

   b. In *Roxana*, the extract we studied showed her *naïve* and optimistic about the landlord. We therefore chose to look at an episode where Roxana develops and argues the opposite, expressing pessimistic cynicism and refusing to trust any man.

From taking these short-cuts and deliberately seeking out the variety and differences within the theme, we feel that we have progressed a little further than we might have done by sticking to exhaustive analysis of extracts. However, our study is still at an early stage, because of the complications that are so abundant in Defoe. We need only remember how Roxana's reply, when her Dutchman invokes religion and law, simultaneously validates and undercuts his attack.

Suggested Work

Gender issues make such a continuous motif within *Moll Flanders* and *Roxana* that you can open almost any page and choose a passage for study. Furthermore, as remarked above, each new page you study will significantly widen and alter your perception of the theme. Consequently, in this chapter we suggest **two further episodes** for study, from each of **the two texts narrated by women**. The following extracts will repay close analysis:

In ***Moll Flanders***:

(1) look at page 175 (from 'It is True that Sick Beds are the times, when such Correspondences as this are look'd on . . . ') to page 177 (' . . . as if I was forsaken of God's Grace, and abandon'd by Heaven to a continuing in my wickedness.'), when Moll is deserted by her penitent gentleman of Bath.
(2) look at page 249 (from 'I never liv'd four pleasanter Days together in my life . . . ') to page 253 (' . . . my Understanding was sometimes quite lost in Fancies and Imagination.'), which tells more or less the whole course of Moll's 6-year marriage to her friend the banker.

In ***Roxana***:

(1) look at the passage on pages 80–2 (from 'At Night, when we came to go to-Bed, *Amy* came into the Chamber . . . ' as far as ' . . . as the poor Girl said, so it happen'd, and she was really

with-Child'), when Roxana puts Amy in bed with her 'husband', the once-landlord. This passage raises perplexing questions concerning Roxana's own opinions, her relationship with Amy, and her motives, which are fascinating to explore.

(2) look at page 117 (from 'But to look back to the particular Observation I was making...') to page 119 ('...for he was extremely fond of it.'). Here Roxana almost goes too far in conjuring the Prince's conscience, and it is interesting to consider her motives within the context of his affection for their child, and the stigma of illegitimacy.

5

Instability and the Outsider

This chapter is an attempt to describe the quality we have recognised in several different contexts during the course of our study that can be called 'instability', and is made up from the unpredictability, improvised adaptations of character, rapid changes of circumstances, and complex motives that abound in Defoe's novels. In Chapter 4, we remarked that 'Defoe's novels partake of the quality of ordinary life: they resist purpose and shaping, they remain stubbornly unpredictable, anarchic'. We will now look at this aspect of Defoe's narratives, and at the same time we will consider his choice of three narrators who are at or beyond the margins of society.

Analysis: *Robinson Crusoe*, pp. 102–3

We begin with the most 'outside' view of the three: that of Robinson Crusoe on his island:

> This griev'd me heartily, and now I saw, tho' too late, the folly of beginning a work before we count the cost; and before we judge rightly of our own strength to go through with it.
>
> In the middle of this work, I finish'd my fourth year in this place, and kept my anniversary with the same devotion, and with as much comfort as ever before; for by a constant study, and serious application of the Word of God, and by the assistance of his grace, I gain'd different

knowledge from what I had before. I entertain'd different notions of things. I look'd now upon the world as a thing remote, which I had nothing to do with, no expectation from, and indeed no desires about: In a word, I had nothing indeed to do with it, nor was ever like to have, so I thought it look'd as we may perhaps look upon it hereafter, *viz.* as a place I had liv'd in, but was come out of it; and well might I say, as Father *Abraham to Dives, Between me and thee is a great gulph fix'd.*

In the first place, I was remov'd from all the wickedness of the world here. I had neither the *lust of the flesh, the lust of the eye, or the pride of life*. I had nothing to covet; for I had all that I was now capable of enjoying: I was lord of the whole manor; or if I pleas'd, I might call my self king, or emperor over the whole country which I had possession of. There were no rivals. I had no competitor, none to dispute sovereignty or command with me. I might have rais'd ship loadings of corn; but I had no use for it; so I let as little grow as I thought enough for my occasion. I had tortoise or turtles enough; but now and then one was as much as I could put to any use. I had timber enough to have built a fleet of ships. I had grapes enough to have made wine, or to have cur'd into raisins, to have loaded that fleet when they had been built.

But all I could make use of was, all that was valuable. I had enough to eat, and to supply my wants, and, what was all the rest to me? If I kill'd more flesh than I could eat, the dog must eat it, or the vermin. If I sow'd more corn than I could eat, it must be spoil'd. The trees that I cut down, were lying to rot on the ground. I could make no more use of them than for fewel; and that I had no occasion for, but to dress my food.

In a word, the nature and experience of things dictated to me upon just reflection, that all the good things of this world, are no farther good to us, than they are for our use; and that whatever we may heap up indeed to give others, we enjoy just as much as we can use, and no more. The most covetous griping miser in the world would have been cur'd of the vice of covetousness, if he had been in my case; for I possess'd infinitely more than I knew what to do with. I had no room for desire, except it was of things which I had not, and they were but trifles, though indeed of great use to me. I had, as I hinted before, a parcel of money, as well gold as silver, about thirty six pounds sterling: Alas! there the nasty sorry useless stuff lay; I had no manner of business for it; and I often thought with my self, that I would have given a handful of it for a gross of tobacco-pipes, or for a hand-mill to grind my corn; nay, I would have given it all for six-penny-worth of *turnip* and *carrot* seed out of *England*, or for a handful of *pease* and *beans*, and a bottle of ink:

> *As it was*, I had not the least advantage by it, or benefit from it; but there it lay in a drawer, and grew mouldy with the damp of the cave, in the wet season; and if I had had the drawer full of diamonds, it had been the same case; and they had been of no manner of value to me, because of no use. (*RC* 102–3)

Let us take an overview of this extract by summarising each paragraph according to our habit. The passage opens when Robinson has made a boat, but cannot launch it. The paragraphs can be summarised as follows:

1. I was upset, and learned the value of planning a project thoroughly beforehand.
2. I celebrated 4 years on the island, and with God's help I saw the world as if from Heaven, as not relevant to me, and felt a gulf between myself and other men.
3. I was separated from lust and pride, I was King without rivals and could have produced large quantities of goods and a fleet to carry them.
4. However, nothing had value that I could not use.
5. I learned that nothing is worthwhile unless it will be used. I had money but it was useless, and I would have given it all for the few trivial things I longed for.

Looking at our summary tells us that there are two strands to Robinson's discourse at this point. First, he tries to convey the distance he feels between himself and the world, and the uniqueness of his perspective. Secondly, he develops a sermon against surplus, expounding the principle that everything must be for use, and nothing else has value. We will look at these two topics of Robinson's thought in turn, and then examine how he knits them together.

The passage begins, ironically, as Robinson learns a practical lesson: he wasted a great deal of effort making a boat, but failed to plan how he would launch it. However, he immediately claims a unique enlightenment for himself, of a different kind from this practical lesson. He claims that his own 'serious application of the Word of God' combines with 'the assistance of his grace' to bring him a sense of distance from the world, and set him free from all worldly desires. He describes his view of the world as 'I thought it look'd as we may perhaps look upon it hereafter.' Robinson imagines himself as Abraham, with a 'great gulph' between him and 'Dives'. This is a reference to Luke, Chapter 16. The story is of 'Dives', a rich man now suffering in Hell, who sees Abraham and a poor man called Lazarus, happy in Heaven. He calls on Abraham for help, but the reply is that 'between us and you there is a great gulf fixed: so that they which would pass from hence to you cannot; neither can they pass to us, that would come from thence'.[1] So, Robinson's references have a twofold resonance. First, he flatters himself, arrogating the purity of a soul in heaven and the patriarchal status of Abraham. Secondly, he casts his island as Heaven, and the world of which he is no longer part, as Hell.

The effect of these claims seems to be equivocal. Robinson succeeds in conveying the unbridgeable distance from which he views the world: phrases such as 'different knowledge', 'different notions', and the words 'remote' and 'nothing' (twice) do convey the strangeness of Robinson's circumstances, as does the description of 'a place I had liv'd in, but was come out of it'; and this promotes our understanding, preparing us for some 'different notions' from the narrator's unique experiences. On the other hand, Robinson both goes too far in claiming God's grace and identifying himself with Abraham-in-bliss; and seems to mis-cast his island as Heaven. We can note a further equivocal element of the context: Robinson is still 'In the middle of this work', that is the futile labour on the boat, when he celebrates his anniversary and spiritual 'knowledge'. So, Robinson is still unaware of his silly mistake (the unlaunchable boat), when he develops grandiose ideas of superiority over 'the world'. Poignantly however, Robinson remembers the 'great gulph' mentioned in the Gospel. Abraham's words 'they which would pass from hence to you cannot; neither can they pass to us, that would come from thence' underline the hopelessness of Robinson's situation.

By the second paragraph of our extract, then, we are already involved in an equivocal set of impressions and ironies. Defoe charts Robinson's mental development as an outsider in a complex ironic context, and our third paragraph increases complexity. Robinson revisits the idea of his detachment from 'expectation' and 'desire' in stronger terms: this time he celebrates freedom from '*lust of the flesh, lust of the eye, or the pride of life*'. This changes the idea from that of freedom from emotional dependence, to glorying in being free from sin. However, Robinson's claim is hollow: his isolation, not his virtue, makes him virtuous. The corollary – that a return to 'the world' would mean a return to sinful living – is hinted by the next stage of his thinking, which he begins by remarking that he is 'lord of the whole manor'. Robinson here celebrates the absence of any higher authority outranking him. However, he moves from 'lord' to 'king' and finally 'emperor', as if he cannot resist adopting ever-grander titles; whereupon he glories in his absolute 'sovereignty' and 'command'. We can appreciate that he may feel an outsider's freedom, liberated from the need to compete that is always present in a human society. On the other hand, Robinson displays hubris, taking pleasure in the concepts of 'sovereignty' and 'command' even though he has nobody to command. A critique of colonialism is suggested, also, by the easy manner in which Robinson assumes ownership of his island and his right to rule over it. This questionable paragraph ends with further grandiose visions, this time visions of commerce: of 'ship loadings of corn', 'a fleet of ships', and enough 'wine' or 'raisins, to have loaded that fleet'. These are a colonist/planter's visions, and we notice Robinson's easy assumption, again: this time that he may exploit whatever nature puts within his grasp.

The third paragraph, then, strikes a succession of discordant notes. First, there is the enforced virtue of isolation; then a series of grandiose titles of rank and power; then, visions of plentiful merchandise; with, additionally, the casual assumption of 'sovereignty' or ownership and rule. Finally, Robinson enjoys freedom from competition, the one possibly liberating element of being outside 'the world' that is conveyed in this paragraph. We must never forget the ironic context: Robinson has plenty of timber for his imaginary 'fleet', but is still working on one canoe that will stay stuck on dry land. Where could this 'fleet of ships' come from? So far, then, the outsider's insight, which Robinson has called 'a different knowledge' and 'different notions of things', tells of a man very ready to think well of himself (as an angelic Abraham, and free from '*lust*', for example) who indulges grandiose daydreams in which he revels in power and possessions.

Paragraph 4 tells us that only useful goods have value. However, the form of the three parallel statements ('If I kill'd . . . ', 'If I sow'd . . . ', 'The trees that I cut . . . ') conjures a picture of overproduction, and of potential plenty and waste, rather than sober restraint. Yet again, although developing a contrary moral, Robinson's mind seems to dwell on visions of plenty and of bulk production, rather than his meagre one-man economy.

The final paragraph of our extract preaches the moral, 'That all the good things of this world, are no farther good to us, than they are for our use.' This is indeed a serious insight and a piece of wisdom that Robinson's isolation, and his use of the island's resources, has taught him. Further, this axiom of 'use' is part of the general correction of his opinions that Robinson claims to learn from his experiences. For example, it opposes that 'rash and immoderate desire of rising faster than the nature of the thing admitted' (*RC* 32), which tempted him to the catastrophic voyage; and so this new axiom of 'use' is related to the 'middle' philosophy Robinson espouses in hindsight. Robinson claims that he learned this 'use' axiom directly from his experience upon the island: for 'if he had been in my case', the 'most covetous griping miser' would have been 'cur'd of the vice of covetousness'.

Robinson's moral is therefore evidence of the benefit his mind draws from his experience. However, the remainder of the paragraph complicates the issue yet again. Showing that he is free from 'covetousness', Robinson describes his money as 'nasty sorry useless stuff'. There is a serious argument here, for we may decide to value nature's bounty above the artificial value of precious metals, which can neither be eaten, nor used for clothing nor for any other natural purpose. We may therefore concur with Robinson's comment that he 'had no manner of business for' his money; for even a drawer full of diamonds would have been 'of no manner of value to me, because of no use'. On the other hand, Robinson encloses regrets within this argument. He describes the money in rather resentful language as 'nasty sorry useless' and exclaims 'Alas!', not because money is intrinsically artificial, but because he cannot go to a shop and spend it. Robinson's argument is becoming confused: he does not prove that money is useless. On the contrary, he desperately wishes to have access to a shop. So, as he argues the virtues of a Rousseau-esque natural life, we are most struck by his longing for the products of a commercial society: 'tobacco-pipes', a 'hand-mill', or a 'bottle of ink'. He yearns for these things, despite having 'infinitely more than I knew what to do with'.

In summary, then, Defoe provides us with a dual picture of the relation between this individual and society. On the one hand, he describes and explores various aspects of an original perspective, that which we may call the 'outsider's' view. Simultaneously, however, Defoe shows us how learned habits of thought, and human weaknesses, are like tentacles that still clutch at Robinson's brain and heart, confusing his ideas and spurring his emotions even while he is cut off from society. The result is that an 'outsider's' perspective presents us with a complex set of insights: the effect of distance on one's view of society; the effect of isolation on the psychology of Robinson; and the relativity of values, according to usefulness on the one hand, and rarity, or supply and demand, on the other.

Analysis: *Moll Flanders*, pp. 330–2

We now turn to *Moll Flanders*. Moll lives an unconventional life, and she tells us that her 'outsider's' experience of sexual morality would have made her 'the better Wife for all the Difficulties I had pass'd thro', by a great deal' (*MF* 182). However, she is at her most 'outside' as a thief, since discovery would mean death. Here is Moll's description of one thieving escapade:

> The next Day I dress'd me up again, but in quite different Cloaths, and walk'd the same way again; but nothing offer'd till I came into *St. James's Park*, where I saw abundance of fine Ladies in the *Park*, walking in the *Mall*, and among the rest, there was a little Miss, a young Lady of about 12 or 13 Years old, and she had a Sister, as I suppose it was, with her, that might be about Nine Year old; I observ'd the biggest had a fine gold Watch on, and a good Necklace of Pearl, and they had a Footman in Livery with them; but as it is not usual for the Footman to go behind the Ladies in the *Mall*, so I observ'd the Footman stop'd at their going into the *Mall*, and the biggest of the Sisters spoke to him, which I perceiv'd was to bid him be just there when they came back.

When I heard her dismiss the Footman, I step'd up to him, and ask'd him, what little Lady that was? and held a little Chat with him, about what a pretty Child it was with her, and how Genteel and well Carriag'd the Lady, the eldest would be; how Womanish, and how Grave; and the Fool of a Fellow told me presently who she was, that she was Sir *Thomas . . . 's* eldest Daughter of *Essex*, and that she was a great Fortune, that her Mother was not come to Town yet; but she was with Sir *William . . . 's* Lady of *Suffolk*, at her Lodgings in *Suffolk-Street*, and a great deal more; that they had a Maid and a Woman to wait on them, besides, Sir *Thomas's* Coach, the Coachman and himself and that the young Lady was Governess to the whole Family as well here, as at Home too; and in short, told me abundance of things enough for my business.

I was very well dress'd, and had my gold Watch, as well as she; so I left the Footman, and I puts myself in a Rank with this young Lady, having stay'd till she had taken one double Turn in the *Mall*, and was going forward again, by and by, I saluted her by her Name, with the Title of Lady *Betty*: I ask'd her when she heard from her Father? When my Lady her Mother would be in Town and how she did?

I talk'd so familiarly to her of her whole Family that she cou'd not suspect, but that I knew them all intimately: I ask'd her why she would come Abroad without Mrs. *Chime* with her (that was the Name of her Woman) to take care of Mrs. *Judith* that was her Sister. Then I enter'd into a long Chat with her about her Sister, what a fine little Lady she was, and ask'd her if she had learn'd *French*, and a Thousand such little things to entertain her, when on a sudden we see the Guards come, and the Crowd run to see the King go by to the Parliament-House.

The Ladies run all to the Side of the *Mall*, and I help'd my Lady to stand upon the edge of the Boards on the side of the *Mall*, that she might be high enough to see; and took the little one and lifted her quite up; during which, I took care to convey the gold Watch so clean away from the Lady *Betty*, that she never felt it, nor miss'd it, till all the Crowd was gone, and she was gotten into the middle of the *Mall* among the other Ladies.

I took my leave of her in the very Crowd, and said to her, as if in hast, dear Lady *Betty* take care of your little Sister, and so the Crowd did, as it were Thrust me away from her, and that I was oblig'd unwillingly to take my leave. (*MF* 330–2)

We easily follow Moll's strategy: she dresses, observes, and researches; then acts up until there is an opportunity; whereupon she strikes, then escapes; and Defoe relates the event in six paragraphs, each one a separate stage. By this time, we are used to Moll being a thief. She begins, in misery and poverty, by taking an unattended bundle. She then follows a 'wicked Impulse' to 'go out again and seek for what might happen' (*MF* 257). Gradually guilt is calmed, until she tells us that the Devil 'prompted me to go out and take a Walk, that is to say, to see if any thing would offer in the old Way' (*MF* 263); and, when her affair with the gentleman ends, she decides to 'look Abroad into the Street again' (*MF* 308). As she becomes more experienced, so the way Moll sees the world changes. By the time of our extract, she is a practiced opportunist. She has learned how to go out and 'seek for what might happen', 'see if any thing would offer', or 'look Abroad'. Notice the emphasis on seeing: 'seek', 'see', and 'look'.

Stage one of Moll's method is her own costume: on her second day in the West End, she is in 'quite different Cloaths'. Later in the extract, we learn that she was 'very well dress'd, and had my gold Watch, as well as she'; so Moll ensures that she will not stand out among a crowd of West End ladies. We have previously heard that she 'had several Shapes to appear in' or that 'to prevent my being known, I pull'd off my blue Apron' (*MF* 308, 309 resp.). Again, the emphasis is on appearance, as Moll seeks to become invisible by blending in. As she recedes from sight, her target – the rest of the world – comes forward into sharp focus. Moll tells us that 'I saw' the crowd in which 'there was' a young girl; then 'I observ'd' a gold watch; 'observ'd' the Footman stop and 'perceiv'd' the order given by the girl. We can follow the process of elimination: from a crowd of ladies, Moll selects the most vulnerable, 12 and 9 years old, then homes in upon the target: the watch. The contrast is obvious: Moll herself becomes invisible, which makes everybody else unusually visible.

The next three paragraphs are reported speech: first between Moll and the Footman, then her talk to the children. The first of these is a paragraph in two parts, hinged at the semicolon after 'Grave', when the 'Fool of a Fellow' tells Moll everything she needs to know in order to pose as a friend of the family. This structure allows the paragraph to move in one sentence from beginning to end, so that the transition from Moll's flattering remarks about the children (who are 'pretty', 'Genteel', 'well Carriag'd', 'Womanish', and 'Grave'), to the Footman's boasts about his master's family (that the girl is 'a great Fortune' and details of all the servants they have), is smooth and seems inevitable. The majority of the paragraph, being either flattery or boast, is in complimentary terms. There are two descents: Moll's contemptuous, alliterated phrase 'Fool of a Fellow', which merely underlines how predictably her flattery and the footman's vanity work; and her final cynical comment 'enough for my business'.

The next two paragraphs tell us how Moll gains Betty's confidence, and in the second (paragraph 4 of our extract), Moll 'enter'd into a long Chat with her' including 'a Thousand such little things to entertain her'. Clearly, Moll cannot allow her mark to answer, or to ask any questions of her own. The sentence moves from 'Chat', to the 'Sister', then '*French*', and finally 'a Thousand' things, and we sense Moll's increasing desperation to keep the conversation going, so there is palpable relief when 'on a sudden' the Guards and the King approach.

The actual theft is beautifully placed in the middle of Defoe's sentence, the first half of which builds increasing speed and height: the ladies 'run' and Moll helps Betty onto the boards, to be 'high', then 'took' the younger girl and 'lifted her quite up'. The culmination of these movements is the climax of the paragraph: echoing the construction 'quite up' Moll manages to take the watch 'clean away'. The second half of the sentence has the three shorter phrases, 'that she never felt it, nor miss'd it, till all the Crowd was gone,' like excited panting, followed by the long phrase when Betty is finally back down on the ground and out of the crowd, and calm. Our final paragraph shows us how thorough is Moll's skill as a performer, as she allows the crowd to seem to part them, and fixes Betty's attention on her sister, even as she escapes.

Our extract, then, tells a story of daring theft by a skilled operator who exploits others' weaknesses: in this case the Footman's vanity about his master's wealth and little Betty's trusting nature. Betty's excitement at the King passing by and the naturalness with which information flows from flattery are both enhanced by the shape of

Defoe's sentences, and we also enjoy Moll's skilful performance. However, at the same time we are being introduced to a new way of looking. In Moll's stories of thefts, Defoe shows how she might 'go out and take a Walk, that is to say, to see if any thing would offer'. Like Moll, we become invisible behind our anonymity and disguise, while the rest of the world appears in a new light: as a series of potential opportunities where, rather than seeing a whole society, certain elements stand out: first, objects that are not watched or not bolted down; and secondly, people with weaknesses, people who are inattentive, trusting, or easily bamboozled by flattery. This is the particular viewpoint to which Moll introduces the reader; and the more professional she becomes, the more we become used to seeing the world from the thief's 'outside' point of view. Defoe turns this aspect of Moll's narrative into a beneficial lesson for the reader, in the following tongue-in-cheek passage:

> . . . [my Governess] observ'd, that a Thief being a Creature that Watches the Advantages of other Peoples mistakes, 'tis impossible but that to one that is vigilant and industrious many Opportunities must happen, and therefore she thought that one so exquisitely keen in the Trade as I was, would scarce fail of something extraordinary where ever I went.
>
> On the other hand, every Branch of my Story, if duly consider'd, may be useful to honest People, and afford a due Caution to People of some sort or other to Guard against the like Surprizes, and to have their Eyes about them when they have to do with Strangers of any kind, for 'tis very seldom that some Snare or other is not in their way. The Moral indeed of all my History is left to be gather'd by the Senses and Judgment of the Reader; I am not Qualified to preach to them, let the Experience of one Creature compleatly Wicked, and compleatly Miserable be a Storehouse of useful warning to those that read. (*MF* 342–3)

We can enjoy the play with which Defoe surrounds this ingenuous digression. So, for example, Moll's conventional repentance in 'compleatly Wicked, and compleatly Miserable' is balanced by the Governess's compliment 'one so exquisitely keen in the Trade'. Notice also that the moral is left to the reader's 'Senses and Judgment', and is practical, not spiritual or ethical, advice. In all of this playful commentary, however, Defoe argues the value of reading Moll's narrative specifically because of her special perspective: 'a Thief being a Creature that Watches the Advantages of other Peoples mistakes', the thief's narrative becomes 'a Storehouse of useful warning' for people to 'have their Eyes about them', all suggesting that Moll's viewpoint is an unconventional and eye-opening perspective.

Some aspects of Moll's 'outsider' perspective may be shocking to us. For example, 'Lady *Betty*' is not the first child she has robbed; and her exploits in the burning house may also strike a reader as morally repugnant. Defoe also makes some fun out of Moll's special way of seeing, however. So, when Moll sees a horse she can remove, she takes it; but 'never was poor Thief more at a loss to know what to do with any thing that was stolen' (*MF* 326), and she has to return the animal to its owner. The idea of Moll walking away with a horse, and then not knowing what to do with it, is very funny; which her thefts from the fire or from children are not.

Analysis: *Roxana*, pp. 198–9

We now turn to *Roxana*, where the protagonist takes an 'outsider's' point of view in a more intellectual manner, and in circumstances – unlike Moll's and Robinson's – where she does not seem to be under duress:

> If I had not been one of the foolishest, as well as wickedest Creatures upon Earth, I cou'd never have acted thus; I had one of the honestest compleatest Gentlemen upon Earth, at my hand; he had in one Sence sav'd my Life, but he had sav'd that Life from Ruin in a most remarkable Manner; he lov'd me even to Distraction, and had come from *Paris* to *Rotterdam*, on purpose to seek me; he had offer'd me Marriage, even after I was with-Child by him, and had offer'd to quit all his Pretensions to my Estate, and give it up to my own Management, having a plentiful Estate of his own: Here I might have settled myself out of the reach even of Disaster itself; his Estate and mine, wou'd have purchas'd even then above two Thousand Pounds a Year, and I might have liv'd like a Queen, nay, far more happy than a Queen; and which was above all, I had now an Opportunity to have quitted a Life of Crime and Debauchery, which I had been given up to for several Years, and to have sat down quiet in

> Plenty and Honour, and to have set myself apart to the Great Work, which I have since seen so much Necessity of, and Occasion for; I mean that of Repentance.
>
> But my Measure of Wickedness was not yet full; I continued obstinate against Matrimony, and yet I cou'd not bear the Thoughts of his going away neither; as to the Child, I was not very anxious about it; I told him, I wou'd promise him that it shou'd never come to him to upbraid him with its being illegitimate; that if it was a Boy, I wou'd breed it up like the Son of a Gentleman, and use it well for his sake; and after a little more such Talk as this, and seeing him resolv'd to go, I retir'd, but cou'd not help letting him see the Tears run down my Cheeks; he came to me, and kiss'd me, entreated me, conjur'd me by the Kindness he had shown me in my Distress; by the Justice he had done me in my Bills and Money-Affairs; by the Respect which made him refuse a Thousand Pistoles from me for his Expences with that Traytor, the *Jew*; by the Pledge of our Misfortunes, *So he call'd it*, which I carry'd with me; and by all that the sincerest Affection cou'd propose to do, that I wou'd not drive him away.
>
> But it wou'd not do; I was stupid and senceless, deaf to all his Importunities, and continued so to the last; so we parted... (*R* 198–9)

In Chapter 4, we studied Roxana's critique of Matrimonial Law and gender-politics, her case being that marriage deprives the wife of all property, power, and independent identity. In this extract, Roxana's hindsight takes a different stand, and she calls herself 'one of the foolishest, as well as wickedest, Creatures upon Earth' for rejecting marriage as offered by her Dutch merchant; and she concludes that because she remained 'stupid and senceless' they 'parted'. This extract, then, argues the conventional point of view Roxana adopts as a retrospective narrator, the repentant attitude she has 'since seen so much Necessity of'. However, when we look more closely at the narrative Roxana encloses in repentant hindsight, we find that her experiences do not support the moral conclusions she foists upon them. We have met this effect before in Robinson's inappropriate adoption of his father's 'middle station' philosophy; or when Moll turns her criminal experience into a practical lesson for her victims. Here, Roxana adopts a pro-marriage opinion, but in a context that undermines any such conventional moral.

Our extract's first paragraph lists the advantages from which Roxana would have benefited had she accepted the merchant's offer. He is 'one of the honestest compleatest Gentlemen' and had saved Roxana from ruin; he loved her so much that he followed her to Rotterdam; he proposed marriage, even after she became pregnant; he would let her keep her money, he was rich, between them they could live in luxury. She could have given up sin and devoted the rest of her life to repentance. It sounds irresistible, but let us consider each item in turn.

He is honest and a well-set-up man, which are advantages to the match. He performed an important service, saving her from ruin. Yes, and she should respond with gratitude; but gratitude is not necessarily a basis for marriage. He loves her so much that he followed her to Rotterdam: yes, but this again is an ambivalent reason. On the one hand, it suggests that he may treat her well after they are married. So, if all she requires is an obedient man, this is a sound reason to marry him. On the other hand, it is irrelevant to her decision, which should take into account her love, as well as his. As for his proposing marriage even when she is already pregnant, and allowing her to control her money – these promises may recall the men she described in her anti-matrimonial discourses as using 'the Pretence of Affection', so that marriage 'takes from a Woman every thing that can be call'd *herself*' (*R* 189). Furthermore, his promises do not answer her objection: he may treat her well, but she has no guarantee, because matrimonial law gives him absolute power. So, all his promises of kindness are only another form of subjection, because 'a Woman is indeed, infinitely oblig'd, where she meets with it; but can't help herself where it fails' (*R* 191).

There are two further items on Roxana's list. First, they are rich enough to live in luxury. This is true, but not a compelling reason for marriage, since Roxana is already independently wealthy: her choice is not between marriage and poverty. Again, we should recall Roxana's objections, when the merchant talked of husbands suffering the cares of financial management while their wives live at ease. Roxana said that a woman's marriage 'was a dear Way of purchasing their Ease; for very often when the Trouble was taken off their Hands, so was their Money too' (*R* 193). So, with her independent fortune, and matrimonial law as it was, her financial self-interest would argue for her to remain single.

Finally, Roxana declares that she could have given up 'Crime and Debauchery' and devoted her life to 'Repentance' had she married the merchant. There are two possible interpretations of this statement. Either Roxana felt a repugnance for her way of life, and would have been happier as a conventional wife; or, she now (i.e. with hindsight) feels that she missed an opportunity to escape into virtue. That the latter motive is the stronger is suggested by her idea of being 'sat down quiet in Plenty and Honour'. Linking these two terms suggests the cynical truth that lies behind much of Roxana's story: that poverty brings dishonour just as surely as 'Honour' only exists where there is 'Plenty'.

What are we to make of this list of advantages, then? They provide a mish-mash of reasons and motives for marrying the Dutch merchant, ranging from gratitude, the temptation of dominance, and some value for his qualities of character, to the desire for social acceptance or 'Honour', together with some rationalisation about financial security. Overall, the list does not convince because the reasons given here in favour of marriage fail to overcome the objections Roxana has herself so cogently argued. In other words, the repentant hindsight of Roxana's retrospective narrative is an ineffectual gloss which displays all the flaws of marriage that Roxana has criticised so trenchantly. Here, then, the narrator pays lip-service to convention, but the 'outsider's' attitude remains disturbing and dominant. The power of Roxana's 'outsider' attitude – her critique of marriage and her choice of profession – can be said to be enhanced, paradoxically, by the very shallowness of conventional hindsight that attempts to lay it to rest.

The second paragraph of our extract begins with another ritual self-castigation: Roxana upbraids herself for persisting in her 'Wickedness', still using the censorious voice of moral hindsight. This voice fades, however, as she describes their parting: she 'cou'd not bear the Thoughts of his going away', and she was 'not very anxious' about their child, as she would bring it up to be a gentleman. When she sees him set on leaving her, Roxana retires – but allows him to see her weeping, whereupon he launches a final appeal, urging four reasons why she should marry him. These are his past kindness, his financial honesty, his generosity in refusing compensation for his expenses in the affair of the Jew, and her pregnancy. He finishes by declaring 'the sincerest Affection' and begs her not to 'drive him away'.

How does each of them behave at this crisis? Roxana calls her own behaviour 'Wickedness'; and Defoe makes no bones about her manipulative performance: she continued to be 'obstinate against Matrimony' but could not bear to lose this man, either. So, she makes light of his scruples about their child's illegitimacy, and watches him carefully, choosing the moment when he is 'resolv'd to go', and beating him to it, while at the same time weeping openly. Clearly, Roxana hopes to keep the man but avoid marriage, and uses all her wiles to achieve this. The merchant responds just as he ought, kissing her and begging her to accept him, and declaring his devoted love; but he does not concede the moral ground, and insists on marriage or parting. Defoe writes this account as a comedy. Roxana's desire to keep her man and her lack of anxiety about the child are both shocking and amusing. We laugh outright at her ingenuous expression when she 'cou'd not help letting him see' the tears she deliberately exhibits. The paragraph then builds in emotional intensity as he 'kiss'd me, entreated me, conjur'd me' in three short breathless phrases which lead in to five clauses introduced with 'by . . . ' and of rising intensity culminating in 'by all that the sincerest Affection cou'd propose to do'. Having reached such a passionate pitch, with her weeping and the merchant kissing and entreating and conjuring, the final phrase is a comic anti-climax: Roxana's manipulations have done everything, except persuade him to live with her unmarried.

Their behaviour, then, is a comedy; and in keeping with this view Roxana calls hers 'Wickedness', while we have described her as 'manipulative' and using 'all her wiles'. As in the preceding paragraph, however, we cannot rest easy with a single interpretation. Just as Roxana's lists of advantages of marriage fail to overcome her previous critique of matrimony; so now, the merchant's failure to escape from his conventional gender strait-jacket and Roxana's attempts to manipulate stereotypes undercut the comic treatment with a sadness that reveals failure rather than laughter. The comedy of this episode appeals to gender-conventions, making laughter out of shock and the stereotypes of manipulative 'femininity'. The sadness of their parting recalls Roxana's critique, which remains unanswered. See, for example,

Roxana's description of an independent woman, who is 'as fit to govern and enjoy her own Estate, without a Man, as a Man was, without a Woman', and who 'if she had a-mind to gratifie herself as to Sexes, she might entertain a Man, as a Man does a Mistress' (*R* 188). Such a vision of equality is beyond the Dutch merchant's intellectual range. Even as he portrays the man's earnest passion, Defoe subtly reminds us of his limitations. With rising intensity, he appeals to Roxana's gratitude, particularly in financial matters; then to her pregnancy; and finally to his declaration of love. Roxana's critique has already answered such appeals: why should she feel obliged, just because he is honest in commerce? What reliance can she place on his affection, when the law gives him absolute power? The dead-weight of moral convention that limits him is underlined when he refers to their child as 'the Pledge of our Misfortunes'.

This extract, then, demonstrates the complexity of views Defoe has built into Roxana's narrative, and shows how unsettled and unstable are the interpretations which are successively encouraged. The two main paragraphs of our extract adopt different standpoints – shallow moral hindsight, and the comedy of gender-stereotypes, respectively – yet neither standpoint survives scrutiny. On the contrary, both fail. Paradoxically, by failing, they enhance the authority of the 'outsider's' perspective Roxana puts forward and her story exemplifies. So, the narrator's superstructure of moral hindsight is swept aside; and our enjoyment of simple comedy is rendered temporary and uncertain, while the trenchant critique of gender-politics that Roxana develops remains an independent 'outsider' view. People, caught up in these complexities, are as sad as they are funny and vice versa.

Comparative Discussion

There is, however, a further and ultimate irony. Roxana rejects the profession of a wife, and is shockingly original in pursuing the alternative profession – that of a whore. This makes her an 'outsider' in the sight of social and religious establishments. However, we should remember that she has joined what is called 'the oldest profession'; that she accepts and acts out a degrading sexual role ascribed to her by men;

and that she assesses her value in terms of sexual commerce. However much of an 'outsider' Roxana may be, then; and however much we may admire her honesty, we must remember that she is a victim in a patriarchal system. She debunks some of that society's hypocrisy, perhaps; but she cannot change or escape from its nature. The reader's responses are therefore further complicated, because the most radical 'outsider' standpoint is really a function of weakness, not a position of strength. What stability can a woman achieve, who has to use sex to make a living?

Moll's experience develops the same point. The account of her first theft lays a heavy emphasis on the fact that she is a victim of poverty. She has little money and 'it wasted daily' while she has 'no way to encrease it one Shilling'. She compares her life to 'only bleeding to Death, without the least hope or prospect of help from God or Man' and she ends 'looking up to Heaven for support' uttering 'the wise Man's Prayer, *Give me not Poverty least I Steal*' (all from *MF* 253–4). Moll is fair in allocating blame: God fails to help, but then 'the Devil carried me out and laid his Bait for me', so Heaven and Hell share responsibility. We know from Roxana that women can make a living from sex – the choice being only between marriage and whoredom. Moll is now 48 and deprived of such means, for 'it was past the flourishing time with me . . . that agreeable part had declin'd some time, and the Ruins only appear'd of what had been' (*MF* 252). The only means of survival open to Moll, therefore, is to become a thief. So, Moll is forced to discover her 'outsider' view, by being driven into crime in order to survive, just as starvation forces Roxana to take up her profession and consequently to develop her devastating critique of matrimony.

In both *Moll Flanders* and *Roxana*, then, a shocking and radically subversive spotlight is turned upon the society and mores of Defoe's time. In both cases, this point of view is remarkable for its honesty and rigour, in contrast to the shallowness of establishment values, and is the perspective of an 'outsider'. On the other hand, in both cases this revelation comes as a function of weakness and failure. Terror of poverty is the catalyst, and the protagonists are not heroic: they are sympathetic, human, and compromise themselves. These circumstances create a particularly unstable and shifting foundation for our judgements of the narrators or their behaviour. Both return from 'outsider' honesty to convention and write with suspiciously pompous hindsight. On the other hand, perhaps a return to the fold is justifiable. Moll and Roxana compromised in order to survive; why should they not compromise again in order to conform when they finally have the chance? Perhaps this is enough to explain the unsettled gulf between their 'outsider' insights and their retrospective moral hindsight.

Studying the perspective on society Robinson Crusoe develops from his distant vantage point, we find an equally complex structure of possible judgements. Remember that we found vainglory and vanity in Robinson's assertion of moral superiority; comedy in his contempt for cash that he nonetheless keeps; and hypocrisy because he advocates a philosophy of use, while longing for the products of a consumer economy. At the same time, there is some persuasive force when, for example, Robinson sees the world as 'I thought it look'd as we may perhaps look upon it hereafter, *viz.* as a place I had liv'd in, but was come out of it'; or when he observes that 'The most covetous griping miser in the world would have been cur'd of the vice of covetousness, if he had been in my case.' We are convinced that Robinson has a genuine 'outsider's' view at the same time as Defoe encourages us in several critical counter-judgements and undercuts his protagonist. We may even suggest that Robinson's 'outsiderness' has nothing to do with his confused meditations on Abraham, lust, or 'use' at all. Instead, it is what Virginia Woolf calls the 'earthenware pot' nature of his island experience, or its sheer narrowness and pragmatism of focus, that has the most lasting effect.

In the cases of all three narrators, there is the further irony: that the protagonist has no choice about achieving 'outsider' status. Robinson is marooned on his island, Moll is terrified of poverty, and Roxana is starved into her immoral profession. For Robinson, the consequences include his discovery of religion and his experience of the detached 'outsider's' view of society; but these were not deliberately sought by him, nor does Defoe suggest that Robinson's is any more than an average intellect. In short, we can conclude that all three protagonists are as much a human mixture of insights, moral confusions, qualities and weaknesses, luck, misfortunes, and mistakes, as each other.

Conclusion

There is, of course, a significant difference between Robinson's 'outsider' viewpoint, developed in distant isolation, and the unconventional perspectives Moll and Roxana develop from within society. *Robinson Crusoe*'s protagonist faces a more consistent series of situations, than do either Moll Flanders or Roxana. So, for example, Robinson is 28 years on his island, where his circumstances do not change radically until a few months before his departure. Moll, on the other hand, lives short periods in London, Virginia, Bath, London, Lancashire, London, and Virginia again before finally London; and her circumstances change radically several times, including spells as respectable wife, mistress, fortune-hunter, thief, condemned prisoner, and transport. None of these different circumstances is stable enough to endure, and Moll herself adopts different perspectives on life, adapting radically to suit new circumstances. Roxana, similarly, passes through a series of different circumstances in her career; and lives in London, Paris, Holland, London, and Holland again, as well as travelling elsewhere in Europe. Roxana also adapts her behaviour radically according to changing circumstances. She gives a series of bravura performances as, for example, bereaved widow, Turkish dancer, or sober Quaker; and she also alters her outlook on life. In other words, circumstances are more subject to sudden change, for the two women, than they are for Robinson. Furthermore, although generations of readers have marvelled at Robinson's ability to adapt and survive, the two women show greater flexibility, and adapt more frequently. Moll and Roxana have to show more fluid responses to sudden shocks or alterations than are called for from Robinson.

This difference raises two possible issues. First, are circumstances in *Moll Flanders* and *Roxana* more unstable, more changeable, because the protagonists are women? Secondly, are circumstances within society more unstable than on an uninhabited island? The first of these questions asks us to focus on gender and raises the controversial issue of Defoe's female narrators. It has been argued that Moll and Roxana are vain, ambitious, manipulative, immoral, dishonest, and flighty: in other words that Defoe's female narrators are no better than an excuse for traditional chauvinist characterisation. Contrarily, it has been argued that the relentless instability of circumstances, and the depiction of fluid, unfixed identity in Moll and Roxana, demonstrates Defoe's success in understanding and adopting the female voice.[2]

The second question focuses on Defoe's critique of society and on the colonising age in which he wrote. In this connection, we may note that all of Defoe's masculine narrators with the exception of H.F. from the *Journal of the Plague Year*, that is, Robinson Crusoe, Captain Singleton, Colonel Jack, and the Cavalier, spend most of their lives overseas; while Moll's visits to Virginia are temporary interludes, and Roxana remains in Europe throughout. What difference does this make? Is there a fundamental difference between Moll, taking what she can on the streets of London; and the colonist or pirate, taking what the wider world has to offer? Is there a meaningful difference between women confronted by danger, instability, oppression and poverty in rapid episodic changes, on the one hand; and Robinson confronted by slavery, wild beasts, shipwreck, starvation, cannibals, and mutinous sailors across half the world, on the other hand?

Each reader will answer such questions for themselves. In this chapter, we have shown that the narrators develop 'outsider' viewpoints, critical of establishment mores; that Defoe builds a structure of undercutting judgements around these viewpoints, fostering a state of uncertainty. Thus, Defoe restrains our judgement so that we draw a complex sympathy from the text, rather than a simplified moral. This chapter has also shown how the protagonists must constantly adapt. We are faced by an ironic structure of undercutting that cannot be resolved. The protagonists are faced by the instability of circumstances that never endure and therefore the disappointment or subsequent irrelevance of their hopes. In short, in the world Defoe portrays in these fictions, complexity of judgements and instability of circumstances are the rule.

This characteristic of Defoe's fictions has been noticed by several critics. It is notoriously difficult to describe, so different critics find different ways to describe it. Virginia Ogden Birdsall, for example, describes Defoe's narrators searching for a 'significant selfhood' in 'an inhospitable and unsustaining world'. She concludes that none of them succeed in creating 'a fiction of identity', their identities remaining 'incomplete' or 'unstable' so that they 'carry on the death-defying struggle to become somebody' right to the end.[3] Katherine Clark remarks on 'the unstable relationship between language and meaning' in Defoe's fictions.[4] Ellen Pollak describes a 'kaleidoscopic effect of shifting perspectives', remarking that Defoe's writing 'ultimately frustrates any effort to locate him stably or decisively anywhere', and suggests that he wrote in order to 'expose truth's always contested and circumstantial nature' rather than to endorse 'particular moral or ideological truths'.[5] The suggestion that Defoe was working paradoxically against the transformation of chaotic life into structured fiction only underlines how relevant and modern Defoe remains.

Our observation is that Defoe's novels deny us the comfort of interpretation, their themes remaining complex and unresolved. It would be a fatal misapprehension to think that Defoe lacks meaning, however. Our conclusion in this chapter, about instability of interpretation, should not in any way take from our studies of particular themes and topics such as society, early colonialism, patriarchy, or religion and ethics. We should never doubt that Defoe 'says' many things. For example, we can confidently assert that he is critical of the gender-stereotypes of his time, and that he regarded them as unjust in themselves as well as cruel and degrading to women. This is not the only thing his texts 'say' about gender, but it is one among many. Our point, then, is not that Defoe's novels lack meaning, but that they multiply and complicate it.

Methods of Analysis

Close analysis of extracts uses the same range of techniques as we have employed in previous chapters. In this chapter, however, we have:

- looked at each extract with the particular aim to define the narrator's viewpoint. This quickly led us to realise that each narrator's viewpoint is neither single nor simple.
- So, for example, in ***Robinson Crusoe*** we found the protagonist both rejecting all the false values of civilisation, and glorying in his lordship, in quick succession; and simultaneously denigrating and keeping his money. In ***Moll Flanders***, we find her both enjoying

her performance skills and using herself as a lesson, at the same time.

- In our analyses, we also found it helpful to characterise the viewpoints of different paragraphs by thinking of different dictions or genres of writing. So we remarked that in ***Roxana***, she adopts a sermon-like moral hindsight in one paragraph, and then passes to comedy of the sexes in the next.
- In this chapter, the additional method of formulating leading questions to interrogate the text, so identifying further episodes for study, is adapted to our particular aim. To explore 'instability' of the narrative, we have kept in mind two kinds of question:
    - How many different interpretations are supported by this part of the narrative, and to what extent do they contradict each other?
    - How soon and how often do other elements of the narrative contradict or undercut interpretations of this passage?
- Pursuing answers to these questions has helped us to find further evidence of how uncertain and short-lived are the interpretations encouraged in parts of the narrative. So, when considering arguments for matrimony in ***Roxana***, we were repeatedly reminded of her arguments against matrimony, set out elsewhere in the text. This underlined the weakness of the moral hindsight Roxana expresses in our extract.

Suggested Work

Considering the interpretative instability we have found throughout our study of Defoe, it will be instructive to study the three Prefaces written in the assumed persona of an editor of these 'true' narratives (***Robinson Crusoe*** p. 3, ***Moll Flanders*** pp. 37–42, and ***Roxana*** pp. 35–6). The addition of a level of narrative frame, and of a voice speaking from within convention rather than as an 'outsider', further complicates the irony.

A further useful study to undertake would be to select a prominent moral assertion from each novel, and then by means of **(a) thinking about the text** to identify likely locations, followed by **(b) selecting**

as quotations other related moral statements, or other observations of fact, either confirming or contradicting the original assertion, **attempt to construct a list** of views, facts, revelations, or events that contribute to the moral issue raised.

In ***Robinson Crusoe***, we could suggest selecting the following: 'I kept the anniversary of my landing here with the same thankfulness to God for his mercies, as at first; and if I had such cause of acknowledgment at first, I had much more so now, having such additional testimonies of the care of Providence over me, and the great hopes I had of being effectually, and speedily deliver'd' (*RC* 181). In this extract Robinson uses several terms that are alive with questionable meanings throughout the text: for example, 'mercies', 'the care of Providence', and 'deliver'd'. Considering other moments in the text when Robinson has employed these terms would lead to a rich study of moral complexity.

In ***Moll Flanders***, we might begin with her statement that 'it seem'd to me that I was hurried on by an inevitable and unseen Fate to this Day of Misery, and that now I was to Expiate all my Offences at the Gallows, that I was now to give satisfaction to Justice with my Blood, and that I was come to the last Hour of my Life, and of my Wickedness together' (*MF* 349). Several significant terms, such as 'Fate', 'Misery', 'Offences', and 'Wickedness', may be rewarding to pursue. Following up this quotation will lead, among other places, to the accounts of Moll's first thefts, and of her repentance, as well as to the novel's final page.

In ***Roxana***, we could start with her observation: 'so with my Eyes open, and with my Conscience, as I may say, awake, I sinn'd, knowing it to be a Sin, but having no Power to resist' (*R* 79). Obvious topic-words here are 'Conscience', 'Sin', and the phrase 'no Power to resist', but it will also be rewarding to consider the concept of sin with 'Eyes open' and 'knowing it to be a Sin', which may prompt you to focus on Roxana's consciousness of guilt during her desperate attempts to silence or escape her daughter. Starting with a consideration of this remark's immediate context, further thought will lead to numerous other moments in Roxana's career.

6

Themes and Conclusions to Part I

Themes are nothing more than topics raised by the text, so they are easy to list, but hard to separate from each other. For example, Defoe's novels are obviously concerned with society and gender, but can we discuss the one without the other? Look back at Moll's rejection by her first lover: how far is their relationship determined by their different social status and birth and how far by gender? The answer, of course, is that the narrative involves both issues and neither can be ignored. We should therefore remember that 'themes', as headings, are only a matter of convenience: topics selected by us rather than by Defoe.

A Discussion of Themes

The Middle Station

The words are from *Robinson Crusoe*, but analogous ideas are present in *Moll Flanders* and *Roxana*. We remember that the elder Crusoe recommends a 'middle station' as opposed to wealth or poverty because they bring 'the calamities of life' (*RC* 6). We suggested that Defoe is being ironic, and noticed that Crusoe *père* is utterly negative in recommending total inactivity with death as the ultimate achievement.

We met references to the 'middle station' philosophy in Chapters 2 and 3, first in relation to Robinson's developing religion, where he seems to identify his father and Providence, and suggests that leaving home was his 'ORIGINAL SIN'; then when he undertakes the disastrous voyage from the Brasils. On both these occasions, the text treats the 'middle station' with complexity and irony. For example, in Chapter 3, we remarked that Robinson's hindsight complicates questions about 'Providence' for the reader. These questions require answers before we can say Robinson was wrong to undertake the voyage, but how can we find answers?

Turning now to *Moll Flanders* and *Roxana*, we can identify aspirations analogous to the 'middle station' philosophy. For example, Moll remarks that she should have sought respectable security, and left off thieving, after 'the many hints I had had . . . from my own Reason, from the Sense of my good Circumstances, and of the many Dangers I had escap'd to leave off while I was well' (*MF* 349); and we notice her respectable middle-class marriage to the banker. In *Moll Flanders*, then, there is a recurrent motif of Moll's ambition to become a 'gentlewoman', a concept which begins as the child's dream of escaping 'Service', but which Moll's hindsight relates to moderate or 'middle' respectability. In *Roxana*, the narrator accuses herself of vanity and ambition, every time she chooses the path of excess instead of settling down. So, for example, she calls herself 'one of the foolishest, as well as wickedest Creatures upon Earth' for rejecting the Dutchman, and remarks that she 'had been really happy' had she married a merchant. So, Roxana's and Moll's retrospective opinions chime with Robinson's.

There is, then, a vein running through the three novels that plays upon an ideal of moderation and security. All three narrators acknowledge this aim, and part of each one's struggle is to achieve membership of that respectable group who exist in the 'middle station'. On the other hand, Defoe treats this concept ironically. First, the protagonists fail to make a consistent case for the 'middle station'. See, for example, how Robinson conflates his father's 'middle station' and the prosperity in Brasil he has achieved through disobedience; or Moll's idea that moderate crime is better than ambitious crime. Secondly, none of the protagonists finds this mythical 'middle station': it is an ideal favoured in retrospect, but there is no sign that it really exists.

On most occasions, the protagonists reject 'middle station' opportunities. When they accept them, however, things are hardly better: 'dreadful . . . calamities' (*R* 379) beset Roxana after her eventual marriage to her Dutchman; and ruin cuts short Moll's most sensible marriage – the safe haven she hoped for with the banker. We are left, then, with a persistent idea, which is undercut whenever it approaches translation into reality.

Gentility, Social Rank, and Class

Defoe is an acute observer of his society, and we have discussed class and social attitudes several times in our study. In *Moll Flanders*, for example, her childish aim of becoming a 'gentlewoman' combines with her terror of poverty to fuel Moll's career, while the family's debates leading to her first marriage, and the reformation of her Bath gentleman, demonstrate how rigidly social boundaries fenced in the fortunate and kept out the likes of Moll. Virginia society is different, for there 'many a *Newgate* Bird becomes a great Man' and 'some of the best Men in this Country are burnt in the Hand'[1] (*MF* 134). In *Moll Flanders*, however, the 'gentility' theme begins as a ribald joke when Moll mistakes the status of the local whore, then passes through misleading appearances such as her second husband the '*Land-water-thing*, call'd, *a Gentleman-Tradesman*' (*MF* 104) and her fourth, the squire/highwayman. Ultimately, apparent social structures in *Moll Flanders* are deceptive and unstable.

In *Roxana* we meet the theme of social rank more directly, for the heroine moves in aristocratic and royal circles. In Chapter 3, we analysed Sir Robert's recommendation of a merchant as the 'best Gentleman in the Nation' (*R* 210), his insights into economic change, and Roxana's description of the Court. In Roxana herself, however, we meet the power of vanity and her enduring snobbery. She persuades herself that she 'could not resist' a 'Prince of such Grandeur, and Majesty; so infinitely superior to me' (*R* 104); and an important element of her final settlement appears when her husband 'saluted me one Morning with the Title of *Countess*' (*R* 307), a purchased honour. Defoe's theme is that of a society in the throes of radical change: in decline is a feudal society founded on land, estates, and titles; while a new order founded on the power of trade, merchants, profit, capital, and expansion is in the ascendant. Roxana is a hybrid: by nature and habit a profiteer, driven to acquisitiveness by her early lesson in poverty, yet impressed by the vanities of rank and title. Does Defoe paint Roxana as really of the 'new' economy, stripping the royals of their last finery as they mortgage their estates to pay for their sins? Or, is she a dupe, foolishly attached to an obsolete order, when she would really have been 'happy' had she taken Sir Robert's advice and married into the merchant bourgeoisie?

Robinson Crusoe adds little to this summary. We remember Robinson's pride that 'if I pleas'd, I might call my self king, or emperor over the whole country' (*RC* 102–3); his easy assumption of sovereignty; and his self-appointment as 'master' of Friday, then of his other 'citizens'. At the same time, Robinson retains a pragmatic wariness. So, he attempts to protect himself by legalistic and contractual means and by extracting promises; and he agrees to use the title 'Governor' to create the impression of state authority.

In all three novels, the protagonists' motives display the full range from pragmatism to idealism, and usually mix the two. Numerous questions about social structures are thus raised; and Defoe extracts much comedy and satire, from this theme. However, none of the three narrators lives consistently. On the contrary, they have to adapt to events. We could say that they are improvising their mores and their relationships within society, as they go along. In Chapter 3, we suggested thinking of Defoe's characters as the colonists of a new society, where behaviours, power, boundaries, the possible, and the impossible are all being re-defined. In other words, society is so much in a melting pot that the protagonists have to 'discover' their identities and their place in society from scratch.

Marriage and the Economics of Sex

In Chapter 4, we concluded that Defoe provides a detailed critique of patriarchy, together with a great deal of material critical of gender politics, and the economics of marriage and sexuality. Robinson shows no awareness and finds his greatest contentment in the relationship with Friday. Above all, however, we remarked on the formidable critical analysis *Moll Flanders* and *Roxana* present regarding the economics of gender. In *Moll Flanders* the relation between being female, poverty, and crime is shockingly exposed; and Moll struggles for wifehood, hoping throughout her life to exchange her sex for security, and only succeeding in old age. Roxana, on the other hand, exposes the economics of sex by choosing the profession of a courtesan.

The most prominent critique is Roxana's analysis of matrimony in her debates with the Dutch merchant. She argues that matrimonial law is cruel in allocating absolute power to the husband. Some of her subsidiary arguments are astonishingly modern. For example, Roxana suggests that being owned 'takes from a Woman every thing that can be call'd *herself*' (*R* 189), and objects to a law which makes a woman 'infinitely oblig'd' to receive mere 'Curtesie and Kindness', that is, civilised treatment to which she is not legally entitled. It is notably ironical that the two eventual husbands – Moll's Jemy and Roxana's Dutchman – both willingly submit to being managed by their wives.

Both Moll and Roxana explore circumstances which exemplify that insoluble paradox, the exploiter-exploited. In other words, they use their femininity for profit and thus exploit men, while at the same time they have no other means of survival, so they are in turn victims exploited by patriarchal society. Defoe plays upon this paradox by multiplying and complicating the situations his female protagonists face, but does not offer a solution. However, the terror of poverty is powerfully presented at the outset of each novel, which enlists our sympathy, and firmly establishes the heroines' victimhood.

Early Capitalism and Colonialism

Robinson remarks that his money is 'nasty sorry useless stuff' (*RC* 103), and apostrophises the coins he finds: 'O Drug! . . . what art thou good for? Thou art not worth to me, no not the taking off of the ground' (*RC* 47). Then, 'upon second thoughts', he keeps the cash; and we are struck by the recurrent counting up of accounts, details of investments and profits, cargoes and products, purchases and sales, and contracts and other business arrangements, which fill all those parts of Robinson's narrative that are not set upon the island. The island part of the narrative is equally dominated by counting and lists, but the investment is in the form of labour and Robinson limits production to suit his needs.

Robinson's island shares certain qualities with his Brasil, and Moll's Virginia, however. Robinson could have 'rais'd ship loadings of corn', 'built a fleet of ships', and made 'wine, or . . . raisins, to have loaded that fleet'. This abundance of natural wealth is true of Virginia and Brasil also, where potential prosperity is unlimited: the only restraint is how much can be invested in implements and servants. In *Roxana*, it is clearly a credible story for Amy to say that Roxana has made her fortune in the East-Indies.

Moll and Roxana are just as addicted as is Robinson, to counting their possessions. We analysed one of Moll's attempted calculations in Chapter 3. We can easily remember similar episodes, such as the account of Roxana, the Jew, and the Dutch merchant (*R* 149–60) extricating Roxana's fortune as bills payable at Rotterdam; or the accounting of Roxana's provisions for her children and the summing up of their wealth when she and her Dutchman marry. In *Moll Flanders* we are told the value of each piece of lace or silver cup stolen and Moll's total profits from crime are regularly rehearsed.

All three narrators become rich in the end, but Defoe maintains a relationship between profit and vice, which suggests that the two necessarily co-exist. We may applaud Roxana's investment of her fortune; we admire Moll's acumen as she expands her plantation; and we are pleased that Robinson's Brasil property has become so valuable. But each success is built upon a morally tarnished stake. Roxana's fortune comes from prostitution; Moll's stake is her profit from thieving; and Robinson's profits began with a slaving voyage. Attitudes to slavery being what they were, Defoe's readers would not be as judgmental of Robinson as about Moll and Roxana. On the other hand, the ironical treatment of the sale of Xury implies some distaste for trafficking in people, and Robinson's disastrous voyage is also illegal. So, in present-day language, we could describe all three narrators as criminals who 'go straight' in the end. Roxana's and Moll's eventual investments are 'money-laundering'.

We have previously remarked that Defoe portrays a society in the throes of transformation from medieval to modern, from a land-based economy to an order in which the merchant becomes society's 'best Gentleman'. In Chapter 3, we also suggested two ways of thinking about Defoe's theme of colonialism.

Our **first suggestion** is that Defoe portrays a contrast between the old societies of Europe and the new colonial world. This way of interpreting the novels lays emphasis on poverty, crime, judicial cruelty, decadence, sin, vanity, and corruption that are seen to thrive in old Europe; and suggests a sense of freedom, opportunity, and an absence of hierarchy and oppression in the colonies. Our **second idea** is that Defoe describes a new society being formed, whether in Europe or in the colonies – so the protagonists are, as it were, colonists exploring this new society's boundaries for themselves, struggling to establish stable identities in an unstable social environment.

Both of these ways of considering Defoe's socio-economic theme are valid and they are not mutually exclusive. All the characteristics we have noted belong to the colonising period in which Defoe wrote and portray the transformation from mediaeval and feudal on the one hand, to bourgeois-capitalism on the other. Defoe never allows our judgements to settle into a rigid pattern, however. He is a wry and ironical writer, and a comic writer. We must never make the mistake of attributing *naïveté* to the writer who can describe Roxana, in a storm at sea, frightened enough to cry out to God, 'tho' softly' because she does not want the sailors to hear her confession (*R* 165).

Convention (Morality and Religion)

Roxana's precisely measured degree of penitence in the storm brings us to the question of morality and religion. In Chapter 2, we describe an author who leaves no ethical or religious assertion without its countercurrent. So, ethical and religious issues in Defoe's novels are always complex: they always consist of a combination of narrative strands, never a single one alone. Roxana's precisely portrayed combination of penitence and self-consciousness exemplifies this ethical complexity, as does Moll's recovery from her penitent passion after the climax of her reprieve.

This complexity, together with Defoe's critique of conventional mores, shows the protagonists improvising their morality and religion as they go along. They have an 'instrumental' relationship to morality and religion, because they adapt and compromise, attempting to reconcile the competing demands of convention, survival, and their own impulses. The idea that Defoe's protagonists 'improvise' their lives connects with their 'outsider' status, and reinforces the metaphor that they live like colonists, because they have almost unlimited room to 'discover' a way of living, just as colonists have a wilderness to cultivate. Robinson, Moll, and Roxana can thus be thought of as living in the moral equivalent of early colonialism, or like early settlers in a virgin morality.

Insecurity, the Anarchy of Experience

We have described the protagonists as 'improvising' their lives. In fact, the impression of Robinson, Moll, and Roxana dealing with unforeseen situations almost on every page is one of the most abiding impressions left by reading Defoe. This characteristic of the fictions implies two further insights: first, Defoe writes about people struggling to develop a stable identity in an unstable world; and second, Defoe depicts a world in an unusually fluid state of unpredictability, perhaps because of the melting pot between medieval and modern.

However, the insistence on insecurity, and the frequency of anarchic events in these novels, is such that there are also implications for the very act of writing a narrative. In Chapter 5, we mentioned Ellen Pollak's description of the 'kaleidoscopic' effect that frustrates any attempt to locate Defoe himself.[2] The three protagonists could also all be considered as existential characterisations, in that they improvise and build their identities within an environment so unstable as to be almost 'absurd'.

For the present, our survey of themes has suggested two parallel strands to our developing thoughts about these texts. **On the one hand**, we have been pursuing **social and environmental topics**, such matters as a society in flux between medieval and modern; the age of colonisation; society's related pillars of conventional ethics, law, and religion; economics and mercantile growth; sexual mores in convention and actuality; and the economy of sexuality as well as matrimony and social gender issues. We have found Defoe's analysis to be acute and satirically effective, wide-ranging, but never static. He is an ironic author who complicates judgements, an effect he achieves by building multiple strands into every situation.

On the other hand, we have considered the **individual protagonists**. In this connection we have thought about such issues as their status as outsiders; their struggles to improvise life and their attempts to develop stable identities; their response to chaotic life-experience; and their inability to achieve mastery of their physical circumstances, their meaning, or that of the world around them.

Both of these strands are fruitful and relevant, and further study will show that there is a long way to go, with a great deal of rich material still to reveal and enjoy.

Conclusions

We have listed interim conclusions in the final part of each chapter, and considered some themes in the first half of this chapter. We now pose supplementary questions, and offer an initial response to each, in the hope that this may act as a bridge towards further investigation of Defoe's novels.

- **What conclusions have we reached concerning emergent capitalism and colonialism as critical themes of Defoe's writing?** These are major themes. All three protagonists have strong acquisitive drives and a consuming interest in financial growth and security; but in the novels there are always mixed motives, and our judgement is often complicated by compromises between the demands of morality and those of survival. Our study of the 'society of two' formed by Robinson and Friday shows how lightly and deftly Defoe weaves together the different issues. The novels are repeatedly concerned with radical changes both to society in Britain and to the world as a consequence of colonial expansion. We have suggested the idea that the instability portrayed by Defoe shows his protagonists improvising their lives in a new world, just as colonists must improvise when they find themselves in a virgin land.

One observation that seems to be justified is that Defoe presents economic activity and moral compromise as necessarily linked. We remember that all three protagonists obtain their financial stake by questionable means, although Robinson's sins would not have been as marked to readers of his time, as are Moll's and Roxana's.

- **Is there a progression from *Robinson Crusoe*, through *Moll Flanders*, to *Roxana*?**

Several critics have suggested why *Roxana* was Defoe's last novel. For example, Michael Shinagel writes that 'Defoe became involved personally in the career of Roxana . . . tried to check himself by occasional moralising and reminders . . . but he was not entirely successful in these endeavours.' Shinagel then observes that Defoe was 'astute enough as a Puritan and as an artist to realise that his fictions were leading him to excesses of the imagination' and consequently stopped writing fiction.[3] Virginia Ogden Birdsall observes that each novel is an account of the narrator's attempt to 'create a fiction of identity' – a struggle in which we are all engaged, fighting to build our own stories against the formlessness of 'an inhospitable and unsustaining world'. In her view, the nightmarish final pages of *Roxana* conclude Defoe's entire fictional quest, for the heroine 'learns that . . . There is no identity that works. When she strikes down that devilish daughter who would expose what she really is in all her earth-bound contingency, she strikes down life itself. In destroying the past, she destroys the future. No wonder that, after *Roxana*, Defoe was to write no more fictions.'[4]

These opinions are no more than opinions, however: Defoe has left no explanation.[5] What we do have is three novels and the question of whether they relate to each other in order of publication. That the female narrative of Moll's career as mistress, bigamist, and thief should then lead Defoe to tell the story of a successful courtesan is no surprise: these are two shocking women, and it seems appropriate that the accidental victim, Moll, should come before the more deliberately ambitious Roxana, whose intellectual challenge is so much more powerful. Alternatively, we may think that Defoe was working through 'outsider' viewpoints. Robinson writes from his isolation on the island, a male outsider; then comes *Captain Singleton* the nomadic pirate – a criminal male outsider. What should logically come next? Why, a criminal female outsider – *Moll Flanders*.

These suggestions may help us to string the novels together in our minds, but this remains an artificial activity. What about *Captain Singleton*, *Colonel Jack*, the *Journal of the Plague Year*, or *Memoirs of a Cavalier*, all of which were written between *Robinson Crusoe* and *Roxana*? Also, Defoe continued to write political, historical, and moral tracts throughout the 5 years he spent writing fiction.

When considering our three texts as a group, the salient feature does seem to be the issue that provokes Michael Shinagel and Virginia Birdsall: the final part of *Roxana*, when she is driven to desperation by her daughter Susan. Shinagel's idea that Defoe became too involved is *naïve* and patronising. Birdsall's insight that Roxana finds 'no identity that works' is all very well, but, what does that actually mean in terms of her character at the end of the book? What remains is the impression that the final part of *Roxana* is somehow different.

The answer to this puzzle lies somewhere in the characterisation of Roxana herself. Three aspects of Roxana seem to be particularly striking and mark her out as radically different from either Robinson or Moll. First, there is the complex relationship between her and Amy, who acts as representative, alternative, agent, and virtually as Roxana's 'alter ego'. From the time when Amy disposes of the children, or when she urges moral compromise against Roxana's virtuous outrage, and the sequel when Roxana strips Amy and puts her in bed with her 'husband', these two women act out elements of each other's desires as if they are two aspects of a single personality. In the final episode concerning Susan, Amy acts the most horrific of Roxana's desires: the murder of her child. There is nothing comparable to this relationship, and the disturbing psychological effects Defoe thereby achieves, in *Robinson Crusoe* or *Moll Flanders*. Robinson's primary relationship with Friday and Moll's with her

Governess simply do not compare to the complex interaction of Roxana and Amy.

The second unique quality of Roxana is her intellect. In Robinson and Moll, Defoe has created two very resourceful people, quick to adapt to new circumstances, as well as resilient and determined. Both of them are clever in the sense that they formulate plans, and have pragmatic cunning, while Moll is also a first-rate actress. However, neither Robinson nor Moll is intellectually gifted, which Roxana is. We have admired Roxana's critique of marriage, which anticipates the insights of twentieth-century feminism. In fact, we are struck by Roxana's intellectual clarity from the moment when she advises 'Never, Ladies, marry a Fool' (*R* 40). Her analysis of a changing society, her attitude to marriage, and her shocking honesty about her career all witness this quality.

The third element of characterisation that marks *Roxana* out from the two earlier texts is Defoe's development of involuntary, or 'subconsciously driven' behaviour, in the final part of the novel. We can see this, for example, when Susan and the Captain's wife visit, and Roxana receives them 'in a kind of *Dishabille*', a 'Morning-Vest, or Robe . . . more shap'd to the Body, than we wear them since, showing the Body in its true Shape' (*R* 330); then, when Susan remembers her ex-mistress's beauty, Roxana 'put in Questions two or three times, of how handsome she was? And was she really so fine a Woman as they talk'd of? *and the like*' (*R* 334); and finally, when she receives the Quaker's warning letter, at Tunbridge, Roxana fails to act: 'I run a greater Risque indeed, than ordinary, in that I did not send *Amy* up under thirteen or fourteen Days' (*R* 357). These behaviours all increase Roxana's risk, and are consequences of the violent inner turmoil she describes so vividly: 'the strange Impression which this thing made upon my Spirits; I felt something shoot thro' my Blood; my Heart flutter'd; my Head flash'd, and was dizzy, and all within me, *as I thought*, turn'd about' (*R* 323). The final part of *Roxana*, in short, shows the narrator in a progressive state of paralysis from inner conflict. She fails to control her self-revealing behaviour and sinks under the horror of her other unacknowledged desire. This is a development of psychological characterisation that is distinctively modern, and it goes further than Defoe attempted in either *Robinson Crusoe* or *Moll Flanders*.

We recognise Robinson's restless nature, and that this is in conflict with the lip-service he pays to his father's philosophy. We meet Moll as a passionate nature, often carried away by her feelings, often against her conscience as well as against her own best interests. The impulsiveness with which Defoe endows these two provides empathy, entertainment, and excitement, certainly, but it does not create the sense of a character whose subconscious drives are dark and self-destructive. This last development of characterisation is reserved for *Roxana* alone.

- **What elements of comedy or tragedy have we found in Defoe's works?**

All three of these texts are repeatedly comic: we are frequently amused and sometimes laugh aloud. The jokes are often ironic and often created by character. So, for example, we are ironically amused that Roxana agrees with Sir Robert, but then cultivates the court; or that Robinson and Moll repent in such intermittent bursts. There is also the comedy of farce, for example when Moll steals a horse; when Roxana pushes Amy into bed with her 'husband'; or when Robinson cannot launch his boat, or keeps the 'nasty' money. Comedy is more than mere amusement, however.

Robinson Crusoe and *Moll Flanders* can be considered comedies because both protagonists end their stories in prosperity and contentment. Robinson is rich, married, and settled (at least, temporarily); and even his mention of the voyage that makes the substance of *The Farther Adventures* is written in comfortable retrospect. Moll is married to her highwayman, the rogue she has loved the best, and they are prosperous, happy, and settled. So, both of these novels fulfil the requirements of a comedy by ultimately arriving at an optimistic and light-hearted view of life and fate.

Both Robinson and Moll encounter darker issues during their narratives. In both cases, moral issues are compromised and behaviour is far from strict; and in both cases, there are unresolved moral issues at the end of the tale. Defoe does not allow these ethical problems to undermine the pleasure of the comic outcome, however. *Robinson Crusoe* and *Moll Flanders* share this quality with many other comedies. Think, for example, of the darker episodes of *The Merchant of Venice*, or *Much Ado About Nothing*, which are not quite allowed to destabilise the endings.

We should insert one caveat, however. Defoe's fictions have carried us through so many unstable vicissitudes that we invest less trust in the prosperous outcomes, than is the case at the end of a less anarchic comic tale. Despite the financial plenty in which Robinson and Moll find themselves, we cannot help feeling, as Virginia Ogden Birdsall does, that these narrators return home, and their identities remain double or unstable. They return to a home that offers them 'no more safety now than it ever did'.[6]

What is the case for regarding *Roxana* as a tragedy? This is a complex and fraught question, and we can do no more than mention three elements of the novel in connection to concepts of tragedy. First, we can consider *Roxana* to be structured along the lines of a classical tragedy, if we regard her eventual misery as an inevitable consequence of 'hubris', that is, her overweening arrogance in pursuing an erroneous and headstrong course. Tragedies of 'hubris' include, for example, *Macbeth* and *King Lear*. This interpretation may be supported by her own remarks that she was the 'foolishest' and 'wickedest' to pursue her career as a courtesan instead of either marrying the Dutch merchant or being well-married on her return to London. Roxana also reflects on the inevitability of her fall, for 'Sin and Shame follow one-another so constantly at the Heels, that they are . . . like Cause and Consequence, necessarily connected one with another' and ''tis not in the Power of humane Nature to conceal the first, or avoid the last' (*R* 345). This is a viable interpretation of the novel, but not fully convincing because Roxana's 'hubris' appears in such complex circumstances (and half-way through her career), and her 'fall' is also an indeterminate, episodic series of events.

A second 'tragic' interpretation of *Roxana* tells how she pits herself, with only her individual strength, against the power of society and its mores, and is ultimately and inevitably crushed. *Hamlet*, Shaw's *Saint Joan*, or Thomas Hardy's *Jude the Obscure* can be seen as tragic in this sense. In Roxana, Defoe proposes a woman who determines to live single in order to be 'Masculine in her politick Capacity' and have 'the full Command of what she had, and the full Direction of what she did' (*R* 188). In doing so, she challenges the immeasurable power of society and convention, all that was 'decreed by Heaven; that it was the fix'd State of Life, which God had appointed for Man's Felicity, and for establishing a legal Posterity' (*R* 191). This interpretation of *Roxana* suggests that she is eventually crushed by the power she has, heroically but hopelessly, challenged.

Our third and final suggestion returns to our remarks about characterisation. We suggest that Defoe creates an inner Hell in her psyche in the final part of her narrative, when she suffers from emotional conflicts she cannot reconcile. Then, as a consequence of Roxana's psychological paralysis, the horrific tragic act is carried out by her surrogate or 'alter ego', Amy. That Roxana recognises her responsibility is apparent in the final paragraph, for 'the Blast of Heaven seem'd to follow the Injury done to the poor Girl, by us both' (*R* 379). When we think of psychological tragedies, of course *Hamlet* springs to mind again.

Defoe's *Roxana* does exhibit some tragic features then. On the other hand, none of the three interpretations discussed above is quite convincing. Do we really believe that Roxana's one paragraph of misery at the end is the 'catastrophe' of a tragedy of hubris? Or, that this is the dominant meaning of the fable? Hardly – the story, episodic and unstable in nature, does not permit such simplification. Do we really think that Roxana is undone by her opposition to the power of patriarchy and social convention? No: her nemesis is the girl Susan.[7] In her conflict with society, Roxana is the victor, for she enjoys independent wealth. Finally, is Roxana's character of a tragic kind? Well, perhaps; but on the other hand, she has twisted and turned, grasped opportunities, adapted herself, and passed through so many changes that her ultimate psychological 'breakdown', as we could call it, is only one episode from a wider, more anarchic, and varied fable.

The above questions are not the only ones possible. For example, we might have asked: 'What conclusions can we formulate about the depiction of people, and therefore character, in Defoe's novels?' This question has been partly broached by our discussion of characterisation in *Robinson Crusoe* and *Moll Flanders*, in contradistinction to the characterisation of Roxana; on the other hand, we have only mentioned in passing the striking character-duality of Roxana and Amy, which would make a fascinating study on its own. Similarly, we might ask: 'Are we justified in drawing modern conclusions from the interpretative instability of Defoe's narratives?' This question arises each time an interpretation proves unconvincing, or is undercut by the shifting nature of circumstances in Defoe's narratives. Then, the dual issues of a narrator improvising an identity, or Defoe making fiction, from chaotic life-experience, are brought into question.

PART II

THE CONTEXT AND THE CRITICS

7

Daniel Defoe's Life and Works

Daniel Defoe lived a busy and varied life about which we have a great deal of information, but do not know everything. He wrote a vast number of works – pamphlets, treatises, poems, travel writing, histories, as well as his few fictions. Much of this output was political, some expounding his own opinions, but a great deal written to order while he was more-or-less secretly employed by politicians. As a result, many of the works attributed to Defoe were published anonymously, or under invented names; and scholars still argue about the authorship of many pieces. This chapter will give a brief account of Defoe's life and some account of his better-known works.

The Life of Daniel Defoe

Daniel was born Daniel Foe, in approximately 1660. His father James Foe had moved to the City of London from the village of Etton, Northamptonshire, served an apprenticeship, became a liveryman, and prospered as a tallow chandler. In 1665, London suffered the great plague; and a year later, the Fire of London destroyed virtually all the houses in the Foes' district. So, as a small child, Daniel witnessed devastating destruction and horror, which arrived without warning.

He also grew up as a Dissenter (a Protestant who refused the sacraments of the Church of England) and therefore belonged to a persecuted minority. Daniel saw Quaker children put in the stocks, gangs of roughs sent to break up Dissenter meetings with violence, and understood that he could never attend university, or serve his country, because of the laws known as the Clarendon Code. His education was therefore finished at the Newington Green Dissenters' academy run by Charles Morton, starting in or around 1674. In 1681, having completed 4 of the 5 years training required, Daniel decided against becoming a minister and chose to set up in business as a hosier.

Defoe's dissenting background brought him into contact with many outstanding characters. Notably, the Defoe family minister was Samuel Annesley, a man of exceptional abilities as well as rigid principles, who resolutely resisted persecution. Charles Morton, Daniel's teacher, was another exceptional man. The Newington Green curriculum was innovative, providing an education superior to that provided by the universities, and Morton's academy was highly regarded. Morton emigrated to New England in 1686, and became the first vice-President of Harvard College.

In 1682, Defoe began to court one Mary Tuffley and presented her with a book made up of anecdotes and stories, called *Historical Collections*, which is the first substantial work he wrote. They were married on 1st January 1684. A daughter, Mary, died in infancy, but there was another girl and a baby by the time of Daniel's bankruptcy in 1693. There is every reason to believe that Daniel loved his wife and respected her intelligence, and that she showed great patience and loyalty to a man who must have been an exasperating husband at times. During his first years in the City, Daniel became a wine and spirits merchant as well as a hosier, acquired properties in various places, and became a responsible citizen in his Ward.

In February 1685, King James II came to the throne: persecution of Dissenters and measures to curtail the freedom of the City of London intensified, and in June of that year Defoe left home, to join the duke of Monmouth's rebellion. Defoe fought against the King's forces at the battle of Sedgemoor, where Monmouth's army was routed. Somehow or another Defoe managed to evade pursuit and so avoid execution or transportation to the colonies. Most of the rebels were discovered and punished, but Defoe managed to stay clear of trouble until the King granted a pardon in 1687. Ironically, it was only a year or so later, in December 1688, that King James himself fled to France in the events of the Glorious Revolution. William of Orange became King, ushering in a much improved situation for Dissenters and those of Defoe's political views.

Defoe's decision to set up in business began with optimism, expansion, and some successes but led to a decade of frenetic commercial activities dominated by ideas for new ventures, projects, and attempts to make headway, together with losses and disasters, increasing debts, too many of which were owed to friends, or his wife's family, and increasingly desperate attempts to stave off court cases. Defoe doubled debts to pay other debts, while at the same time putting yet more borrowed money into yet more hopeful schemes. He sold property to his mother-in-law that he had already sold to somebody else, tried to fight court cases with counter-writs: generally, he tried every slippery dodge to stave off the final collapse. Defoe had a house and warehouse in Freeman's Yard, but between 1692 and 1694 his family had to give up the house, turn away their five servants, and move in with his wife's mother Joan Tuffley, while Daniel was repeatedly in Fleet Prison, then committed to the King's Bench Prison for debt.

Defoe eventually negotiated a settlement with his creditors and was released. The next few years were a little more secure financially, although he was still attempting to settle debts, and was not above accruing new ones. He achieved some measure of security from a government post as an accountant for the glass duty, which lasted until 1699; and he still had a property in Tilbury where he ran a profitable brick and tile factory. During this period, Daniel Foe added the genteel 'De' prefix to his surname, suggesting his desire to present himself as a born gentleman; and during these few years he also began writing political polemic. He published pamphlets arguing one or the other side of contemporary controversies. In particular, he scored a huge success with his *The True-Born Englishman* (1700) and he became famous when his *Legion's Memorial* (1701) led Parliament to release four Kentish petitioners who had been unjustly imprisoned and to vote the funds King William needed for the army. In early 1702, however, William unexpectedly died, and Queen Anne came to the throne. She quickly displayed High Church, anti-Dissenter, and High Tory sympathies, which were an ominous sign for a writer such as Defoe.

In 1702, Defoe entered the controversy over Dissenters who occasionally took Church of England communion. He published *The Shortest-Way with the Dissenters*, an ironic response to the vitriolic anti-Dissenter writings of one Reverend Henry Sacheverell. With tongue in cheek, Defoe recommended the massacre of Dissenters, hoping in this way to ridicule High Church extremists. Unfortunately, many readers missed the irony, the Dissenters felt that Defoe had inflamed the issue dangerously, and the Church party (which was the new Queen and her government) issued a warrant charging Defoe with 'seditious libel'. In short, Defoe found himself without supporters and a fugitive from justice. Various attempts to arrest him were made, starting in the late autumn of 1702, and culminating on 21 May 1703, when he was seized and taken to Newgate. After a short period of bail, Defoe returned to court and was tried in July. The law did not allow the jury to decide the question of libel: the prosecution had already decided that question. The jury was asked merely to determine whether the defendant wrote those passages, and of course Defoe could not contest this. He pleaded guilty and was given a heavy exemplary sentence: a large fine, three appearances in the pillory, and further imprisonment until he could produce surety for his future good behaviour. Defoe's was something of a show trial, and his sentence showed him publicly humiliated for having offended the government. However, the most frightening elements of the sentence – his appearances in the pillory – were turned into a success for Defoe. A collection of his writings and a poem *A Hymn to the Pillory* were handed out to bystanders, and it appears that supporters surrounded him, so that he was not struck by rotten eggs and other filth, or injured by rocks and stones. The fine, and imprisonment, remained; and Defoe wrote of his surroundings in Newgate in the same horrified terms he would later put into *Moll Flanders*.

During his months as a fugitive, Defoe tried to negotiate with the Earl of Nottingham, who was responsible for the prosecution, even going so far as to send his wife to plead his case. He now offered his service to Earl Godolphin and Robert Harley, Speaker of the House of Commons, but he was left to languish in Newgate for several more months, becoming increasingly depressed and desperate. Possibly, Harley left him in jail to ensure that Defoe was 'softened up' for his subsequent use. At the end of October, Godolphin acted, at Harley's suggestion, and arranged Defoe's release. The fine was settled using government secret service funds, and Daniel returned to rejoin his wife and, by this time, seven children (five daughters and two sons, between 2 and 15 years old), at his mother-in-law's house in Kingsland. He was now in his mid-forties, no longer able to dream of success as a merchant or a career in the City, and with a large family to support.

Defoe's life continued to be busy and chaotic as he threw himself into the task of supporting his numerous family with the income from writing and political service to Robert Harley. Defoe wrote and published *The Review*, a periodical which came out twice or three times a week for the next 9 years. Periodicals were eagerly followed, and Defoe introduced the question and answer format in a feature called the 'Scandal Club', like a problem page but canvassing public issues, which became very popular. During 1704, Defoe became a spy for Harley, following his own suggestion for the gathering of intelligence. He travelled around England, meeting with local people, noting local influential personalities, assessing local opinions on political matters, and reporting in detail to Harley. Meanwhile Defoe's enemies the High Church Tories continued to harrass him, so that his writings always had to tread a tightrope on the edge of danger. He was repeatedly threatened with a new prosecution and another spell in jail. In this maelstrom of a life, Defoe was away from home for most of the time, maintaining a punishing schedule of travel and work, and still bedevilled by debts, worries about his family, and anxiety about how he could educate his children.

Towards the end of 1706, Defoe was sent to Edinburgh to work for the Act of Union (1707) that would incorporate Scotland and England into a 'United Kingdom'. He made numerous friends and contacts in Scotland, became involved in some small business ventures, worked tirelessly to persuade the Scots that Union would benefit their country, while anti-Union mobs rioted. In 1708, he enrolled his eldest son, Benjamin, in the University of Edinburgh. Being in Scotland, Defoe was unable to attend the funeral of his father or, a few months later, of his little daughter Martha.

When Robert Harley lost power in February 1708, Defoe continued to work for the government, but under the patronage of Earl

Godolphin. As 1710 began, there was a further political upheaval. The Reverend Henry Sacheverell published more vitriolic sermons, but this time Sacheverell himself was charged with seditious libel. Defoe was delighted, but the government made a hash of the prosecution. Sacheverell was given a light sentence, and became a Tory hero whose triumph was celebrated all over the country. There followed a disastrous election, a parliament full of Tory extremists, and the fall of Godolphin. Queen Anne recalled Robert Harley to form a government, and Defoe returned to serve his original patron. During the next 4 years Defoe tried to defend policies Harley had to adopt because of the Tory majority, but which went against his own beliefs. In 1713, Defoe was again facing prosecution both for debts and for his inflammatory writings, and needed money and then a royal pardon, both provided via Harley, to keep himself out of prison. Difficulties intensified: the government was unravelling, Harley was drinking heavily, and then, the Queen died.

One would have thought that the accession of George I, a Lutheran protestant Whig and Britain's first Hanoverian King, would be a happy event for Defoe. This was not the case, however. King George was hostile to the previous government, several Tory journalists were prosecuted, and Defoe, propagandist for the Harley administration, had to be careful. He wrote publicly in support of George I, and in moderate terms called for unity and tolerance from his fellow-countrymen. At the same time, he wrote a *Secret History* of Harley's ministry,[1] in a loyal attempt to defend his old patron. However, the arguments that could be marshalled on Harley's behalf were not convincing, and little could be done to resurrect the statesman's ruined reputation.

Defoe had now moved his family into a spacious house with a large garden in Stoke Newington, a prosperous and genteel suburb outside the City. He owned several periodicals which, together with his journalism, brought in a good income, and he began writing conduct-books. These proved successful and a reliable source of income for the rest of Defoe's life. The first of these, *The Family Instructor*, came out in 1715, with volume 2 in 1718. Most biographers and critics note that these works make use of imagined characters and naturalistic dialogue, dramatising day-to-day domestic situations. It is argued that the conduct-books thus enabled Defoe to develop his novelistic techniques. We should also note that Defoe had practised imagined characters' first-person narratives. For example, in 1716, he wrote as a hanger-on at the French court, giving an account of the secret peace negotiations; and in 1715, he probably wrote as a woman, the 'Countess of....' for *Memoirs of the Conduct of her Late Majesty*.[2] Then, in 1719, Defoe published *Robinson Crusoe*, and all of the novels were written in the next 5 years.

Roxana came out in 1724. Defoe continued to write throughout his final 7 years. His travel writing, conduct-books, treatises on the supernatural, a world atlas, and an ambitious work describing Britain's opportunities for world economic domination, all flowed from his pen. However, any ease and prosperity associated with the move to Stoke Newington was short-lived. Defoe suffered from gout and bladder-stones from his fifties onward. He underwent an operation removing the bladder-stones in 1725, but gout continued to plague him. Then, he succumbed to the same temptations that had led to catastrophe 40 years before. Together with his daughter Hannah he bought a parcel of land near Colchester, and there followed a litany of bad decisions and disastrous mismanagement. Defoe dreamed of starting another brick factory there, like his former property in Tilbury. What with debts, mortgages, arrears of rent, and legal threats, Defoe was eventually forced to seek help from his son Daniel, who took the liability off his father's hands, and made something of it while settling the debts and rents, by means of some complicated but astute manoeuvres. The dreadful saga of the Colchester land lasted from 1722 to 1728.

Three other matters should be mentioned to give a flavour of Defoe's final years. First, his brother-in-law Tuffley died and left a substantial fortune to Mary Defoe and their children. However, the will pointedly ensured that Daniel could not touch any of the money. This must have caused ambivalent feelings: relief that his family was finally quite well provided for, but also shame and anger at his brother-in-law's evident mistrust. Secondly, Defoe's youngest daughter Sophia became engaged to one Henry Baker, in 1727; a happy event, but unfortunately it led into 2 years of angry wrangles as Baker demanded a dowry and Defoe pleaded poverty. This acrimonious business was only settled when the young couple took over the Stoke Newington house and Defoe moved out, in May, 1730. Thirdly, in 1728, two widows of past business associates of Daniel's, a Mrs Brooke and Mrs Stancliffe, filed suit against Defoe for a debt dating back to his bankruptcy in 1691. Defoe claimed this ancient debt had been settled at the time, but he could not prove this, and the legal threats continued. When Defoe died in 1731, of a 'lethargy' (probably what we would call a stroke), he was hiding in lodgings in Rope-Maker's Alley in the City of London, avoiding arrest and creditors again, as he had done so often throughout his life. His final letter bemoans the fact that in hiding, 'I have not seen Son or Daughter, Wife or child, many Weeks, and kno' not which Way to see them.'[3]

Such was Daniel Defoe's life. We may be tempted to try out a number of different interpretations. We could say that his troubles were his own fault; that he was the unfortunate victim of disrupted times; or that he was a resourceful survivor. What we can certainly conclude is that he could never settle or relax, and that he experienced virtually continuous financial and personal insecurity. In short, Defoe's life was a lesson in instability, as were the lives of his fictional protagonists. We can also conclude that the period during which Defoe lived was one of the greatest melting pots of English history: he was born in the year of the Restoration, after Civil War and Commonwealth; when he was five and six came plague and fire; and in his lifetime he watched the Glorious Revolution, William, Anne, two Georges, the Act of Union, and by the end of his life Britain was governed by Parliament, on the modern format of a constitutional monarchy. At the same time, the world was changing and opening up to colonists and pirates, merchants and criminals, as the old landed authorities decayed and faded. Through such a period did Daniel Defoe duck and weave and survive.

The Works of Daniel Defoe

Defoe wrote a wide range of works, and the full list of his productions runs to several hundred titles. We will list only one or two of the more important from each genre, while giving a slightly fuller account of the novels.

As a young man, Defoe wrote some verse ***Meditations*** and the ***Historical Collections*** scrapbook of stories for his future wife. His political journalism, and emergence as a public purveyor of opinion, began gradually. Defoe published one or two pamphlets and a poem in the 1680s, then in the 90s he wrote pamphlets on the controversy over a standing army, and his ***An Essay upon Projects*** was published in 1697. This is a collection of ideas to improve production and inventions intended to benefit society. This book joined an existing trend, and Defoe hoped to profit both from the subscription sale of the book and possibly from the development of the 'projects' themselves. Defoe invested in a diving-bell in the 1680s and was always interested in money-making schemes. *An Essay upon Projects* is significant in that Defoe obviously regarded this venture as a way of earning a living, which connects the *Essay* with the later historical accounts, lives of criminals or soldiers, conduct-books, and travel-writing which helped Defoe to make authorship a paying occupation. ***The Storm*** (1704) is a collection of anecdotes and facts written as a documentary, describing the freak hurricane that devastated England in November 1703, again an example of Defoe writing to exploit a market: accounts of wonders and extraordinary events were popular.

Defoe's most successful political writing was ***The True-Born Englishman*** (1700), a poem in support of William III. Defoe ridicules the concept of a 'true-born Englishman' by reminding his readers of the invasions and immigrations that make the English a mish-mash of foreign ancestry. This of course implied that King William, a Dutchman, is just as English as everybody else. This poem was so successful that Defoe put 'by the author of *The True-Born Englishman*' on other title-pages, for at least another 20 years. We have mentioned the further fame and success of ***Legion's Memorial*** (1701) in our account of Defoe's life, where we also gave a brief account of how ***The Shortest-Way with the Dissenters*** (1702) led to his conviction, pillorying, and imprisonment for seditious libel. In passing, however, we should remark that the tone of *The Shortest-Way* ironically parodies the fulminations of a High Church extremist so accurately that it is too accurate, too believable. Consequently, many of Defoe's readers missed the point and read the pamphlet literally. This is worth noticing, both because it was a problem that recurred with the ironically titled ***Reasons against the Succession of the House of Hanover, And What if the Pretender Should Come?*** and ***An Answer to a Question That No Body Thinks of, viz. But What if the Queen Should Die?*** for which he suffered prosecution for libel again, in 1713; and because his irony often seems so close to ingenuousness in the novels.

We cannot give even a highly selective summary of Defoe's hundreds of political writings. Any appreciation of his writing life should remember, however, that he wrote three issues each week of his newspaper ***The Review***, between 1704 and 1713. He also contributed to many other periodicals, and sometimes wrote and edited other periodicals also, even while he was still bringing out *The Review*. Defoe also owned periodicals: there was a time when he owned and edited virtually all the newspapers and magazines in Edinburgh; and at the start of the 1720s Defoe owned a significant proportion of London's periodicals. Paula Backscheider remarks that around 1720 Defoe's eight London periodicals earned 'together perhaps as much as £1,200 a year'.[4]

In 1715 and 1718, Defoe brought out the two volumes of ***The Family Instructor***, a conduct-book featuring dialogues, characters, and domestic situations, often thought a pre-cursor to the novels. This brings us to the golden 5 years, beginning in 1719 with the publication of ***The Life and Strange Surprising Adventures of Robinson Crusoe***, Defoe's first 'novel' and arguably one of the few most read and best-known stories that have ever been.[5] We know *Robinson Crusoe*, so we will pass straight on to ***The Farther Adventures of Robinson Crusoe*** which was also issued in 1719. In the *Farther Adventures* Robinson returns to his island, gives an account of the wicked behaviour of the English mutineers and good behaviour of the Spaniards he had left there; invasions by hundreds of cannibals and how they were repulsed; and then continues on an episodic voyage around the world, returning by means of an overland trip from China through Tartary and Muscovy, then by ship from Archangel to Hamburg and finally back to England. There are marvels and details of foreign customs, adventures, and crises; but there is not the extended account of Robinson that makes the first volume so rivetting. It is an enjoyable read, but it is arguable that Defoe dashed off the *Farther Adventures* largely to capitalise on the popularity of the first novel.

Memoirs of a Cavalier (1720) was the next fiction, an account of the military career of an English gentleman who takes part in the Thirty Years War on the continent of Europe, in the army of the Swedish King Gustavus Adolphus, then returns to England to take up arms in the English Civil War. In this tale of adventure the Cavalier reveals his knowledge of modern military strategy, analysing campaigns and battles; and describes the horrors of the battlefield in vivid and feeling passages. In the same year, Defoe published ***Captain Singleton*** (1720), the fictional memoir of a successful pirate. This narrative is one of the three Defoe novels to begin with a destitute or orphan childhood, *Moll Flanders* and *Colonel Jack* being the other two. Bob Singleton is stolen from his nursemaid at age 2, then used by a beggarwoman who is hanged, and then placed with a ship's master by the parish. When their ship is taken by pirates, Singleton's career begins. He is a wild and violent youth, and becomes a pirate captain in his own right. Singleton and his crew are marooned on Madagascar, make their way to the mainland, and walk across Africa. Following this exploit, Singleton continues as a pirate and amasses a vast treasure. The character of Singleton's friend, the quick-witted Quaker William, becomes increasingly influential: he repeatedly proves, using the arguments of self-interest, that violence or cruelty is not the best tactic; and that moderation will achieve better results. Finally, despite their notoriety, Singleton and William manage to retire by adopting new identities and returning to England incognito, where they purchase an estate and Singleton marries William's sister.

To bring the *Robinson Crusoe* fiction and the busy year 1720 to an end, Defoe brought out ***Serious Reflections During the Life and Surprising Adventures of Robinson Crusoe, with His Vision of the Angelick World***, supposedly a series of meditations written by Robinson and drawn from his wandering life. No fictions appeared during 1721, but Defoe was undoubtedly still writing them, for three appeared in 1722. ***The Fortunes and Misfortunes of the Famous Moll Flanders*** was published in this year, as were ***A Journal of the Plague Year*** and, in December, ***The History and Remarkable Life of the Truly Honourable Col. Jacque, Commonly Call'd Col. Jack***. As we know, *Moll Flanders* follows *Captain Singleton* by taking as its narrator a destitute orphan, daughter of a transported felon, brought up by parish charity.

A Journal of the Plague Year is narrated by one H.F., who supposedly lived in the City of London and remained there throughout the terrible infection of 1665. Defoe was about 5 years old at the time, but researched the events and gives a vivid, convincing, and moving account of fear and mass deaths, while at the same time reflecting on the human qualities and weaknesses shown during the visitation. H.F.'s observations praise some London authorities and criticise others. He discusses which measures were effective and which were not, among the attempts to contain the plague. This subject-matter may have been of political interest in 1722; but above all the *Journal* is remembered, and still widely read, for its vivid evocation of scenes of horror, of silent frightened streets, carts and pits full of bodies, and for its moving representation of human grief, sympathy, and kindness.

Colonel Jack, the third novel of 1722, is also the third in Defoe's series of destitute orphan stories. Jack's earliest memory is of sleeping among the ashes outside the glasshouse with a band of abandoned, rough boys. He is less of a stalwart or violent criminal than his fellows, but becomes a thief in the inevitable way of Defoe's poor characters, that is, because it is either that or starvation. Following his lowly beginning, Colonel Jack's career is episodic as he is transported to Virginia, earns his freedom, returns to England as a prosperous merchant, marries four times miserably then re-marries his first wife (who has since learned the error of her ways) happily, takes part in military action on the continent, joins the Jacobites at Preston, returns to Virginia, is pardoned, and finally undertakes illegal trading voyages to Mexico. At the end of a long life of wandering, Jack is able to settle in England again, with his wife and in prosperous circumstances, while his trusted agent manages their Virginia estate. The structure of this novel is extremely loose, and the final episode about an illegal Spanish trade seems particularly 'tacked on', and unrelated to the earlier events.

It is worth noting three elements of *Colonel Jack* before we move on, however. First, in one episode Jack becomes a plantation overseer, and persuades his master to sanction an experiment on the black slaves. Jack theorises that fair treatment will encourage them to work harder than would cruel punishments. Jack treats the blacks with justice, and shows mercy; the plantation prospers, and Jack has proved his point. Secondly, Jack's wife, who was a brazen whore when he first married her, reforms her character as a result of severe hardships, and arrives in Virginia as a criminal transport. When they are re-united, Jack and his wife love and support each other, and their marriage becomes an ideal of conjugal contentment. Thirdly, Jack's story is also the story of a social climber. In Virginia, Jack employs an educated transport to be his tutor, and this, together with his prosperity, turns him into a gentleman. This is a story and an aspiration shared with *Moll Flanders*, who periodically impersonates and eventually achieves the status of a 'gentlewoman' to which she so ignorantly aspired as a child.

In 1724, Defoe brought out (to give it its full title): ***The Fortunate Mistress: Or, a History of the Life and Vast Variety of Fortunes of Mademoiselle de Beleau, Afterwards Call'd the Countess de Wintelsheim, in Germany. Being the Person known by the Name of the Lady Roxana***. We have mentioned two theories, as to why *Roxana* was the last of Defoe's fictions, and other critics make other suggestions. Certainly, *Roxana* has the darkest and most ominous final episodes of any of Defoe's novels. However, this is no reason why Defoe should not have written more. In this chapter, we focus on Defoe's life and his career as a writer of a variety of genres. We know that he wanted to earn a living, and was usually in need of money; and Paula Backscheider remarks that 'he probably made less than £100 on any of the novels, even *Robinson Crusoe*'.[6] It is thus quite believable that Defoe simply turned away from fiction to more lucrative writing projects.

During his final 7 years Defoe continued to manage a prodigious output. In these years, he penned the enormous three-volume ***A Tour Through the Whole Island of Great Britain*** (1724–6), which describes each local area, giving both a physical description and information, whether historical, anecdotal, or in the form of an account of local trades and industries: a vast collection of observations and a blueprint for the travel-writing genre. Defoe had noticed the popularity of his fictional criminals, so during this period he also probably produced lives of the notorious pirate Captain Avery, and the London gang-leader and master-criminal Jonathan Wild. Defoe also wrote further conduct-books, such as ***Conjugal Lewdness or Matrimonial***

Whoredom and ***A New Family Instructor*** (both 1727); and developed plans for English expansion around the world in ***The Complete English Tradesman*** (1725–7) and ***Augusta Triumphans: A Plan of the English Commerce*** (1728). A prestigious and lucrative project which cost subscribers three guineas each was Defoe's explanatory atlas of the world, a large-format publication with impressive maps and charts entitled ***Atlas Maritimus*** (1728). These publications show that Defoe continued to earn a living from his writing, producing volumes that would appeal to popular taste. There is no reason to seek further explanation for why *Roxana* was the last fiction: Defoe was, as usual, pressed for money; and there were quicker and better ways to earn than writing more 'novels'. Finally, remember that the novel is a recognised form in our culture. To Defoe, his fictions had no particular label: they were simply some of his many writings, and less lucrative than others. In the next chapter, we will consider a question Defoe would not have asked: what place do these novels occupy in the development of English prose fiction, or, as Ian Watt put it in the title of his seminal study, in *The Rise of the Novel.*

8

The Place of Defoe's Novels in English Literature

Defoe's fictions have attracted attention from literary historians, because they appeared among the first prose fictions in English. Arguments therefore often circle the question: were these the first 'novels' in English? Or, were they forerunners of the 'novel' which only developed later in the works of, say, Richardson and Fielding? Such debates can be enlightening, but will never be settled because opinions depend so much on the question of definition. What is a novel? Do we list Defoe's characteristics and call them a 'novel', or list a 'novel's' characteristics and seek them in Defoe?

Defoe's Innovations 'Evolutionary'

In our brief look at these questions, then, we will be wary of reaching conclusions. Our aim is to appreciate both what can be called the 'evolutionary' nature of Defoe's innovations: that is, how his fictions adapted and synthesised existing forms into a new whole; and the startling originality of the whole Defoe distilled from his antecedents. We begin by re-visiting some remarks we have already made.

First, we remember that Defoe began to develop novelistic techniques during the years before writing *Robinson Crusoe*. Among these were creating imagined people or 'characters', in his conduct-books, particularly *The Family Instructor* (1715). Equally, naturalistic dialogues within a context of everyday domestic life, and with a cast of ordinary people rather than heroes or aristocrats, were practised in the conduct-books. Secondly, we noticed that Defoe demonstrated a facility for the kind of writing his fictions would entail. For example, remember that he imitated a High Church extremist too successfully in *The Shortest-Way with the Dissenters* (1702): he was a talented mimic, able to adopt an imaginary personality in his writing. Finally, we know that Defoe wrote several factual accounts of particular events, memoirs, and lives, which required him to project his imagination and deploy narrative skill. Furthermore, in the years immediately prior to writing *Robinson Crusoe,* Defoe had several times adopted the persona of an imagined witness, such as the 'Countess of... ' who recounts the life and behaviour of Queen Anne,[1] or the lowly French official 'Monsr. Mesnager' who tells of the secret negotiations leading to the Treaty of Utrecht. Slipping into these narrative personae was practice for the viewpoints of Robinson, Moll, and Roxana, not to mention Bob Singleton, Jack, the Cavalier, and H.F. So, Defoe was ready to write prose fictions, having pioneered and practised many of the techniques he would need.

Our next observation suggests the 'evolutionary' theory of literary development. In Defoe's time, there was a popular enthusiasm for stories of wonders from all around the world; and the publishing industry supplied a stream of travellers' memoirs to satisfy this appetite. There was an equally lively curiosity for the lives of famous criminals, or people of scandalous reputation. Defoe probably contributed biographies of the pirate Captain Avery (*The King of Pirates,* 1719) and the master-criminal Jonathan Wild (1725)[2] to these genres; and one of the sources of *Robinson Crusoe* probably was Captain Woodes Rogers' *A Cruising Voyage Round the World* (London, 1712). So, one might not have noticed the difference between *Robinson Crusoe* and other accounts of voyages; or between *Moll Flanders* and the lives of such notorious female criminals as Moll King, Betsy Careless, or Mary Raby. Furthermore, Defoe's Prefaces claim to introduce true stories. The difference, then, is between fiction dressed up as fact, on the one hand, and fact enlivened by the use of imaginative technique, on the other. Defoe merely took the documentary form, and invented the content.

Precursors

It is wrong to suppose that there was no fiction beforehand, and then suddenly *Robinson Crusoe* burst upon the world. This is simply not true: there was a rich tradition of fiction before Defoe. We can mention in passing the romances popular in medieval times; Boccaccio's *Decameron* and Chaucer's *Canterbury Tales*; Cervantes' *Don Quixote* (1605) or M. de la Fayette's *La Princesse de Clèves* (1678); as well as the fact that the *One Thousand and One Nights* was first published in England between 1704 and 1715. We can broaden our understanding of the varieties of fiction being produced at the time, by mentioning four of Defoe's contemporaries: Mrs Delarivière Manley (1663 or c. 1670–1724); Aphra Behn (1640–89); Eliza Haywood (1693–1756); and John Bunyan (1628–88).

Mrs Manley was the author of *Secret Memoirs and Manners of Several Persons of Quality of Both Sexes, from the New Atlantis, an Island in the Mediterranean* (1709), a satirical fiction in which recognisable political figures appear lampooned in an imagined setting and take part in imagined (and scandalous) events. She also wrote *The Adventures of Rivella, or the History of the Author of The New Atalantis* (1714), a supposed autobiography of her scandalous life; and a collection called *The Power of Love in Seven Novels* (1720). Mrs Manley was in danger of being charged with libel for her *New Atlantis*, but argued that the work was fiction, and therefore not libellous: one may wonder how such a defence appealed to Defoe, with his experience of the libel laws. In addition to her fanciful, satirical, and amatory prose fictions, Mrs Manley wrote a comedy and two tragedies for the stage.

Aphra Behn was, like Mrs Manley, a playwright. Also like Mrs Manley, she led an adventurous life, working as a spy abroad for Charles II, visiting Surinam, and being scandalously open about her bisexuality. She wrote numerous successful plays during the Restoration period, and her most famous novel *Oroonoko*, a romantic tale about an African Prince, his royal behaviour, and devotion to his consort during and after being taken to the Americas as a slave, was published in 1688. The slave-prince's story ends tragically and is one of the first 'tear jerkers', in addition to its early characterisation of a 'noble savage'.

Eliza Haywood's first romantic novels were published at the same time as Defoe launched *Robinson Crusoe*. So, *Love in Excess or The Fatal Enquiry* came out in 1719 and 1720; and the improbable, melodramatic, and sentimental *Idalia; or The Unfortunate Mistress* (1723) not only appeared the year before *Roxana*, but clearly inspired the title *The Fortunate Mistress* that Defoe gave to his novel. Haywood's works were popular and successful.

If we seek antecedents for the psychological interiority, that confessional quality found in Defoe's first-person narratives, then another earlier contemporary comes to mind. John Bunyan's most celebrated work is *The Pilgrim's Progress* (1678 and 1684), which tells a story of spiritual revelations in an allegorical form; but perhaps Defoe owes more to Bunyan's *The Life and Death of Mr. Badman* (1680), an imaginary biography, or *Grace Abounding to the Chief of Sinners* (1666), a spiritual autobiography.

Manley's, Behn's, Haywood's, and Bunyan's works do not compare with Defoe's, but they do demonstrate that a variety of fictional writing was already happening. Social historians also point to an increased audience of literate middle-class professionals and tradesmen, and their families: middle-class women would rather read stories with scandalous, amorous, or romantic content, than the sermons and religious tracts their clergymen recommended; there was thus a growing market for 'novels'. At the same time, the publishing industry expanded, so the printed book became easier and cheaper to produce.

We must also avoid the absurdity of thinking that there was no psychological subtlety of characterisation, or powerful subjective experience, in English literature before Defoe. It would be ridiculous indeed to ignore Chaucer and Shakespeare, to name only the two most prominent. In the centuries before Defoe, English literature rehearsed everything the novel was to do in later centuries; but it did so in poetic and dramatic form, not in prose.

Defoe's Originality

So far our discussion has emphasised that the novel did not materialise out of thin air; that, to Defoe and his contemporaries, it may have appeared little more than a refinement of forms that were already widespread. We will now take a different direction. By whatever alchemy Defoe managed to synthesise elements into the imagined wholes that are his novels, we must acknowledge the outstanding originality of the three novels we study in this book. What, then, are the new qualities Defoe brings to fiction? Then, what are the features that are the most influential, that are the most developed in later novels? In attempting to answer these questions, we will consider how Defoe treats **character**, how he structures **plot**, how he depicts **society**, and how the text may be **significant**.

Defoe's fictions are told in the first person, and all three of his main **characters** write memoirs from a retrospective old age. This gives opportunities for analysing, philosophising about, and judging the character's motives, actions, emotions, beliefs, and impulses. We can be treated to the protagonist's psychology as events occur – as for example when Moll tells us that she 'had much ado, to avoid sinking down, for indeed I lov'd him to an Extravagance'(*MF* 99); or to explanations of character informed by later wisdom – as when she remarks that 'I had a most unbounded Stock of Vanity and Pride' (*MF* 63–4); or to plain hindsight – as when Roxana calls her younger self the 'foolishest, as well as wickedest' (*R* 198). Much of the fascination of these confessions arises from the interaction between such different self-views, and the play of irony between experiences as they occur and as they are remembered. What Defoe presents can be called the play of an individual's mind as it analyses itself and seeks to reveal, understand, and ultimately judge its own identity. No resolution of our three narrators' psychological complexity is offered; and no judgment will adequately distinguish a consistent ethic for any of the three texts. We see, for example, that Robinson's conversion to his father's philosophy does not fit the events of the story; that Moll's repentance is a passing phase; and that Roxana's self-condemnation is not adequate to contain either her original distress, or her challenge to patriarchal values. Indeed, retrospective moralising may be a personal emotional event, rather than an ethic. Defoe's narratives, then, offer an insoluble fascination with individual psychology. In particular, he creates a tension between ethics and individual character: where ethics fails to dominate: experience, impulse, emotion, and psychology force necessary compromises.

We could argue that, in suggesting that individual experience may not be containable in terms of morality, Defoe's characters and their subjective experiences prefigure the arrival of a Romantic outlook towards the end of the eighteenth century.

Defoe's **plots** are in the form of successive and varied episodes. So famous is *Robinson Crusoe* that his life on the island has become a story everybody knows, virtually a myth. However, the story moves through several very different environments: home; on his first voyages; the voyage of escape; the Brasils; then, the island; after that England, Portugal, and the overland journey through the Pyrenees; and finally, England. Each episode is introduced either by some headstrong act on the part of Robinson, or some uncontrollable event (such as storm or shipwreck). *Moll Flanders* is even more episodic: despite her desire for security, each episode crashes to the next, including six episodes of married life and two as a mistress, in a series of events most of which are catastrophic. In *Roxana* there are not quite as many changes of circumstances, and each episode is investigated more fully; but the fundamental structure is the same: the protagonist passes from one situation, via cataclysmic change, to the next, at the whim of circumstances. Each new circumstance becomes simultaneously a test, a revelation, and a complication of character, so that the seemingly random succession of episodes furthers the fascination with character we have discussed in the preceding paragraph.

We have suggested that the plots of our three texts are a loosely connected series of episodes, mimetic of the uncertainty and instability of living; and that none of our texts shows a satisfactory ethical superstructure. However, there are some elements of Defoe's stories that suggest a unifying or 'shaping' structure. Clearly, each text focuses on the consciousness of its narrator; and each text relates one life, from youth (childhood in Moll's case) to old age. There is, therefore, the natural shape of a life which begins energetically and hopes for a settled ending; and as all three protagonists are ambitious, the plots are driven by that energy, and measurable throughout in terms of aims, progress, success, and failure. It could be argued that the three narrators achieve their ambitions, for all three are wealthy in the end. Even this observation is complicated, however: Robinson mentions his 'farther adventures' on the final page of his novel; Roxana tells of falling into 'a dreadful Course of Calamities' (*R* 379) without specifying what these were; and even Moll's report of living in 'the greatest Kindness and Comfort imaginable' (*MF* 427) is not fully convincing. Readers react with differing degrees of scepticism to the idea of Moll becoming penitent and contented. One critic feels that Moll's identity remains 'incomplete, or double and not integrated, or unstable' when she returns to a home country that offers her 'no more safety now than it ever did'.[3] The argument that Newgate is structurally significant, in that it begins Moll's life and is one of her ultimate destinations and therefore stands over her life like an 'arch' does not work either, since Newgate is a final destination Moll manages to evade. She and her story continue for some time after Newgate has retired into memory.

The paragraph above argues back and forth. The very form of Defoe's novels – being a narrator's first-person memoir from youth to old age – provides a powerful unifying force which maintains a tight hold on the reader. On the other hand, no such unifying structures appear in the seemingly accidental succession of circumstances that are the novels' plots. Neither have we found any adequate overarching ethical structure. In conclusion, then, we would argue that Defoe's novels have only a loose plot structure, emphasising instability; and that the unity and the driving fascination of these books lie in characterisation: in individual improvisation and experience, not in plot or morality.

We realised, in Chapter 3, that Defoe depicts the **society** of his time critically, satirically, and with a serious analytical purpose. Various social themes are clearly major concerns in these texts: we may mention economics, changing social hierarchies, decadence, poverty, snobbery, the new colonies, crime and punishment, and gender politics / economics. At this point, we should also stress that the loose and picaresque movement from episode to episode, from place to place, and company to company allows Defoe to present a particularly wide-ranging social panorama. People appear from all walks of life, engaged in various activities, in settings including half-way around the world. This feature may be considered a major element of many later novels. For example, consider the French novelist Honoré de Balzac (1799–1850) who hoped his novels might present a 'Comédie Humaine' – an inclusive picture of human life and society; or look at the novels of Charles Dickens (1812–70) which depict a society made up from different classes hardly aware of each other, yet describing individuals and groups from the bottom to the top of the social scale: from Fagin to Mr. Brownlow; from Magwitch to Lady Havisham; or, unfortunately, from Little Emily to Steerforth. The presentation of a 'social panorama' as a broad and detailed descriptive canvas, then, became a prominent feature of many novels. However, a little thought tells us that yet again Defoe had antecedents: Geoffrey Chaucer's *The Canterbury Tales* (circa. 1380–1400) was a scheme as ambitious as Balzac's; and although the full range of *Tales* was never completed, the *General Prologue* provides portraits of a cross-section of medieval society, all the way from Plowman to Knight. Chaucer in turn was elaborating on Bocaccio's *The Decameron* (1349–52), and was familiar with his contemporary William Langland's *Piers Plowman* (written circa. 1360–87) with its world depicted as a 'fair field full of folk' between a tower (Heaven) and a dungeon (Hell). Another attempt at portraying a 'panorama' of humanity was the Italian poet Dante Alighieri's *Divine Comedy* (1308–21), in which the poet's dream journey through Hell, Purgatory, and Heaven enables him to meet all from the worst sinners to the most holy. Clearly, the desire to represent the whole of society in a panoramic form had a long and distinguished history by Defoe's time. Nevertheless, he was arguably the first to convey this social 'overview' in an English prose fiction.

Finally, we should consider in what way these texts may lay claim to **significance** as works of literature. This is a question to which there is a blindingly obvious answer: *Robinson Crusoe* remains one of the world's most widely read books, and has been translated into virtually every language; *Moll Flanders* and *Roxana* are also established classics, still widely read both for pleasure and for study. Defoe would not still be with us in this way, if his works did not have some **significance**. Any other answers to such an amorphous question are fraught with difficulty, however, since the so-called meaning of any work of literature is a matter of contentious argument. In these circumstances, we will confine ourselves to three observations that are really no more than suggestions.

Our first observation is that Defoe's novels do have qualities that make them enduringly relevant, and that therefore encourage us to apply the words 'literature' and 'significant' to them. It is far more difficult to say what these qualities are. Various kinds of pleasure are experienced as we read: for example, we enjoy the practical resourcefulness of Crusoe, and at the same time the novel is funny enough that we sometimes laugh at him; then, we can identify sympathetically with Moll even as we enjoy her series of antics; while her misfortunes are so many and so bizarre that we are entertained as they unfold. Finally, we can appreciate the beauty of Roxana's arguments, the elegance of her mind, and her challenge to convention. In the most general terms, however, the stories of *Robinson Crusoe*, *Moll Flanders*, and *Roxana*, hold and provoke our interest because of something we can call 'universal'. The three characters concerned claim a connection with us, and the significance of the novels lies in the way these three people are placed in their world, between sky and earth, so that their circumstances and their struggles represent a universal picture of life, of people struggling with uncertain circumstances and moral compromise.

Our second observation is more specific. Defoe wrote at a particularly volatile time: he lived between the Restoration and the second Hanoverian George, through extraordinary changes including the Glorious Revolution, the reigns of William and then Anne, and the progressive establishment of Parliamentary power in a constitutional monarchy. At the same time, society was a melting pot between old attitudes and hierarchies dating back to medieval times, and a new, more open, and opportunistic society founded on a growing merchant bourgeoisie and the untapped wealth of the colonies in a rapidly expanding world. Defoe's three stories are set within these cataclysmic social changes and are all exemplary. That is, as we have suggested in Part I, Defoe's figures struggle for identity, and improvise their own characters and mores, within a context of social upheaval in progress. In this sense, then, Defoe's novels are stories of significant human experiences within a significant social critique.

Thirdly and lastly, we may refer again to a persistent insight of Defoe criticism: that these novels deliberately deny or undercut interpretation. This is variously described: some say that Defoe's world is anarchic, or that events are unpredictable. Some complain about loose ends, while others point out ironies that are structured to counter each other and so to deny conclusions we might otherwise reach. Virginia

Ogden Birdsall describes a 'hostile and unsustaining world' due to life's 'viscous formlessness and lack of significance' as she depicts the protagonists struggling to create their own identities[4]. Ian Watt describes how 'Defoe flouts the orderliness of literature to demonstrate his total devotion to the disorderliness of life'.[5] Katherine Clark remarks on 'the unstable relationship between language and meaning';[6] while we, in our analyses, have remarked on the unrelenting, carefully ironised instability of motives, events, ideas, morals, and so forth. Due to this characteristic 'disorderliness', 'formlessness', call it what you will, Defoe's novels leave us with teasing yet always unresolved conundrums. It can be argued that their continuing fascination may reside in this quality. Equally, we may be tempted to define a necessary quality of literature in such terms: that it will stimulate sympathy, emotion, and thought; and that it will never foreclose these faculties.

Defoe's Successors and Influence

Where, then, does Defoe fit into the history of English Literature? A simple answer is that he sits at the top table, together with the great writers of our culture. A more explanatory answer, and one that has been indicated by the discussions in this chapter, is that Defoe can lay claim to the title of the first English novelist; or at least, that of the first writer of recognisably modern novels: fictions that display the characteristics that became common in the later flowering of the genre. These are fictions driven by character and individual, subjective experience, set within a loose and wide-ranging structure and a panoramic overview of social context. However, Defoe's claim to this title rests on his originality in making a new synthesis from existing elements, combining them in a way that had not been done before. Our argument has therefore been that Defoe's new prose fictions should be seen in terms of literary evolution, in terms of synthesis and development of literary forms, and not as a sudden novelty. At the same time, Defoe's synthesis is an original whole: a new literary form of surprising modernity.

Ian Watt titled his influential book *The Rise of the Novel: Studies in Defoe, Richardson and Fielding*, and we will briefly consider the two novelists thought of as Defoe's immediate successors, before discussing his influence in a broader context.

Samuel Richardson (1689–1761) was a printer and publisher who wrote three novels, all in epistolary form: *Pamela: Or, Virtue Rewarded* (1740), *Clarissa: Or the History of a Young Lady* (1748), and *The History of Sir Charles Grandison* (1753). Pamela is a servant whose master, 'Mr. B', attempts to seduce her. She clings steadfastly to her virtue until he is eventually brought to reform his character under the influence of her principles, whereupon he proposes to her and they marry. Clarissa, on the other hand, is abducted and oppressed by her seducer Lovelace, and eventually starves herself to death. In Sir Charles Grandison, Richardson created a virtuous male hero for the first time. The novel follows the story of Harriet Byron, who is rescued from kidnap by Sir Charles Grandison. After his appearance, the novel focuses on his history and life, and he becomes its central figure. Richardson's novels became extremely popular, and the content of his stories caused controversy from the start. While both *Pamela* and *Clarissa* supposedly show the purity and virtue of idealised heroines, and Mr B and Lovelace display the predatory depravity of libertines, Richardson's text actually presents a different story. Certainly, many modern readers consider Pamela an insufferable prude as well as a calculating social climber; and it can be argued that Clarissa is another over-bred hysteric, one of the first anorexics in literature. Meanwhile, the character Lovelace, for all his villainy, is an attractive and passionate creation who grows far beyond his villainous role, contradicting the author's condemnation. Finally, it was also argued that both *Pamela* and *Clarissa* had a prurient, voyeuristic element that verges on the pornographic. After all, both tell of the sexual pursuit of beautiful women and gratification is constantly delayed. In the case of *Pamela* gratification waits for about 800 pages in a normal edition. Standard editions of *Clarissa* run to around 2000 pages.[7] Both books were accused of stimulating sexual excitement, particularly in the young female readers for whose morals society was most concerned. Richardson carried on extensive correspondence with his readers and critics, and revised later editions, always asserting that his intentions were moral.

Henry Fielding (1707–54) seems to have begun writing novels as a satirical response to Richardson. His first, *An Apology for the Life of*

Mrs. Shamela Andrews (1741), purports to tell the true story of Pamela, whose name turns out to be Shamela. In Fielding's version of the story, she is a lustful and scheming manipulator who inveigles Squire Booby into marriage. Fielding followed up the success of this first satire with the story of Pamela Andrews's supposed brother, *Joseph Andrews* (1742). This novel tells of a young man so handsome that his virtue is assailed on all sides, but he remains chaste. Fielding's satirical intention is obvious, as he reverses the genders to re-tell Richardson's tale of chastity rewarded. However, *Joseph Andrews* developed into a full-fledged novel in its own right. It is a comic novel, playing on degrees of innocence in both Joseph, and his companion Parson Adams, but it is much more than merely a satire on Richardson. In 1749 Fielding wrote the novel considered his masterpiece, *Tom Jones*. In this work, the hero is, again, a young man of exceptional attractions. However, Tom is unlike Joseph Andrews because he is warm-hearted and does not resist temptation. Consequently, after being forced to run away from home, he has sexual relations with a number of women on a picaresque journey through the English countryside to London, before the villainy of the hypocrite Blifil is revealed, and Tom finally wins the hand of Sophia Western, the girl he has always adored. In *Tom Jones*, Fielding carried on from *Joseph Andrews* by creating a further group of memorable comic characters, most of them grotesques such as Tom's two tutors, Thwackum and Square; or Sophia's father, the hard-drinking, hard-hunting, and oath-shouting Squire Western. The unchaste young man who is nonetheless honest, kind-hearted, and warm is a further satire on the morals promoted in Richardson's works, of course; and it appears that Richardson wrote his final novel about the virtuous male Sir Charles Grandison in response to *Tom Jones*.

Our summary of Richardson's and Fielding's works has shown how closely these two writers were indebted to each other, and thrived on the competition and debate between them. They can be said to have developed novels of seduction and novels of courtship, in readiness for the popular prominence of Gothic fiction (its villains clearly inheritors of Lovelace's mantle; and its heroines' chastity always threatened) and the perfected version of eighteenth-century courtship in Jane Austen's six works. Equally, they demonstrated the potential for psychological detail and investigation of emotion, in Richardson, and for comic writing and the invention of grotesques, in Fielding. In short, by the middle of the eighteenth century, the novel was already demonstrating that it could become almost anything, in the hands of each different author. This truth was most magnificently demonstrated by Laurence Sterne's *The Life and Opinions of Tristram Shandy, Gentleman* (1759–70), a most idiosyncratic, trivial, rambling, and comic collection of minor incidents and reflections. One novel's ability to be completely different from any others has continued to be demonstrated by the outstanding originals of the genre. The unique *Wuthering Heights* of Emily Brontë (1847) and James Joyce's massive stream-of-consciousness *Ulysses* (1922) are two such.

Turning our attention back to the beginning of the novel genre, we can suggest that Defoe's three most celebrated works opened up a significant field that was then variously exploited by Richardson, Fielding, and subsequently many others. Both *Moll Flanders* and *Roxana* tell of the sexual adventures and amorous lives of beautiful women. It can be argued that the immorality of both Moll and Roxana, in contrast to the chastity of Pamela and Clarissa, hardly matters: all four novels stimulate sexual and amatory excitement in the reader. Defoe's directness may be very different from Richardson's vicarious thrills, but the idea that a prose fiction can explore love relationships, gender-conflicts, and sexuality, and that this will be a theme of endless fascination to the reading public, was certainly encouraged by the success of *Moll Flanders* and *Roxana.*

Robinson Crusoe suggests a different literary inheritance. Many critics have remarked on the manner in which Defoe's first novel rapidly became a myth, so that the story and the character of Robinson himself were quickly better known than their author; and that Robinson's life cast away on his island soon became common knowledge among people who knew nothing of the rest of the novel. The rapid translation of the story into many languages, and the extraordinarily rapid spread of its fame and readership, indicate that there was and is a potent connection between Robinson's isolation on his island and something responsive in us, something fundamental that was waiting for this particular story. *Robinson Crusoe* thus indicated the potential for prose fiction to tell an archetypal or epic story: the potential for prose fictions to achieve a deep universal appeal like that of a myth. Some later novels may also come to mind as resonating with mythic archetypes. For example, we may consider Mary Shelley's *Frankenstein* (1818), Brontë's *Wuthering Heights* (1847) again, Joseph Conrad's *Heart of Darkness* (1902) or even a modern contribution like William Golding's *Lord of the Flies* (1954). Notice that many people who have not read the novels know about Robinson, Frankenstein (confused with his monster), and Heathcliff.

It would be possible to continue tracing Defoe's literary descendants for a long time. What is already clear is that Defoe's novels had and have a wide-ranging influence on English literature. Most of all, however, we admire Defoe for writing fictions that are relevant, as well as fascinating and entertaining, in the present day; and for developing both the overpowering sense of a character struggling, searching, changing, and improvising through the vicissitudes of life; and the structure of counter-cutting ironies that leaves the issues that are raised by his stories as complex, interesting, and unresolved as when they first reared their problematic heads.

9

A Sample of Critical Views

The Scope of this Chapter

This chapter cannot attempt to survey the critical history of Defoe's novels: we only have space for a sample. For an overview you need to go to Paul Baines' excellent *Daniel Defoe*: Robinson Crusoe/Moll Flanders*; A Reader's Guide to Essential Criticism.*[1] Instead, this chapter has a deliberate aim: to show that a range of different approaches and different interpretations exist, in order to encourage readers and students to develop your own ideas with confidence, and to be stimulated by debate. We make no pretence that the critics represented here are typical. They are only representative of critics in general, in that they hold different opinions from each other. We begin by noting how three twentieth-century novelists responded to Defoe, and with some remarks on Ian Watt's hugely influential work, as a form of background. We will then sample six critical arguments in the form of summaries and extracts.

Background

Three Novelists: Woolf, Forster, and Joyce

Virginia Woolf wrote two essays on Defoe.[2] Regarding *Robinson Crusoe*, she argues that all great novels force us to see the world through their own 'perspective',[3] which is often different from our own. Because Defoe has kept 'consistently to his own sense of perspective', he 'thwarts us and flouts us at every turn', upsetting our preconceptions. The grand themes we expect from a castaway's story – God, man, Nature – are 'snubbed back with ruthless commonsense' until we find our expectations are 'contradicted on every page. There are no sunsets and no sunrises; there is no solitude and no soul. There is, on the contrary, staring us full in the face nothing but a large earthenware pot.' Robinson's 'perspective' is so ruthlessly pragmatic that everything is reduced to a basic 'Reality, fact, substance'. So man 'must be reduced to a struggling ... animal' and God 'shrivel into a magistrate' (all from W285). Paradoxically, we become willing to accept almost anything Robinson tells us – we even swallow improbable scenes such as the 'vast great creatures' that swim out from the coast of Africa, because we have come to trust Robinson's lack of imagination and therefore his accuracy. Furthermore, in *Robinson Crusoe* 'he comes in the end to make common actions dignified and common objects beautiful. To dig, to bake, to plant, to build – how serious these simple occupations are.' Robinson's matter-of-factness extends to characterisation also: he 'describes the effect of emotion on the body, not on the mind'. Woolf concludes that 'the solidity of the pot and its earthiness' is Defoe's 'perspective' which enables him to bring 'the whole universe into harmony' (all from W287). Bearing in mind Woolf's initial definition of a novel, Defoe has thus written a 'masterpiece'.

When commenting on *Moll Flanders* and *Roxana*, Woolf points out that they, in common with Bob Singleton and Colonel Jack, are reduced to utter penury at the start.[4] Moll finds that 'from the outset the burden of proving her right to exist is laid upon her. She has to depend entirely upon her own wits and judgement, and to deal with each emergency as it arises by a rule-of-thumb morality which she has forged in her own head'; and Defoe 'makes us understand that Moll Flanders was a woman on her own account and not only material for a succession of adventures' (both from WBxiv). With regard to the 'feminism' of Moll and Roxana, Woolf argues that 'Defoe not only intended them to speak some very modern doctrines upon the subject, but placed them in circumstances where their peculiar hardships are displayed in such a way as to elicit our sympathy' (WBxvi). Finally,

Woolf claims that *Moll Flanders* and *Roxana* succeed because Defoe does not subscribe to the shallow morality of the prefaces: 'Poverty was their task-master. Defoe did not pronounce more than a judgement of the lips upon their failings. But their courage and resource and tenacity delighted him' (WBxviii).

E. M. Forster's idea of a novel is a work 'in which a character is everything' and plot may be loose and subsidiary.[5] *Moll Flanders* is a perfect example of this because 'everything she does gives us a slight shock . . . the thrill that proceeds from a living being'. However, novels are not the real world, for they provide perfect understanding of the character's inner world – a knowledge that never exists in reality. Moll's completeness as a character is therefore a kind of pleasing illusion the novel gives to its readers.

James Joyce's comments are from the perspective of an Irishman in exile.[6] He sees Defoe's characters, female and male, as forerunners of English types: the women have the 'continence of beasts' and the men are strong and silent: 'English feminism and English imperialism already lurk in these souls.' Furthermore, Crusoe himself is the 'true prototype of the British colonist, as Friday . . . is the symbol of the subject races'. Joyce's list of Crusoe's character traits may ring a series of bells for us: 'The whole Anglo-Saxon spirit is in Crusoe: the manly independence; the unconscious cruelty; the persistence; the slow yet efficient intelligence; the sexual apathy; the practical, well-balanced religiousness; the calculating taciturnity.' Joyce therefore sees *Robinson Crusoe* as a work 'prophetic' of subsequent imperial history.

Together with this devastating critique of Robinson's imperialist Englishness, Joyce called Defoe 'father of the English novel' because he was able to 'devise for himself an artistic form'. Alongside his ability to 'infuse into the creatures of his pen a truly national spirit', Joyce seems to have regarded 'matter-of-fact realism' as the outstanding quality of Defoe's fictions.

Ian Watt

We now turn to academic critics, beginning with Ian Watt. In a remark of extraordinarily patronising insouciance, Paula R. Backscheider calls

Watt a 'scholar without a Ph.D' and ranks him with a Scotsman, and 'women', as equal contributors to Defoe's continuing reputation.[7] Watt's essay '*Robinson Crusoe* as a Myth' came out in 1951, and *The Rise of the Novel: Studies in Defoe, Richardson and Fielding* in 1957. The latter is an ambitious and hugely influential attempt to turn literary history into an intelligible story about society, philosophy, publishing, writers, and culture. Watt suggests that England was prepared, receptive, and ready for the 'rise of the novel' when it happened: he argues a kind of perfect fit between society and writers, the one desiring and the other providing the same product. Reading expanded and tastes changed, in the new middle class of tradesmen, professionals and merchants, and their wives and daughters. This readership turned away from aristocratic and classical forms such as epic poetry, and from a theological diet of tracts and sermons, and sought entertainment: they were a ready-made market for novels. All of the manifold historical trends and changes Watt discusses are, he says, 'merely reflections of a larger and even more important feature of their time – the great power and self-confidence of the middle class as a whole'.[8]

At the same time, self-conscious individualism and empiricism were on the rise due to the philosophy of Locke (1632–1704) and the science of Newton (1642–1727). This new emphasis on truth discovered by the individual through his or her senses encouraged or coincided with the characteristic that Watt called 'formal realism': formal because it is a distinctive feature of the new novel 'form'; and realism because it is the narrative expression of the premise that 'the novel is a full and authentic report of human experience'. 'Formal realism' therefore provides the reader with 'such details of the story as the individuality of the actors concerned, the particulars of the times and places of their actions'.[9]

Watt's analysis of *Robinson Crusoe* discusses the hero under the three headings of 'Back to Nature', 'Dignity of Labour', and 'Economic Man', all three of which Watt believes have mistakenly grown up around the Crusoe 'myth'. Crusoe did not go 'Back to Nature': on the contrary, he had a toolbox, and imposed the orderliness of production onto his environment. Crusoe works hard, yes; but a proper reading shows that the 'Dignity of Labour' is, when possible, for others such as Xury, the slaves to be brought from Guinea, or Friday.

Crusoe is a capitalist and not a labourer: he owns the means of production and his Brasil plantation goes on earning even while he is absent. Considering Crusoe as 'Economic Man', Watt develops a Marxist idea about the 'process of alienation by which capitalism tends to convert man's relationships with his fellows, and even with his own self, into commodities';[10] so we should understand Crusoe as a fully alienated man rather than some heroic 'Economic' individual.

Watt finds *Moll Flanders* troubling. His major complaints are threefold. First, he believes that Defoe became too close to his narrator: his 'identification with Moll Flanders was so complete that, despite a few feminine traits, he created a personality that was in essence his own'.[11] This charges that Defoe failed to create a true feminine voice or perspective, having insufficient control over his character. Consequently, Watt's second serious charge is that there is no intentional irony to preserve distance between Defoe and Moll. Watt argues that where there seems to be irony it is rather 'accidents which unwittingly reveal'[12] the serious ethical contradictions from which Defoe suffers. Finally, Watt complains that Moll's narrative has to retail events at the time they happen; provide a retrospective moral reflection; and perhaps be the editor's covert voice as well. For Watt, these different roles are insufficiently distinct, and as a result the novel's didactic purpose is confusing and unstable. Watt also seems dissatisfied because Moll gets away with her crimes, and becomes penitent and happy without having to sacrifice her ill-gotten gains.

We can think of numerous answers to these complaints – not least Watt's own comment that 'Defoe flouts the orderliness of literature to demonstrate his total devotion to the disorderliness of life',[13] which pictures Defoe as an intentional, not accidental, leaver of loose ends. However, the wide range and ambition of Watt's thesis provided material for multiple controversies, investigations, endorsements, and disagreements, which stimulated critics and scholars as Defoe studies surged into the second half of the twentieth century.

A Sample of Six Critical Views

We now turn to a sample of six critics from the latter part of the twentieth century and the beginning of the twenty-first. We provide a summary of all or part of each critic's argument, with the reminder that this is merely a sample where the variety of approaches and views is intended to stimulate argument. In no sense is this sample intended as representative or as embodying a survey of the criticism.

Miriam Lerenbaum

Ms Lerenbaum can stand as one example from the hundreds of reactions to *The Rise of the Novel.* Ian Watt had charged that Moll was not truly a feminine narrator: she was Defoe with a couple of 'feminine traits' tacked on. Leaving aside the question of what a 'feminine trait' might be (natural or learned?), Miriam Lerenbaum takes Woolf's description of Moll as 'a woman on her own account' as the title for an essay arguing that Defoe succeeded in portraying female experience and consciousness.[14] Lerenbaum suggests that Defoe gives us 'an exceptionally accurate rendering of his heroine's involuntary involvement in the feminine role' (L37). Moll's early experiences are traumatic as she discovers what it is to be female: 'Before the age of twenty, all of Moll's romantic hopes are dashed, and all of her options are foreclosed.' Her response is to withdraw into sickness: 'Her severe illness in the face of this crisis is therefore a plausible and significant emblem of her involvement in the feminine role' (L41). Lerenbaum then enters into a discussion of Moll and motherhood, concluding that, beset by manifold difficulties and threats, Moll's treatment of her children was not unnatural. She also shows different degrees of affection for her children, favouring those from her happier liaisons, for example. After remarking how the change of life led Moll to become a criminal, Lerenbaum makes a connection between Moll's early trauma and her arrival in Newgate, where she describes her state 'of "the compleatest misery on earth" in terms very reminiscent of her earlier withdrawals into extreme passivity,' which 'must be seen as a significant part of a lifelong pattern' (L49): in other words, a pattern in which Moll becomes passive, paralysed, and withdrawn when subjected to persecution or suffering as a woman, what Lerenbaum calls her 'involuntary involvement in the feminine role'.

Virginia Ogden Birdsall

V. O. Birdsall published *Defoe's Perpetual Seekers* in 1985. Broadly, this is one of several studies that focus on the struggling characters Defoe created. As we will see, one task Birdsall performs is to take Miriam Lerenbaum's emphasis on Moll's subjective experience much further, in her study of both Moll and Roxana. She begins, however, with *Robinson Crusoe.*

Birdsall begins with a discussion of Robinson's conversion. Hobbes pointed out that 'no man will subordinate himself either to another man or to any power higher than himself unless he stands to gain thereby' and Robinson eventually turns to a supernatural other because he does not have power over 'the nature that dictates his own death'.[15] Robinson's dealings with Providence are like a negotiation where he seeks to 'control the controller or to make the God he serves serve him' by 'figuring out quite rationally what he needs to do to insure that God will take his side' (B27), and Robinson also casts himself in the role of an all-powerful controller:

> The fact is that Crusoe often sees himself, or suggests that others see him, as a powerful and even a godlike figure, the center of a perfectly ordered and wholly nourishing life. (B30)

However, Robinson's own feeling of security is most boosted by controlling 'that most impressive of all tributes to human scientific ingenuity, gunpowder . . . He often feels, in fact, omnipotent' (B31). The terms 'astonishment' and 'admiration' repeatedly describe natives' reactions to gunfire: it seems to confer a supernatural power on Robinson, and Birdsall compares the musket's flash-and-bang with the fiery explosions in Robinson's delirious dream.

However, the power on which Robinson relies most consistently is the power of his reason, which he uses to plan and order nature around him and to keep his terrors at bay. Birdsall perceptively analyses Robinson's moments of helplessness, for example, during his swim from the wreck to the island, or during his illness, saying that 'Confusion of thought carries with it a sense of impotence; presence of mind is associated with control and hence with power' (B34). So, his feeling 'easy' depends on how he can 'master his own fears... order his own confusions' (B35) by using reason, and he makes more use of reason than of faith, even after his conversion. Just as Robinson progressively tames outward nature, so too he uses reason to control despair and helplessness, inner threats that he must also tame in order to survive. Birdsall sees his exploration of the cave where he finds a dying goat as symbolic of 'this conquest of inner space' (B36). It presents as a terrifying place, with shining eyes that watch Robinson enter the 'mouth'. Then knowledge transforms it into a womb-like place of security and storage. For Robinson, 'to name is to know, and to know is to feel in control' (B38). Birdsall then remarks that 'the ultimate self-created world in which he is both orderer and ordered' is Robinson's autobiography; and his remarks about his journal, where he was at first in too much hurry, mean 'In other words, only when reason is in control can one make one's experience seem anything but pointless or meaningless' (B38).

Birdsall's analysis, then, has described Robinson's effort to tame his world, his God, and himself. However, his 'oral fixation' undercuts the idea that 'his adventures truly involve a progressive mastery of his environment':

> What they do involve are alternating periods of shelter and of exposure, and what Defoe implicitly concedes is that the choice Crusoe seems to have amounts, in reality, to no choice at all. For whether he chooses home or restless wandering, the underlying and inescapable reality is always death. He knows that he must leave the womb if he is to live, and that he is born to die – and that no power, whether human or divine, can change that deadly fact. (B39)

Birdsall then elaborates on the recurrent circle motifs (e.g. Robinson's palisades) and notices the narrative's recurring surges of dominance and terror. She concludes that Robinson records, actually, a hopeless struggle against what she calls 'exposure', the 'yawning abyss, the primal night which originates all and to which we all return' (B40).

Birdsall begins her chapter on *Moll Flanders* by observing similarities between Moll and Robinson: so, for example, 'life for Moll is a power game. And the game, Defoe again recognizes, is in the final analysis a losing one'; like Crusoe, 'she fears for her own physical survival' (both B73). This terror drives her to control and order her environment; to secure herself so she 'knows her present and future food supplies to be assured' (B74); to enter manipulative relationships with others, and use generosity as a form of investment; and to glory in her successes. She 'loves making fools of people, proving them less clever and hence less powerful than she' (B77). Reason is as significant for Moll as for Robinson, witness the disastrous passions that turned Moll's head when she was first seduced, as well as the 'Brutish and Thoughtless' hell into which she temporarily degenerates in Newgate.

Moll's terror-fuelled drive towards assuring security, like Robinson's frantic imposition of order, is compulsive, as shown by her addiction to continuing as a thief beyond necessity. However, money is not an end in itself for Moll. Money is sensual in the scene when her Bath gentleman puts her hand among the guineas; or when she gambles with a gentleman's money, keeping some in her lap. It is ironic that many of Moll's thefts are associated with reproduction, such as baby clothes and wedding rings. For Moll, money is a solution not because 'money is God' but because 'money negotiates immortality and therefore is God'.[16] In other words, Moll's quest is spiritual because what she pursues is freedom from the terror of starvation, and a promised land as a 'gentlewoman'. Money is merely the means to these ends.

Birdsall then turns to the question of irony, mentioning Dorothy Van Ghent's opinion that *Moll Flanders* is either consciously ironic, or Defoe's value system is utterly corrupt. *Moll Flanders* is not 'an indictment of capitalism', but is 'an examination of just what money has come to mean to civilized man. And therein lies the irony' (B82). Birdsall discusses several of the passages that have inspired critics to comment on Moll's hypocrisy or ethical contradictions, such as her advice to the parents of the little girl she robs, or her diatribe against drunkenness. These are not unlikely or wicked at all, but the natural products of Moll's agile self-excusing reason, founded on the principle that survival is an absolute motive. Moll's repentance is similar, being a form of religious self-interest. Moll says of her young self that she had 'very little stock of Virtue'. When she spends her old age with Jemy 'in sincere Penitence for the wicked Lives we have lived', she now wants to increase her stock of virtue:

> ... there is no conflict, no incongruity between what she does and what she says about what she does ... For Moll – and for Defoe – morality is a way of dealing with mortality: it is a matter of self-interest. (B93)

Birdsall qualifies her 'Defoe' as 'at least the voice of the preface', avoiding the suggestion that Defoe's own values were corrupt. However, she goes on to explain that Moll has no natural impulse towards good, but instead a lively fear of punishment. In Moll's reaction to her first theft, three fears are expressed: fear of starving, fear of punishment in Newgate, and fear of sin and therefore damnation. The fears must be faced in order, and 'at present starvation is the most immediate of the three punishments she stands to suffer' (B97). Moll's penitence is thus an instrumental thing: not insincere, but serving the purpose of warding off eternity and its fears.

Birdsall begins her analysis of *Roxana* by emphasising the narrator's desire to be someone, in contrast to the fool husband who 'was a meer motionless Animal, of no Consequence in the World', and of whose life she says 'I omit it'. Roxana identifies with the houses in which she lives, and with precious objects, which represent her value, as for example when she remarks 'I seem'd like an old Piece of Plate that... comes out tarnish'd and discolour'd' after her royal affair. True to her need to preserve her selfhood, Roxana rejects 'the sentimental twaddle about marriage as a merging of identities' because a couple's identity becomes that of the man, with the woman as a servant, and 'for Roxana as for Moll, to be a servant is to be nobody' (B145). However, the individual identity Roxana develops and attempts to preserve is problematic. She constantly dresses, putting on costumes to act a part, culminating in her favourite costume and performance as 'Roxana'. Birdsall comments that 'To be stripped is, for Roxana, to be nothing' (B153). Her favourite scenes are those 'in which she most clearly holds centre stage and hence the ones in which she has the most definite sense of being somebody' (B154).

Roxana's reception of the Prince at the start of their affair, and her performance of the Turkish dance, is the climaxes of her acting. Birdsall agrees that Amy acts as Roxana's 'alter ego': 'What Amy seems to represent, then, is the essential self behind all the parts that Roxana acts in her life ... One might say that Amy stands for the underside of Roxana, the earth-bound side' (B158). In putting Amy in bed with her own lover, Roxana 'is attempting to become dissociated from this aspect of herself – that is to say, from her own corruption' (B160); and Birdsall collects various references to 'the Jaws of Hell', 'the Devil', and so on, as well as Amy's epithets as 'Slut' and 'Jade', to support this analysis, establishing the idea of Roxana's divided identity. Crises in which Roxana's survival or the concealment that is necessary to that survival are threatened are often accompanied by imagery of storms or shipwreck, centering on the storm scene itself, but also in the Jew's frightening passion and the threat posed by Susan. Susan's role further complicates Roxana's fragmented identity: Susan 'stands for ... the earthbound self':

> Regarded in this way, Susan is an inner voice that seeks to reelevate what we may call Roxana's Roxana identity – that past which the current Roxana, clad in modest Quaker dress ... looks upon as guilty and criminal and wants to deny ever existed. (B164)

In the final part of the novel, then, Susan and Amy are closely identified linguistically, by 'Slut', 'Jade', and 'Hussy' epithets and demon references. So, 'although it may seem that Roxana hides behind Amy, it is, in a deeper sense, the other way around' (B165), which leads Amy to panic as she did in the storm, and consequently 'Roxana's "Amy nature" becomes, at the end of the narrative, so desperately bent on avoiding recognition and exposure that it is driven to strike out in terrified uncontrol' (B167). Meanwhile, Roxana's 'Quaker friend, whose honesty she often extols, takes over the protective function that has heretofore been Amy's alone,' (B165) in another complication of the identity story.

In the end, Roxana's 'true "Shape" ' cannot be concealed, because in *Roxana* Defoe finally faces the fearful irony, that man is driven to deny his earthbound or animal nature; yet:

> In trying to outwit death – to rise above his own earthboundness – he ultimately outwits himself. (B170)

Birdsall concludes that all the protagonists engage in 'the lonely and futile search for a significant selfhood in an inhospitable and unsustaining world'. Faced with the 'formlessness' of nature, Defoe's narrators are always driven to carry on 'the death-defying struggle to become somebody who matters' (B171). We are also struck by Defoe's 'sense of the predatory nature of his world', with images of devouring and the insecurity of that 'exposure' all the protagonists are desperate to avoid. 'In the fictions ... Defoe has dealt with the existential terrors of an irrational world ... for there the protagonists must cope not only with the chaotic energies outside themselves but with those making up their own lower natures' (B173). Defoe wrote two sequels as Robinson, and Roxana's Quaker and Roxana roles are never integrated, so 'We are left in each case with not one identity but two. There has been no integration of experience. Not order but disorder prevails', but Roxana is singled out because she 'learns at last that there is no hiding place anywhere. There is no identity that works' and 'Nowhere else does he [Defoe] concede so unblinkingly that the world, the flesh, and the devil are parts of a single inescapable fate' (B174).

Birdsall has thus drawn together some prominent elements of character shared between Robinson, Moll, and Roxana, highlighting their drives towards control, and their use of reason; counterpointed by their terrors of exposure, poverty, and starvation, which are the fear of death. We could complain that parts of Birdsall's analysis seem to treat the narrators as real people – particularly in her discussion of irony in *Moll Flanders*. On the other hand, Birdsall's work is enlightening particularly in relation to Robinson's means of gaining control, and in her valiant attempt to divide the personae in *Roxana* into aspects of a single character.

John J. Richetti

Our third critic, John J. Richetti, published his study *Daniel Defoe* in 1987[17] and chapters 4, 5, and 6 deal with our three novels in order of publication. He begins his study of *Robinson Crusoe* by referring to the innovation 'formal realism' noticed by Ian Watt, adding that Defoe's 'realism' presents the individual and particular, not general philosophic truths. This is in keeping with the influence of Descartes and Locke. Furthermore, Defoe is not merely writing a spiritual autobiography:

> The discovery of providential direction and support gives Crusoe peace of mind and allows him to work more efficiently. But [it also has] a material, nearly palpable immediacy that marks the beginnings of realistic fiction in English. (R56)

However, the developing religious story is always in counterpoint with the randomness of mere phenomena. For example, the hats and shoes that are all that remains of his shipmates: 'as he begins his meditation on the fate that put him on the island, Crusoe brings us reports of that world of mere phenomena, things and events that are real precisely because they have no meaning beyond their random factuality' (R58). Equally, Robinson's efforts and spiritual progress (and his gun and toolkit) save him from the alternative outcome, of returning to a primitive beast-like existence as he must have done had he saved nothing from the wreck.

Crusoe's original sin was not wanderlust, or disobedience: it was 'the dynamic tendency of capitalism itself, whose aim is never merely to maintain the status quo, but to transform it incessantly' (R62).[18] In fact, Defoe creates Crusoe as an adventurer, survivor, capitalist, and colonist: 'Defoe's instinctive acuteness, then, makes Crusoe both historically and psychologically meaningful' (R62). Crusoe tames nature, and is simultaneously terrified of it; he is master of his island, but is tormented by loneliness. He describes 'alternations of contentment and despair' which capture the pathos of his life. Defoe proposes two solutions to this dreadful ambivalence. First, Crusoe finds religious thoughts, and his piety is convincing because it is clearly a means of survival born of his 'psychological stress'. Secondly, as soon as he sees the footprint, Crusoe turns from his introspective phase, to 'the external world of adventure and conflict with others' (all from R63). Crusoe turns into a shrewd and successful action hero in the final part of the novel. He ends as 'an aggressive adventurer and domineering colonial overlord' and casts himself as 'deus ex machina' for the English Captain (R66–7).

Turning to *Moll Flanders*, Richetti raises his most persistent doubt at the start: Defoe, he says, is good at incident but weak at coherent plots; and *Moll Flanders* looks 'like the most formlessly episodic of Defoe's books, with over a hundred separate scenes tied together by rapid synopses of other events' (R87). However, this novel is conferred some unity by Moll's gender: 'As a woman... she has a unifying and recurring problem: female survival in a masculine world' (R87). Furthermore, Moll becomes much more than an account of a criminal life because of Defoe's innovatory narrative viewpoint: she is 'an old woman looking back on her life . . . The reader is conscious, in effect, of two characters, one narrating, the other acting' (R91). Richetti finds Moll's moral inconsistencies 'endearingly human' and the narrative therefore tends to 'ethical neutrality' which is a vital ingredient in its illusion of realism. Furthermore, the fact that the story of sin and repentance is intermittent, and not consistently pursued through all the episodes, makes *Moll Flanders* more like a novel and less like a conduct-piece – although this may be due to Defoe's rushed composition rather than design:

> With all its clumsiness and inconsistency and to some extent because of them, *Moll Flanders* conjures up a personality, a character claiming quite aggressively to be a unique individual with a history entirely her own, not simply a moral or social type. (R93)

Richetti then takes on the question of gender, saying that Western literature has habitually characterised women as having 'a turbulent, compulsive sexuality'. This is a 'patriarchal myth' to which Defoe's characterisation of Moll does not subscribe. Calculation and manipulative profit-motive dominate most of Moll's dealings with her lovers and husbands, while sexual desire is barely mentioned, despite her frankness about all else. There are, however, occasions when she admits an emotional involvement, and Richetti seems to counter his own argument, saying that Moll 'acquires skills at survival and manipulation by painfully repressing emotions that the book identifies as specifically female susceptibilities' (R98).

Finally, Richetti turns to the moment in Newgate when Moll records herself going 'brutish and thoughtless, and at last raving mad' so that she is 'no more the same thing that I had been'. This is a crucial moment in the context of Defoe's fiction, because:

> All his narratives challenge the notion of simple or stable identity. His characters record nothing less than the fluid and dynamic nature of personality, a matter of changing roles, wearing masks, responding to circumstances, and discovering new possibilities of self-expression. (R101)

Defoe may intend an irony here. Moll has continued so long in crime that, despite her expertise as a deceiver and actress, she has become 'hardened' in vice. So her becoming a 'meer Newgate-Bird' is a revelation of the 'real Moll formed by a life of crime, 'harden'd' in a sort of moral stupor long before she arrived in Newgate' (R101). Whether this idea is valid or not, two influences then help her to recover: the minister and her repentance; and the reunion with Jemy. Moll's outrageous gratitude to Providence, when she receives her inheritance, shows how Defoe complicates ethics and character:

> For some readers, this particular inconsistency and adamant inability to become simply moral types are what make Defoe's characters a uniquely living collection. (R104)

Richetti argues that *Roxana* is a more developed novel. He discusses the roots of both *Robinson Crusoe* and *Moll Flanders* in popular forms such as spiritual autobiography; accounts of voyages; and criminals' lives; and distinguishes how far Defoe adds to the blueprint. In a discussion of randomness in *Robinson Crusoe*, Richetti remarks that the plot is secondary to an 'autobiographical memoir' because Defoe highlights 'the sequences of individual experience' (R59); and on *Moll Flanders* he finds that this novel is 'formlessly episodic', and complains that Defoe wrote in such a rush that he left the spiritual theme intermittent.

Roxana is 'a uniquely self-conscious and revealingly honest figure' whose 'commentary on her past has an analytic penetration that Moll sorely lacks. Roxana reaches for an intensity Moll is incapable of' (R109–10), because she sees through her rationalisations and feels revulsion from her sins, even while she commits them. Her account is thus more intellectually aware than that of Moll. Therefore, the different episodes are more integrated as parts of a single life-story, and are more tightly connected than in the earlier novels.

The relationship between Roxana and Amy is 'the most profoundly personal link between two people Defoe ever imagined'. When Roxana declares she cannot sin, and Amy 'puts the case for survival at its most brutal', Richetti suggests that this is a place that supports the critic G. A. Starr's theory that Defoe's novels are organised as 'moral dilemmas resolved by the traditional method of "casuistical" analysis' (R111). On the other hand, Roxana does not settle for casuistry: she recognises her own crimes for what they are. So, Roxana goes ahead 'with open eyes' and 'knowing and owning it to be a crime'. Defoe's originality lies in this relation between Roxana and the plot of the novel:

> ... in Roxana's oscillations and defining inconsistencies as she relives her life in the telling of it. Her story has an eddying motion ... And yet, *Roxana* is more than a whirlpool of episodes and incidents. It has a narrative pattern, a unified plot more coherent than Defoe had ever managed. (R113)

Richetti here uses the terms 'oscillations', 'eddying motion', and 'pattern' to suggest that this novel is unified in a way that the series of scenes in *Moll Flanders*, or the succession of interior experiences of *Robinson Crusoe*, are not. The relationship between 'two sequences, which in the end are crucially linked' (R113) exemplifies the point. These are the Turkish dance in Roxana's Pall Mall apartments, which seems the moment of her greatest triumph; and Susan's visit when she tells the story of the Turkish dance, when 'Roxana's tangle of conflicting emotions emerge again in a scene that ties the novel's events and themes together in masterly fashion' (R117). This is a level of narrative composition not attempted or approached before *Roxana*: 'Fate is expressed in character; what appear at first to be freely chosen and self-expressive acts become part of tragic destiny. Roxana's carefully acquired poise and sophistication turn out to be nothing less than the instruments of her destruction' (R118).

Ellen Pollak

Our fourth critic is Ellen Pollak. Her 'Gender and fiction in *Moll Flanders* and *Roxana*'[19] begins with the observation that it is impossible to pin down Defoe, because of the moral and narrative 'instability' of his novels. They 'can be an interpretative nightmare for those trying to locate in them a stable authorial voice or point of view' (P139). Defoe achieves a 'kaleidoscopic' effect by playing first-person experience against memory and retrospect, and uses 'the device of the narrative frame to expose truth's always contested and circumstantial nature' (P140–1). Moll and Roxana are even more unstable than the male narrators, however, and are controversial:

> Critics have long debated whether *Moll Flanders* and *Roxana* celebrate the resourcefulness and cunning of their proto-feminine heroines, provide cautionary lessons about the debasing and debilitating effects of female vice and debauchery, or simply exploit the titillating pleasures of representing female immorality under the pretence of exposing its wickedness. (P142)

Pollak turns to analysis of the prefaces, beginning with the observation that in Defoe's time, 'A woman on her own, uncontained by the neutralizing force of male authority, is spiritually and materially tainted' (P144) and consequently Moll and Roxana become 'embodiments' of the tainted nature of their texts. Meanwhile, in both prefaces 'the excesses and indecencies of the female textual body threaten to undermine the performance of male editorial discipline' (P145).

In both prefaces the editor uses the same figure regarding the female text he must supposedly control. For *Moll Flanders* he 'must put it into a Dress fit to be seen' and for *Roxana* he apologises that he has toned down the 'beautiful' authoress's finery by 'dressing up the story in worse Cloaths than the *Lady*, whose words he speaks, prepared it for the World'. In the prefaces the editor is uncertain whether he can contain or control these transgressive female texts, while Defoe is 'peeking out from behind the editorial mask to suggest that his editors themselves are naïve or overly credulous readers' (P155). Notice, for example, that Roxana's editor claims that her first husband has vouched for the truth of the first part of her story: we can hardly take such a witness seriously.

Pollak sees the 'taint' surrounding these two women as proceeding from a deep contradiction in the ideology of economic individualism that drove the emerging market economy of England at the time. As the old land-based economy and emphasis on birth gave way to commerce, 'capital accumulation and individual desire' began to dominate, and the old determinants of kinship and birth were less important. However, women still had to operate 'first and foremost as members of a family unit' (P148), governed by obsolete determinants, while at the same time occupying an increasingly capitalist society. When Moll tries to exploit her sexual value as an independent agent on her own behalf, she 'crosses over into outlaw territory' (P149). Both Moll's and Roxana's attempts to act on their own account run up against the power of kinship:

> ... both narratives enclose their dramas of class ascent within stories of kinship that work to neutralize or temper the subversive force of the heroines' transgressions, circumscribing the fates of both women within a range of narrative possibilities that seem to have the force of biological imperatives or to be built into the Providential order of the universe. (P150)

The crucial moment in Moll's kinship drama occurs when she succeeds in catching a good husband. This is 'The moment of Moll's fullest realization of her agency as a woman', but it is simultaneously 'the point at which she is most thwarted and defiled' (P151) because her marriage turns out to be incestuous, a transgression against the facts of kinship Moll has attempted to escape or ignore. In the case of Roxana, the crucial moment occurs when she triumphantly dances at her Pall Mall apartments: 'at the moment when the heroine seems to hold sovereign control over the gaze of the crowd, her daughter and namesake, Susan – who happens to be a servant in her employ – is standing by' (P153). Pollak concludes:

> Like Moll's story of self-making, in which kinship returns powerfully and inescapably to delimit the quest for autonomy, Roxana's story is contained by a confrontation with family and fixed social identity. (P154)

Finally, noting the consensus that *Roxana* is Defoe's 'best' novel because Roxana has the most tortured inner life, Pollak asks what that tells us about the 'development of the novel as an institution in the eighteenth century with respect to its construction of the psychological and moral lives of women'; and comments that the development of the novel, at the least, 'was tied up with problematic norms of female interiority' (both P156). Although kinship defeats the aspirations towards agency of both women, this does not represent a patriarchal limitation in Defoe. He has the ironic distance to show such gender norms as 'historical, constructed, and only provisional' (P156).

Michael Seidel

Michael Seidel's article '*Robinson Crusoe:* varieties of fictional experience'[20] is divided into three sections subtitled 'Island supplements', 'Island replicates', and 'Island allegories'. In the first of these, Seidel points out that 'Crusoe's imagination generates many more fictions than the one he experiences'. Much of the text of *Robinson Crusoe* deals with possibilities and imagined alternative realities, plans, anticipations, or speculations. So, for example, Robinson passed 'whole Days' imagining 'how I must have acted, if I had got nothing out of the Ship'; terrified, he guesses about his fate if, instead of one footprint, he had 'seen fifteen or twenty Savages, and found them pursuing me'. Seidel quotes a lengthy passage in which Robinson sees a ship in distress and speculates what the sailors on board are thinking or will do. The passage proves to be much more imagination than fact, and Seidel emboldens terms such as 'I imagin'd', 'as I thought', or 'I fancy'd' in order 'to illustrate just how riddled Robinson's prose can be with imagined recreations within the fiction that Defoe gives us' (S184).

The complications of fictions within fictions, and fictions that are likely rather than factual, become even more interesting when the English mutineers appear on the island; and Seidel provides a commentary, starting when Robinson guesses that the mutineers will abandon their fellows, saying 'I imagin'd it to be as it really was', and going on to remark on the fiction Robinson creates by shouting: 'That is, he creates a contrived action within the presumably real fiction to make something actual happen.' This commentary continues, noting the fiction of Robinson as Governor, or Governor's emissary; and the invention of a garrison of 50 soldiers. This final episode of Crusoe's island life is 'a kind of Prospero-like finale near the end when Crusoe as forest wizard directs the pageant that takes place when Europeans come ashore' (S185–6). Seidel asks why Defoe should bother with so much fictive elaboration, and replies that this is related to the 'innovative nature' of the novel form: 'The way that Defoe tells the Crusoe story becomes a kind of primer on the new art of realistic novel writing in the period' (S186).

When Defoe insists that his work is not a 'romance' but is historical or true, he does not necessarily mean factually true. He means that it is natural or likely rather than improbable:

> At the heart of Defoe's theory of fiction is the notion that the mind expands upon circumstance to engage reader interest only if the 'wonders' described do not depart from the temporal and spatial laws of nature and are perceived as probable. (S188)

Charles Gildon famously attacked *Robinson Crusoe* as a tissue of lies, and in the preface to the *Serious Reflections* Defoe answered the charge by absorbing it, affirming that Gildon's objection is 'false in Fact' whereupon he goes on to 'affirm, that the Story, though Allegorical, is also Historical, and that it is the beautiful Representation of a Life...' Fiction, then, has the ability to be 'true' in the important sense of relevant and believable, despite never having happened. Defoe, in Robinson's voice, says his story is 'a just History of a State of forc'd Confinement' and could have been set on an island or in any other kind of prison, because it is reasonable 'to represent any Thing that really exists, by that which exists not'. It is to reinforce this point about the nature of fiction that Defoe 'has Crusoe live fictionally inside the story; that is, Crusoe reflects on the relation between what he experiences and what he imagines, dreams, or hallucinates' (S189).

In 'Island replicates' Seidel begins by pointing out some of what he calls 'doubling'. When in Brasil, for example, Crusoe feels isolated 'like a Man cast away upon some desolate Island', pre-figuring what will happen; and his dream of rescuing a savage pre-dates the arrival of Friday. Seidel then cites examples of verbal 'doubling' and 'doubling' in the structure of sentences. He shows Crusoe building a 'replicate universe' by calling his cave his 'home', 'castle', 'residence', and so on. Thus, the 'worlds Crusoe builds on his island extend to the fabricated nature of the language he uses' (S191); and verbal doubling is insistent in portraying Crusoe's alternations of mood which oscillate between confidence and terror. Seidel refers to the two-column list of miseries and hopes Robinson draws up, and quotes numerous examples such as 'my Reign, or my Captivity, which you please'.

The narrative also reveals 'doubling' of narrative form. The prime example is that Robinson's first year on the island is told to us twice – in the journal and then as a memoir. There are also other 'replicate' forms and documents in the novel including 'charts, lists, contracts, memoranda, affidavits'. The finished canoe Robinson could not launch now sits on the island, as Robinson says, as a '*Memorandum* to teach me'; and another memorandum is the parrot, like a time capsule, repeating the bemoaning tone of Robinson's earlier miseries. After waking in shock, Robinson 'realises that the voice is a version of his own... [that] we, as readers, had never heard before in the narrative' (S194).

Seidel's final section, on 'Island allegories', elaborates the obvious remark that Crusoe's story is allegorical because he represents a kind of 'Everyman', and the island setting gives Defoe 'a chance to recreate and speed up the story of the race' (S196). So, we notice that Crusoe pulls gold, silver, iron, and lead from the wrecked ship; he lives first in a tree, then surrounded by things, then in a tent, then a room, and soon begins to talk of his 'Settlement'. This may elucidate the significance of those occasions when Crusoe muses on being sole ruler or emperor, and satirises rank and power. Seidel then goes a stage further by remarking: 'The idea of the island experience as speeding the development of the species and cataloguing the occupations of humankind makes *Robinson Crusoe* a kind of modern encyclopedia, a role that novelistic narrative generally grows to take over from the older epic forms' (S196).

However, after seeing the footprint, Crusoe's simple progress towards representing mankind seems to be interrupted. In place of the single allegory, Seidel sees Crusoe in 'a series of renegotiated status roles' and mentions 'all the variety of fictions the mind produces to survive, to fill time, and to endure' (S198) as his concluding observation.

Katherine Clark

Chapter 6 of Clark's *The Whole Frame of Nature, Time and Providence* is called 'Robinson Crusoe: Orthodox Penitent', and she begins her assessment by remarking that Crusoe 'learns, as Defoe wished his readers to do, that the natural world, and one's place within it, can make no sense without acceptance of the supernatural in the shape of revelation and redemption'.[21] She argues that Defoe was an orthodox believer in the doctrine of the Trinity, and that in '*Robinson Crusoe* and its two sequels' his 'central concern' was to defend belief in 'revelation and redemption' (C113) against contemporary attacks from deists and government-sponsored supporters of natural religion, such as Benjamin Hoadley, Bishop of Bangor, whose sermon *The Nature of the Kingdom or Church of Christ* (1717) ignited a vitriolic argument that became known as The Bangorian Controversy. Defoe sought to portray a victory of 'salvation and redemption' over Hoadley's and the deists' 'natural religion'. Clark sees this as 'a theme found in the first volume and defended more explicitly ... in the two *Crusoe* sequels' (C118). Defoe's adoption and development of a Muslim persona in *The Conduct of Christians made the Sport of Infidels* (1717) and *A Continuation of Letters Written by a Turkish Spy at Paris* (1718) demonstrate his commitment to and active participation in the argument for Trinitarianism and against deism and natural religion.

The controversy over belief in the Trinity divided the Dissenting community: in Defoe's own parish a minister was ejected, and a meeting of Presbyterian ministers, at Salters' Hall, voted by a narrow margin to rely on scripture alone and not require specific beliefs such as in the Trinity. Crusoe comments that 'the bare reading the Scripture' was enough to lead him to repentance and salvation, and 'few readers today can be unaware that *Robinson Crusoe* has a religious message', but Clark argues that the 'Christological core' of that message is 'often marginalized or ignored'. This religious message becomes even clearer 'if one considers the three Crusoe volumes as a whole', and she argues vigorously for conceiving the Crusoe trilogy as a unified whole, and as polemical history imparting 'general lessons, practical, moral, or both'; rather than taking the traditional approach and considering the first two volumes as novels, a concept that was always 'an uncomfortable fit' (all C123). Clark quotes at length from the *Serious Reflections*, where Crusoe asserts that his 'Allegorick History' is intended to promote belief in the divinity of Christ and 'the doctrine of special providence which asserted God's direct and continuing role in human history' (C124).

Clark then commentates Crusoe's conversion, mentioning his dream, sickness, and the concoction of rum and tobacco before suggesting that 'the end of his spiritual crisis only occurs when a biblical passage leads him to embrace Christ as his Saviour and thereby to understand the true depths of God's mercy' (C125). She notices that Robinson 'continues to suffer the occasional spiritual setback', but despite this she argues that from this one moment on, 'his days of spiritual bankruptcy are over' (C126). Furthermore, Robinson's difficulties in teaching Friday show that deducing religious belief from nature and reason (i.e. natural religion) can only take you so far, for 'nothing but divine Revelation can form the Knowledge of *Jesus Christ*' (*RC* 173). She points out that Defoe makes Robinson 'unerringly identify Trinitarianism as the basis . . . of an understanding of God's providential care of the world' (C127).

True to her declared approach, Clark then discusses material from the *Farther Adventures* and the *Serious Reflections*, showing that Defoe celebrates the civilising influence of monotheism and particularly Christianity, in contrast, for example, to his depiction of an idolatrous and uncivilised China; and that the essays in *Serious Reflections* comment on contemporary religious and moral issues of heterodoxy that concerned their author: 'Like many of his contemporaries, Defoe worried that his age was one of general moral decline. If left unchecked, he feared that the proliferation of heresy and vice would... endanger the very soul of the nation' (C136). Finally, Clark re-iterates her primary thesis, arguing that it is misleading to approach *Robinson Crusoe* as a novel because Defoe wrote it 'at a time when his overriding preoccupations were the threats posed to Trinitarian religion', rather than 'the dynamism of economic life, the possibility of recreating it from first principles, or the privileged position of the emotions' (C136). On the contrary, we should think of the story as a 'sacred drama that involved the redemption of Crusoe and Friday alike' and as providing a 'framework for human history that Defoe explicitly and didactically applied to China, Muscovy, and continental Europe' (C137). Those who identify Defoe as 'an egalitarian, a spokesman for a rising middle class, and an architect of a new and secular national identity' are misled by 'the need of modern scholarship to find ancient antecedents for present-day positions' (C210).

Clark's reading draws upon a thorough investigation of the history of ideas – historical, philosophical, and religious – of the time when Defoe was writing the Crusoe volumes. However, at the same time it leans heavily upon certain assertions. For example, the argument for taking the trilogy as a single work depends on passing over the glaring differences, both in quality and authorial intention, between the first volume and the rest. Then, the whole of Clark's thesis depends on the assertion that Defoe – a man always multifariously busy – was thinking more about religious doctrine than about any other aspect of life, when he wrote his novel. Finally, we may also find the evidence of the text, with regard to the religious controversies of the time, more equivocal and complicated, with more potential for ironic interpretation, than does Clark. We remember how Crusoe dismisses 'all the disputes, wranglings, strife, and contention' caused by religious controversy as 'all perfectly useless to us' (*RC* 175).

Concluding Remarks

We have summarised six critical views: three of them from the second half of the twentieth century; and three more from the recent or contemporary criticism. From all six we could select at least one comment that chimes with insights we developed in Part I of this book. The reader will already be well aware that Ellen Pollak's comments on a 'kaleidoscopic' effect and the difficulty of locating Defoe himself, echo our own observations of how Defoe's ironic text and narrative of unstable events act to 'complicate' all themes and issues. Equally, the connection is obvious between our finding that Defoe's protagonists 'improvise' their ethics and their lives, and V. O. Birdsall's remarks about 'the . . . struggle to become somebody who matters' (B171) in a context of life's 'formlessness'. To add one further instance, we could compare Michael Seidel's comment that the 'worlds Crusoe builds on his island extend to the fabricated nature of the language he uses' (S191), with our own remarks on Crusoe's language when he 'moves from 'lord' to 'king' and finally 'emperor', as if he cannot resist adopting ever-grander titles' (see Chapter 5 above).

In almost every other respect, however, these critics display differences rather than common ground. This is not to say that they disagree violently. On the contrary, there are consistent themes, such as the alternations of Defoe's protagonists between a drive to control their environments or their lives, and their underlying terrors, versions of which interpretation can be found in Lerenbaum, Birdsall, Richetti, Pollak, and Seidel. Two critics seem to take a patronising view of *Moll Flanders*, and praise *Roxana* on the dubious grounds that it is more constructed (but is it more realistic?). Nonetheless, these samples of criticism show that there are many different ways to focus upon Defoe's novels; and demonstrate that stimulating ideas and perceptive insights can abound, even if Defoe's celebrated 'kaleidoscopic' effect and 'moral instability' render all interpretation either complex or, at the very least, contingent.

The limited aim of this chapter has been to show that there are many different approaches and interpretations. This is strikingly demonstrated by juxtaposing two quotations we have just read. First, a basis for V.O. Birdsall's analysis is Hobbes's assertion that 'no man will subordinate himself either to another man or to any power higher than himself unless he stands to gain thereby', and that self-interest is therefore the foundation of Robinson's religious belief. Then, Katherine Clark founds her analysis of Robinson's conversion upon the premise that he 'learns, as Defoe wished his readers to do, that the natural world, and one's place within it, can make no sense without acceptance of the supernatural in the shape of revelation and redemption'. We should draw encouragement from the sheer variety of opinions: mine the richness of the text, and develop your own responses and insights, allowing your mind to be stimulated by controversies between critics, and then returning to the text to measure their reactions beside your own.

We admitted at the start that this chapter cannot pretend to provide an overview of the vast array of opinions and analyses of Defoe that exists. We chose instead to give a readable summary of only a few, believing that a clear understanding of how these six arguments have been developed will stimulate your own thinking more than would brief references to 40. The next and final part of this book consists of suggestions for further reading, which should act as a bridge for those wishing to read around the three novels, and includes a number of suggestions for pursuing your interest in the critics.

Further Reading

Your first job is to study the text. There is no substitute for the work of detailed analysis: that is how you gain the close familiarity with the text, and the fully developed understanding of its content, which make the essays you write both personal and convincing. For this reason it is better to avoid critical works about the text you are studying until you have studied it for yourself.

Once you are familiar with the text, you may wish to read around and about it. This brief chapter is only intended to set you off: there are hundreds of relevant books and we can only mention a few. However, most good editions, and critical works, have suggestions for further reading or bibliographies of their own. Once you have begun to read beyond your text, you can use these and a good library to follow up your particular interests. This chapter is divided into 'Works by Daniel Defoe'; 'Reading Around the Text', which lists some works which are contextually relevant either by date, content, or genre, by other writers; 'Biography', which lists some of the many accounts of Defoe's life; and 'Criticism', which gives a selection of suggested titles that will introduce you to the varieties of opinion among professional critics.

Works by Daniel Defoe

Defoe wrote eight novels. In this book we have focused on *Robinson Crusoe* (1719), *Moll Flanders* (1722), and *Roxana* (1724).[1] These are the most famous three works of fiction, and arguably the most successful and accessible as novels. Two of Defoe's other fictions would be the next ones to read: first, *The Farther Adventures of Robinson Crusoe* (1719) connects naturally, as the sequel which tells of Crusoe's final voyage and his journey around the world. Secondly, *A Journal of the Plague Year* (1722) is a moving account of the great plague of 1665, told by one 'H.F.', a supposed citizen of London who observed the terrible events at the time (when Defoe himself was a small boy). Masquerading as both documentary and fiction, this work is a novel fine enough to rank alongside the three we have studied. Defoe's three other fictions are *Captain Singleton* and *Memoirs of a Cavalier* (both 1720) and *Colonel Jack* (1722).[2] These are generally acknowledged to be less like what we would call 'novels'. *Memoirs of a Cavalier* partly indulges Defoe's interest in military strategy, and the narrator's character is barely sketched; on the other hand, there are some shocking and vivid descriptions of the battlefield. *Captain Singleton* is a rollicking adventure story, and its high points are the trek across Africa in the first half, then the relationship with Singleton's friend William the Quaker, towards the end. *Colonel Jack* contains the narrator's theory and experiment in the humane treatment of slaves, and some interesting Virginia scenes, as well as his five disastrous, and one eventually happy, marriages. These are all readable, fast-moving, and full of incident, even acknowledging that they are not equal to the three we have studied, or *A Journal of the Plague Year*.

Defoe's other writings are too numerous to list here. A full list of 'Works by or attributed to Defoe' can be found in the Bibliography at the end of *Daniel Defoe: His Life*, by Paula R. Backscheider (pp. 617–25),[3] or in 'Works Cited' at the end of *Daniel Defoe: Master of Fictions* by Maximilian E. Novak (pp. 712–25),[4] but such exhaustive lists include the hundreds of periodicals and political pamphlets Defoe wrote during his long and extremely busy life, which will largely be of interest to dedicated scholars and historians. Defoe was always lively and readable, however, and it is rewarding at least to dip into some of his non-fiction works. The obvious first candidates for this would be *The Storm* (1704), Defoe's documentary account of the freak hurricane that attacked Britain in 1703; and *A Tour Through the Whole Island of Great Britain* (1724–6) and so on. Defoe's *Tour* became a model for travel writing, with its informative mixture of information, anecdote, and description of background and people. Both of these works are available in Penguin Classics editions, but note that the Penguin *Tour* is abridged from Defoe's original three volumes. Anyone wishing to sample Defoe's other writings, in particular his conduct-books and his political polemics, would until recently have needed to gain access to a university library. Since the advent of the print-to-order industry, however, a vast number of rare works can now be ordered and bought through online services such as Amazon.com. Kessinger publishing has a range of titles by Daniel Defoe, including particularly Defoe's early successes *An Essay upon*

Projects (1697); *The True-Born Englishman* (1700); and the conduct-book *Conjugal Lewdness or Matrimonial Whoredom* (1727). The celebrated pamphlet that landed Defoe in Newgate and then in the pillory, *The Shortest Way with the Dissenters* (1702) can also be ordered online, published by Gale Echo Print Editions. In addition, one can read a wide range of Defoe's writings online, free, from such Web sites as Project Gutenberg (www.gutenberg.org). It is suggested that you may 'dip' into some of these titles to gain an idea of the range of Defoe's works.

Reading Around the Text

Defoe is often regarded as the first English novelist, and the fictions we have studied as the first English novels. Some reading in the area of background or source materials may be relevant to each. For *Robinson Crusoe*, you can read accounts of Alexander Selkirk's sojourn on his uninhabited island both from Woodes Rogers' *A Cruising Voyage round the World* (1712) and from Sir Richard Steele in *The Englishman No. 26* (1713), both of which are re-printed in the Norton Critical Edition of *Robinson Crusoe*. In connection with *Moll Flanders*, it may be interesting to read Defoe's lives of two famous criminals, available as *Defoe on Sheppard and Wild* edited by Richard Holmes (Harper Perennial, 2004), or Henry Fielding's life of *Jonathan Wild* (1743), if only to marvel at Defoe's success in transforming a criminal life into a novel. Similarly, Defoe's extraordinary innovation in making a moving novel from a scandalous life in *Roxana* may be appreciated by looking at Delarivière Manley's *The Adventures of Rivella, or the History of the Author of The New Atalantis* (1714), the scandalous autobiography of an already notorious author.

With regard to that famous process Ian Watt called 'The Rise of the Novel', you cannot do better than to bracket Defoe's fictions by reading his immediate precursors and successors. Of those who came before, you can look at Delarivière Manley's *The New Atlantis* (1709),[5] a satire in which recognisable contemporary personalities appear in compromising situations; Aphra Behn's tale of a noble African taken to Venezuela in slavery, *Oroonoko* (1688); or Eliza Haywood's *Idalia; or The Unfortunate Mistress* (1723), an unlikely romantic 'bodice-ripper' which clearly provided Defoe with the title *The Fortunate Mistress* (which we have been calling by its shortened modern title *Roxana*).

The most significant of the novelists who followed Defoe were Samuel Richardson and Henry Fielding. Samuel Richardson wrote three epistolary novels, *Pamela: Or, Virtue Rewarded* (1740), *Clarissa: Or the History of a Young Lady* (1748), and *The History of Sir Charles Grandison* (1753). Of these,

Pamela is the one to start on, but any serious lover of English Literature should also read *Clarissa*, Richardson's enormous masterpiece and one of the finest novels in the canon. Henry Fielding's novels seem to have been inspired by a reaction against Richardson. Fielding the comic satirist clearly found Richardson sentimental. He ridiculed *Pamela* in *An Apology for the Life of Mrs. Shamela Andrews* (1741), changed the unbelievably chaste and virtuous heroine to an unbelievably chaste and virtuous hero in *Joseph Andrews* (1742); and finally created an unchaste but sympathetic hero in *Tom Jones* (1749).

In connection with the sub-genre island stories, initiated by *Robinson Crusoe*, it is surely important to follow this kind of fiction to its less novelistic but more allegorical end by reading Jonathan Swift's classic *Gulliver's Travels* (1726), brought out only 2 years after the appearance of *Roxana*, and written by one of Defoe's contemporaries, a political journalist and therefore rival. The island idea, of course, can be followed much further: even to such modern examples as Aldous Huxley's *Brave New World* (1932) and, of course, William Golding's *Lord of the Flies* (1954). If you are following the development of the novel, however, your subsequent task will be to dive into the complicated evolutions of the middle and later eighteenth-century, when the path of development branched into several. Mentioning only three, you may wish to look at, first, *Roderick Random* (1748) by Tobias Smollet, starting in a direction, with a gentle subjective hero surrounded by comic grotesques, that would strongly influence Charles Dickens in the following century. Second, you could sample a Gothic novel such as Mrs Radcliffe's *The Mysteries of Udolpho* (1794) and consider the influence of this genre on such nineteenth-century novels as *Frankenstein* or *Wuthering Heights*. Finally, try *The Life and Opinions of Tristram Shandy, Gentleman* (1759–69) by Laurence Sterne, which many regard as a more avant-garde experiment in the novel form, than those of the twentieth century. As the novel genre branches out into its several but related lines of development, we leave the business of 'reading around' Defoe.

Biography

There is a great deal of published material about Daniel Defoe's life. Two huge recent biographies have traced Defoe as a writer and include virtually everything that is known about him, particularly as a writer, spy, and journalist. It is interesting to note, however, that these thorough and scholarly works are still very light on information about, for example, Defoe's family life, or even the names and dates of birth and death of his children. These two works are Maximilian E. Novak's *Daniel Defoe: Master of Fictions: His Life and Ideas*

(Oxford and New York, 2001), and Paula R. Backscheider's *Daniel Defoe: His Life* (Baltimore and London, 1989). Both of these are difficult reading. This is partly because of the nature of Defoe's life, which was episodic and filled with catastrophic changes and uncertainty, much like the lives he chronicles in his fictions; and partly because of the rapid succession of writings Defoe continuously produced, and the biographers' attempts to draw together his opinions, as expressed in hundreds of texts, into a coherent whole. Some further primary material can be found in *The Letters of Daniel Defoe*, Ed. George Harris Healey, Oxford, 1955.

There are numerous other biographies of Defoe on the market. John Richetti's *The Life of Daniel Defoe* (Oxford, 2005) is a third scholarly and respected work; then, *A Political Biography of Daniel Defoe* (London, 2006) by P. N. Furbank and W. R. Owens takes a specific slant as its title suggests; and an evocative, story-telling account of Defoe can be found in Richard West's *The Life and Strange Surprising Adventures of Daniel Defoe* (London, 1997). Finally, there are fringe contributions on Defoe's life, such as John Martin's *Beyond Belief: The Real Life of Daniel Defoe* (Bedlinog, 2006), which asserts that he was a homosexual. Is this conjecture or history? There is some more respectable psychoanalytic corroboration, although not supporting John Martin's gay thesis as such: look at Leo Abse's *The Bi-Sexuality of Daniel Defoe: A Psychoanalytic Survey of the Man and His Works* (London, 2006).

Criticism

The six main critical works sampled in Chapter 9 are Miriam Lerenbaum's 'A Woman on Her Own Account', 1977, reprinted in *Modern Critical Interpretations: Daniel Defoe's* Moll Flanders, Ed. Harold Bloom (New York, New Haven and Philadelphia, 1987, pp. 37–51); Virginia Ogden Birdsall, *Defoe's Perpetual Seekers: A Study of the Major Fiction* (Lewisburg, London and Toronto, 1985); John J. Richetti, *Daniel Defoe* (Boston, 1987); Ellen Pollak, 'Gender and Fiction in *Moll Flanders* and *Roxana*'; and Michael Siedel's '*Robinson Crusoe*: Varieties of Fictional Experience', both from *The Cambridge Companion to Daniel Defoe*, Ed. John J. Richetti (Cambridge and New York, 2008); and Katherine Clark's *The Whole Frame of Nature, Time and Providence* (Basingstoke & New York, 2007).

Anthologies of critical essays and articles are a good way to sample the critics. You can then go on to read the full-length books written by those critics whose ideas and approaches you find stimulating. The *Cambridge Companion* in which Ellen Pollak's and Michael Seidel's articles appear also has other interesting contributions such as Srinivas Aravamudan's 'Defoe, commerce, and empire', Hal Gladfelder's 'Defoe and criminal fiction', and Deidre Shauna Lynch's 'Money and character in Defoe's fiction'. Other anthologies of essays and articles on Defoe include *Critical Essays on Daniel Defoe*, Ed. Roger D. Lund (1997); *Twentieth-Century Interpretations of* Moll Flanders, Ed. Robert C. Elliott (New Jersey, 1970) and *Twentieth-Century Interpretations of* Robinson Crusoe, Ed. Frank H. Ellis (New Jersey, 1969); *Modern Critical Interpretations: Daniel Defoe's* Moll Flanders, Ed. Harold Bloom (New York, New Haven, Philadelphia, 1987). Harold Bloom also edited another anthology of criticism, *Major Literary Characters: Robinson Crusoe* (New York and Philadelphia, 1995). Most of these collections of critics contain a range of contributions from the usual suspects, including the background standards such as Woolf, Ian Watt, or Dorothy Van Ghent, and the more recent mainstream such as Novak, Backscheider, Richetti, and Starr. A very different anthology has been edited by two professors of French literature: this is *Robinson Crusoe: Myths and Metamorphoses*, Ed. Lieve Spaas and Brian Stimpson (Basingstoke, London, and New York, 1996).

The following full-length critical works may also be of interest and should be stimulating whether you agree or disagree with the writer's analysis. In Chapter 9, we sampled V. O. Birdsall's *Defoe's Perpetual Seekers*, John J. Richetti's *Daniel Defoe*, and Katherine Clark's *Daniel Defoe: The Whole Frame of Nature, Time and Providence*. Then you may look at *Defoe's Fiction* by Ian Bell (London, 1985); *Defoe's Art of Fiction* by David Blewett (Toronto, 1979); Maximilian E. Novak's *Realism, Myth, and History in Defoe's Fiction* (Lincoln, Nebraska, 1983); Michael Seidel's *Robinson Crusoe: Island Myths and the Novel* (Boston, 1991); and George Starr's *Defoe and Spiritual Autobiography* (Princeton 1965). These are all major contributions from the latter part of the twentieth century. Then, you may try Katherine A. Armstrong's *Defoe: Writer as Agent* (University of Victoria, 1996), with its interesting chapter on 'Moll Flanders: Urban Guerilla'.

There are numerous other full-length critical studies of Defoe, not to mention the many articles and essays to be found in learned periodicals. You may well wish to begin by seeking some guidance on the different critics' main ideas or particular approaches, before attempting to locate and read their work. The best way to do this is to read Paul Baines's volume *Daniel Defoe: Robinson Crusoe/Moll Flanders* in the *Reader's Guide to Essential Criticism* series published by Palgrave Macmillan. Most studies of Defoe will also discuss *Roxana*, so this guide will automatically help with that text as well as the other two. Such a guide provides an ideal short cut: when you find that Paul Baines's text summarises an approach you find stimulating or interesting, then you can go to that particular critic to read in full detail.

Some of the most influential studies of Defoe's novels have appeared within critical works with a wider scope than the one author or text, or as articles in anthologies or periodicals. In this connection, it is worthwhile to use the subject-index in a library, and references and bibliographies which appear in the critical works you try first, both of which will point you towards many valuable contributions to the critical debate that you would not otherwise find. For example, if you look under Eighteenth-century Fiction, or History of the Novel, or Crime in early Fiction, or indeed any of the subject-headings that occur to you as relevant, rather than just under Defoe, you will find many works with chapters or sections which discuss Defoe. So, for example, you might discover the excellent analysis of Defoe's sentences in *The Evolution of English Prose, 1700–1800: Style, Politeness and Print Culture* by Carey McIntosh (Cambridge, 1998); or the equally excellent (and superbly titled) chapter 'Mushrooms, Subjects, and Women' with its stimulating discussion of *Roxana*, in *Ingenuous Subjection: Compliance and Power in the Eighteenth-Century Domestic Novel* by Helen Thompson (Philadelphia, 2005); the section on 'Roxana's Contractual Affiliations' in John P. Zomchick's *Family and the Law in Eighteenth-century Fiction: The Public Conscience in the Private Sphere* (Cambridge, 1993); or James Thompson's *Models of Value: Eighteenth-century Political Economy and the Novel* (Durham and London, 1996), with its chapter on 'Defoe and the Narrative of Exchange'. So, when you are in a library, use the catalogue system resourcefully. There are numerous books which appear to be on different subjects – English prose, the rise of the novel, eighteenth-century fiction plus law or money or society or women or colonies or dissenters or voyages or criminals or – and so on. A large number of these may contain chapters or essays about Daniel Defoe, which bring an illuminating angle to bear upon one or more of the three novels we have been studying.

Notes

Setting the Agenda

1. Birdsall, Virginia Ogden, *Defoe's Perpetual Seekers: A Study of the Major Fiction*, London and Toronto, 1985, p. 171.
2. Clark, Katherine, *The Whole Frame of Nature, Time and Providence*, Basingstoke and New York, 2007, p. 137.
3. McKeon, Michael, 'Defoe and the Naturalisation of Desire', from *Robinson Crusoe, A Norton Critical Edition*, Ed. Michael Shinagel, New York and London, 1994, pp. 422–3.
4. This is the Penguin Classics Edition of *Robinson Crusoe*. Future references to this edition will appear in brackets as the page-number(s) preceded by the abbreviation *RC*, thus: (*RC* 6–8).
5. For an illuminating discussion of Defoe's long sentences and their consequent 'psychological and rhetorical connections between different ideas and emotions', see McIntosh, Carey, *The Evolution of English Prose, 1700–1800: Style, Politeness and Print Culture*, Cambridge, 1998. Quote is from p. 94.
6. Future references to this edition will appear in the text in brackets as the page-number(s) preceded by the abbreviation *MF*, thus: (*MF* 46–8).
7. Future references to this edition will appear in the text in brackets as the page-number(s) preceded by the abbreviation *R*, thus: (*R* 39–40).

Conscience and Repentance

1. See e.g. McKeon, Michael, 'Defoe and the Naturalisation of Desire', from *Robinson Crusoe, A Norton Critical Edition*, Ed. Michael Shinagel,

New York and London, 1994, pp. 402–23. McKeon suggests that Robinson's simple fable is 'repeatedly threatened' by a 'never-articulated' cynicism (op.cit., p. 423).
2. 'Casuistry' became an ambivalent term from debates within the Catholic Church, notably those involving the Jesuits. The quoted dual definition is typical, and comes from *www.thefreedictionary.com*.

Society and Economics

1. For example, see the importance of the term 'Auctoritee' in various of Chaucer's *Canterbury Tales*; the principle that 'after the tyme moste be temperaunce/To any wight that kan on governaunce' (Chaucer, Geoffrey, *The Franklin's Tale*, ll. 77–8); or the exploitation of these terms and concepts in Shakespeare's ubiquitous theme of order.
2. For a discussion of Robinson's attitudes towards women, see Chapter 4, 'Women and Patriarchy'.
3. *The Bible*, King James Version, Romans, ch. 2, Vs. 12–15.
4. From Isaiah, ch. 45, V. 9, we read: 'Shall the clay say to him that fashioneth it, What makest thou? or thy work, He hath no hands?'; and in Jeremiah, ch. 18, V. 6, we find: 'Behold, as the clay is in the potter's hand, so are ye in mine hand' (both *The Bible*, King James Version).
5. It is revealing and amusing that the parrot is taught the familiar 'Robin' while Friday is immediately taught 'Master' (see *RC* 163).
6. This character, claimed as a friend and adviser by Roxana, was an actual historical person. Sir Robert Clayton (1629–1707) was a British merchant banker, politician, and Lord Mayor of London.
7. A point made in Defoe's *Complete English Tradesman*, where he suggests that vice is inevitably part of the basis on which prosperity and civilisation thrive.

Women and Patriarchy

1. The only other way for a woman to avoid poverty and starvation is found in *Moll Flanders*, when she makes her living as a thief.
2. 'A Woman on her Own Account', from *Modern Critical Interpretations: Daniel Defoe's* Moll Flanders, Ed. Harold Bloom, NY, New Haven and Philadelphia, 1987, pp. 41, 49.

3. A brief discussion of tragic characteristics in *Roxana* can be found in Chapter 6. See pp. 166–168.

Instability and the Outsider

1. *The Bible*, King James Version, Luke, ch. 16, V. 26.
2. For example, Ian Watt (*The Rise of the Novel*, 1957) thought Moll a sexless or masculine narrator. Miriam Lerenbaum (*A Woman on Her Own Account*, 1977), on the other hand, argues that Defoe 'gives us in *Moll Flanders* an exceptionally accurate rendering of his heroine's involuntary involvement in the feminine role' (op.cit., p. 37).
3. *Defoe's Perpetual Seekers: A Study of the Major Fiction*, Lewisburg, London and Toronto, 1985. Quotations are from pp. 171–4.
4. *Daniel Defoe: The Whole Frame of Nature, Time and Providence*, Basingstoke and New York, 2007, p. 210.
5. From 'Gender and Fiction in *Moll Flanders* and *Roxana*', *The Cambridge Companion to Daniel Defoe*, Ed. John Richetti, Cambridge, 2008, pp. 140–1.

Themes and Conclusions to Part I

1. That is they have been branded as convicted criminals then transported to the colony.
2. 'Gender and Fiction in *Moll Flanders* and *Roxana*', *The Cambridge Companion to Daniel Defoe*, Ed. John Richetti, Cambridge, 2008, p. 140.
3. Shinagel, Michael, *Daniel Defoe and Middle-Class Gentility*, Cambridge, Massachusetts, 1968. Quotations are from pp. 193 and 196, respectively.
4. Birdsall, Virginia Ogden, *Defoe's Perpetual Seekers: A Study of the Major Fiction*, Lewisburg, London and Toronto, 1985. Quotations are from pp. 171 and 174, respectively.
5. A further brief consideration of this question can be found in Chapter 7 below.
6. Birdsall, Virginia Ogden, op. cit., p. 174.
7. Ellen Pollak suggests that Susan represents an unbreakable value of 'kinship' that finally defeats Roxana's individualism, just as Moll cannot transgress the same absolute when she discovers her incest. See Chapter 9 below, and 'Gender and Fiction in *Moll Flanders* and *Roxana*', *The Cambridge Companion to Daniel Defoe*, Ed. John Richetti, Cambridge, 2008.

Daniel Defoe's Life and Works

1. *The Secret History of the White Staff*, London, 1715.
2. Attribution of this work to Defoe is under question.
3. *The Letters of Daniel Defoe*, Ed. George Harris Healey, Oxford, 1955, p. 475.
4. Backscheider, Paula R., *Daniel Defoe: His Life*, Baltimore and London, 1989, p. 465.
5. Others might be such works as, for example, *Don Quixote* and *Candide.*
6. Backscheider, Paula R., *Daniel Defoe: His Life*, Baltimore and London, 1989, p. 465.

The Place of Defoe's Novels in English Literature

1. In *Memoirs of the Conduct of her Late Majesty*, although the attribution of this work to Defoe is under question.
2. Although attribution of these works to Defoe is under question.
3. Birdsall, V. O., *Defoe's Perpetual Seekers: A Study of the Major Fiction*, Lewisburg, London and Toronto, 1985, p. 174.
4. Birdsall, V. O., op.cit., p. 171.
5. *The Rise of the Novel*: *Studies in Defoe, Richardson and Fielding*, London, 1957, p. 118.
6. *Daniel Defoe: The Whole Frame of Nature, Time and Providence*, Basingstoke and New York, 2007, p. 210.
7. E.g. my own four-volume Everyman edition.

A Sample of Critical Views

1. Basingstoke and New York, 2007.
2. In two essays: 'Defoe' (written 1919), *The Common Reader*, 1925, and 'Robinson Crusoe', *The Second Common Reader*, 1932.
3. Quotations are from 'Robinson Crusoe' as reprinted in *A Norton Critical Edition: Daniel Defoe:* Robinson Crusoe, Ed. Michael Shinagel, p. 285. Subsequent page-references will appear in the text in brackets preceded by W, thus: (W285).
4. 'Defoe' by Virginia Woolf, reprinted as the Introduction to the Modern Library edition of *Moll Flanders*, with notes by Audrey Bilger, New York, 2002, pp. xi–xviii. Subsequent page-references will appear in the text in brackets preceded by WB thus: (WBxi).
5. In *Aspects of the Novel* (1927).

6. Joyce delivered a lecture on Defoe in Italian, to the Universita Popolare Triestina, in 1912. Quotations are from Joseph Prescott's translation from the original Italian text, copyrighted in 1964, as abridged and printed in *A Norton Critical Edition: Daniel Defoe:* Robinson Crusoe, Ed. Michael Shinagel, New York and London, 1994, pp. 320–3.
7. Backscheider, Paula R., *Daniel Defoe: His Life*, Baltimore and London, 1989, pp. 540–1.
8. Watt, Ian, *The Rise of the Novel: Studies in Defoe, Richardson and Fielding*, 1957, edition of 1987, p. 59.
9. Op.cit., p. 32.
10. Watt, Ian, '*Robinson Crusoe* as a Myth', reprinted in *A Norton Critical Edition: Daniel Defoe: Robinson Crusoe*, Ed. Michael Shinagel, New York and London, 1994, p. 301.
11. Watt, Ian, *The Rise of the Novel: Studies in Defoe, Richardson and Fielding*, 1957, edition of 1987, p. 128.
12. Op.cit., p. 146.
13. Op.cit., p. 118.
14. 'A Woman on Her Own Account', 1977, reprinted in *Modern Critical Interpretations: Daniel Defoe's* Moll Flanders, Ed. Harold Bloom, New York, New Haven and Philadelphia, 1987, pp. 37–51. Page-references to this work will appear in the text in brackets preceded by 'L' thus: (L37).
15. Birdsall, Virginia Ogden, *Defoe's Perpetual Seekers: A Study of the Major Fiction*, London and Toronto, 1985, p. 25. Subsequent page-references to this work will appear in the text in brackets preceded by 'B', thus: (B25).
16. V. O. Birdsall here quotes Ernest Becker (B84).
17. Richetti, John. J., *Daniel Defoe*, Boston, 1987. Subsequent page-references to this work will appear in the text in brackets, preceded by 'R' thus: (R56).
18. Richetti here quotes Ian Watt from *The Rise of the Novel* etc.
19. Richetti, John, Ed., *The Cambridge Companion to Daniel Defoe*, Cambridge and New York, 2008, pp. 139–57. Page-references to this article will appear in the text in brackets, preceded by 'P', thus: (P139).
20. Richetti, John, Ed., *The Cambridge Companion to Daniel Defoe*, Cambridge and New York, 2008, pp. 182–99. Page-references to this article will appear in the text in brackets, preceded by 'S', thus: (S182).
21. Clark, Katherine, op.cit., Basingstoke and New York, p. 113. Subsequent page-references to this work will appear in brackets in the text preceded by 'C', thus: (C113).

Further Reading

1. For simplicity's sake we use the common shortened versions of Defoe's titles.
2. *Captain Singleton* is available from Dodo Press, *Memoirs of a Cavalier* from Nonsuch Publishing, and *Colonel Jack* from Kessinger Publishing.
3. Baltimore and London (1989).
4. Oxford and New York (2001).
5. The full title is *Secret Memoirs and Manners of Several Persons of Quality of Both Sexes, from the New Atlantis, An Island in the Mediterranean.*

Index